Bordeaux

Also by Paul Torday

Salmon Fishing in the Yemen

Bordeaux

Paul Torday

Houghton Mifflin Harcourt
BOSTON · NEW YORK
2009

For information about permission to reproduce selections from this
book, write to Permissions, Houghton Mifflin Harcourt
Publishing Company, 6277 Sea Harbor Drive,
Orlando, Florida 32887-6777.

www.hmhbooks.com

First U.S. edition published by Houghton Mifflin Harcourt, 2009

First published in Great Britain by Weidenfeld & Nicolson as
The Irresistible Inheritance of Wilberforce: A Novel in Four Vintages

Library of Congress Cataloging-in-Publication Data
Torday, Paul, date.
[Irresistible inheritance of Wilberforce]
Bordeaux / Paul Torday.—1st U.S. ed.
p. cm.
"First published in Great Britain by Weidenfeld & Nicolson
as The Irresistible Inheritance of Wilberforce: A Novel
in Four Vintages"—T.p. verso
ISBN 978-0-15-101354-8
1. Businessmen—Fiction. 2. Leisure class—Fiction. 3. Friendship—
Fiction. 4. Entertaining—Fiction. 5. Wine tasting—Fiction.
6. Wine cellars—Fiction. 7. England—Fiction. I. Title.
PR6120.O73B66 2009 823'.92—dc22
2008024726

Printed in the United States of America

MP 10 9 8 7 6 5 4 3 2 1

To Piers & Nicholas,
Jonathan & Charles

Wilberforce's eyes went up to the ceiling, so that he did not seem to know how his glass went up full to his mouth and came down empty.

—W. M. THACKERAY, *Vanity Fair*

2006

One

I stepped out of the taxi too quickly. I rocked back on my heels to slow myself down and found that the best way to maintain my balance was to lean against the side of the taxi and look up. The sky was hard and black and a few stars glittered, though I could not see as many as I used to see. Once I had looked up, it was hard to look down again.

'Are you all right, squire?' asked the driver. A younger man might probably have abused me for bumping against the side of his taxi; this man belonged to an age when drivers were called 'cabbie' and customers were called 'squire' or 'guv'nor'.

The question was difficult to answer. Was I all right? It was a very good question. It required thought before I could answer. I gazed at the stars and thought about the question.

'That'll be fifteen pounds, squire,' the driver said.

I realised I had not managed to answer him. I peeled some notes from a bundle I kept in a money clip and paid him a sum of money. I cannot remember how much it was, but he seemed pleased.

'God bless you, guv'nor,' he said, as he drove off.

I rocked on my heels again. It was a pleasant feeling. I took in a bit more night sky, while I found my balance, and a bit of the front of the restaurant as my weight shifted back to my toes. A small, discreet sign announced: 'Les Tripes de Normandie'. It was a very successful restaurant, I had heard. I had never been before. I did not like to go to the same restaurant more than once; perhaps twice if it was very good. There always seemed to be issues, these days, when I went back to places where I had eaten before. I liked the sign. I thought the font used was probably Arial, and the lighting was clever: the lettering was done in neon tubing in an off-white, almost a cream colour, against a polished black-marble fascia.

They said the chef was brilliant. He had constructed a menu which took rustic French dishes and elevated them to art forms. He had appeared on a number of television programmes and was admired and loved by the public. I am quoting from the restaurant's web site. I am not especially interested in cooking. It is the wine list in a restaurant that catches my attention. When I had inspected Les Tripes's web site, I'd clicked straight away on to the wine list and seen that they offered a Château Pétrus 1982. I don't remember the weather in 1982 in western France, but I have read about it. It was a cool spring and then a warm summer that extended into September: long hours of sunshine and not much rain. Conditions were ideal for the Bordeaux vineyards that year. As a result, 1982 is a vintage that seems to have lasted practically for ever. It is a classic. But, you will not be surprised to learn, it is becoming harder and harder to find.

Finding Pétrus 1982 on a wine list is like discovering a diamond lying on the ground. The vineyard only covers 28 acres and produces about twenty-five thousand bottles annually. The grapes are picked, then fermented for twenty-four days, then macerated in concrete tanks. After that the young wine is aged in oak barrels for twenty months, and then bottled. After that, all you have to do is wait between fifteen and twenty years, and it will be ready to drink. It is rare now to come across a Pétrus 1982 or indeed any of the earlier vintages; but if you do find a bottle, you need to make the most of the opportunity. It is not cheap: the restaurant web site indicated a price of £3000 a bottle; but, if you are an enthusiast, the price is irrelevant if you find what you are looking for. That is what I always say.

It wasn't as if I could drink that particular year of Pétrus at home. I have rather a large amount of wine now, which I obtained from Francis Black. Some people would say it is an incredible amount of wine. But it did not include Château Pétrus 1982.

I found I had finished rocking on my heels and decided to enter the restaurant. As I came through the door, they took my coat and said, 'Mr Wilberforce?'

I nodded and the waiter asked if he could show me to my table. The restaurant was quite empty. It was still opening up, it being just a few minutes after seven in the evening. I liked to go to restaurants early. It meant that I could stay in them a very long time, if I felt like staying – for example, if there were several different wines on their list which I wanted to try. Then again, if there was only one wine I was interested in, I liked to eat my dinner and drink my bottle or two of claret and be out again before the place filled up and I risked being distracted from what I had come to taste.

I entered a warm, softly lit room. The tables were of dark oak, with squares of white linen laid upon them. Two waiters were still lighting the candles on the tables. Another waiter was straightening the knives and forks with microscopic attention to their alignment, and picking up and inspecting the great, bowl-like wine glasses for specks of dust. A girl was putting the final touches to a large flower arrangement in the centre of the room. An important-looking person in an im-maculate navy-blue suit, whom I took to be the head waiter, was standing at the double doors into the kitchen and talking to the chef. A waiter in a white shirt and black waistcoat was standing behind the bar, arranging the bottles on the shelves and flicking them with a duster, so that they gleamed and sparkled in the reflected light from the mirrors behind them. The bar counter was a deep pool of mahogany, on which crystal ashtrays sparkled. This too was given a final polish as I watched, and the ashtrays, which were already clean, were picked up and wiped again.

'Would you like a drink at the bar, sir, or shall I show you straight to your table?'

I realised I had come to a standstill in the middle of the empty restaurant, drinking in its potent spell, as one does when the curtain rises on a stage set, revealing a perfectly ordinary drawing room which is yet latent with a drama that will soon unfold. I love the early evening in a nearly empty restaurant. I love the hushed silence, the whisperings of the waiters as they wait to be called, the distant clatter and shouts that come from the kitchen as the doors swing open for a moment, and then swing closed again, cutting off the intrusion of noise. I love the glitter of the glasses and the cutlery in the candlelight, the purity of it all, the orderliness.

'I'd like to go straight to my table,' I said.

The waiter led me to a corner table and drew the chair back so that I could be seated. Then he gave me a copy of the menu and asked if I would like anything to drink. I asked for a glass of water and the wine list.

'The sommelier will be with you in a moment, sir,' said the waiter. I looked anxiously around the room. So much of my happiness depended on the sommelier. Did he really know how to keep his wine? Did he know how to open it? how to decant it? how to pour it? I have known a perfectly good bottle of Margaux be ruined by a careless wine waiter who managed to slosh it into my glass, accompanied by small pieces of cork, as if he were pouring out lager.

My eye chanced upon a large man in a black apron, with a tasting bowl on a chain around his neck. He was advancing slowly in my direction, carrying the leather-bound wine list.

6

As he approached I could see he was a serious-looking man, with a thick grey moustache, and his complexion bore the noble tints of a man who has spent much of his life engaged with the subject of wine. I felt sure he would look after me. He handed me the list, bowed and withdrew.

After a moment's thought I selected some things to eat, and then sat and turned the pages of the wine list. My heart was thumping. The possibility had just occurred to me that the Château Pétrus 1982 might still be on the web site only because no one had bothered to update the list. When I thought of it for a moment, it seemed very likely that all the 1982s would long ago have been ordered and drunk. In that case, what was I going to do? I turned the parchment-like pages of the wine list rapidly until I found the page headed 'Red Bordeaux'. I saw that the Château Pétrus was still listed and breathed out in my relief. I had been holding my breath. I beckoned to the sommelier. Supposing someone else were to come in, and decide to order it, and took the last bottle?

The sommelier came back to my table and asked, 'Monsieur has decided? Or perhaps I may advise you on something?' He was French – another good sign in a wine waiter.

'No, I'd like the Château Pétrus. The 1982.'

The sommelier took a step back from the table. He looked at me. I could see him looking at my clothes, which were not of the newest. I have not been paying much attention to personal grooming recently, though I still do wash. Then he looked at me again and decided I meant it. He said, 'The Château Pétrus? Monsieur is quite certain?'

'Yes, very certain.'

'And, excuse me, but Monsieur has seen the price? It is our most expensive wine.'

'I have drunk the 1975, the 1978 and the 1979. I have never drunk the 1982.'

The sommelier gave me a very deep bow and said, 'I must

go and bring up the wine. It is a very great wine. It is not to be drunk in a hurry.'

I smiled at him and he smiled back. We understood one another. Price meant nothing. This was a great wine, one of the great classics of the last century, perhaps of all time. Drinking it was in itself an act of passion, of great artistry. The money was irrelevant.

'One moment,' I said, and put out my hand again for the wine list. 'I am going to start my dinner with escalope de foie gras. So I think I shall have half a bottle of a good Sauterne to accompany it. The Château Rieussec 1986.'

'Of course, monsieur,' said the sommelier, bowing low again. Then he took the wine list from me and took a few steps backwards, as if retreating from the presence of royalty, before treading softly away. I saw him having words with the head waiter on the other side of the restaurant, and I saw the head waiter look sharply across the room at me.

A moment later he was at my side, all smiles. 'Have you decided on what you would like to eat?' he asked me. 'Or is there something I could recommend? I understand you have chosen the wine already.'

I ordered the foie gras and something else. I think it was rack of lamb and the menu said '(min. 2 persons)', but I wasn't going to eat much of anything I might order. It was just that I felt the savoury lamb would set off the taste of the glorious claret I was soon to drink.

The head waiter tried to make conversation for a moment. 'I imagine you are a great connoisseur of wine,' he said. 'We sell very few bottles of that particular vintage. As a matter of fact, if I remember rightly, there are only two bottles left in the cellar and Jacques will be bringing one of them up for you now.'

'I don't know about that,' I said, 'but I do collect wine. I have quite a few bottles in my cellar now.'

'A large collection, I imagine, as Jacques says you are already familiar with several vintages of the Pétrus.'

'I don't know what you would call large,' I said. 'Perhaps one hundred thousand bottles of one sort or another.'

When I tell people this – and I don't go out of my way to mention the fact – I find they often think I am joking, or that I might be mad. If it is mad to own one hundred thousand bottles of wine, then I am mad. But I look on it as an investment: not so much a financial investment as an assurance that I will spend the rest of my life drinking delicious wine whenever I want to. I inherited most of it from Francis Black.

The head waiter certainly thought I was mad. He straightened up and the smile left his face. 'Indeed, sir,' he said. 'That is certainly what I would call a large collection. Enjoy the rest of your evening with us, sir.'

He left, which was a relief. I find on evenings like this it takes all my concentration to get the most from the experience of drinking the wine. Conversation can be a tremendous distraction, and anyway I have got out of the way of small talk these days. But then the head waiter came back, with a little silver tray.

'If I could just take an impression of your credit card, sir,' he said apologetically. 'I wouldn't normally trouble you, but as the sum of money is so very large . . .' and his voice trailed away into a deferential whisper.

'I don't use credit cards,' I said, and I pulled out my roll of banknotes. I knew I usually had between five and ten thousand pounds in cash when I went out. The bank always had an envelope full for me when I called on them once a week for my walking-around money, and I would make sure I had a bit extra if I thought I might come across an interesting wine. I put the roll on the plate. 'Take what I spend out of that and give whatever's left back to me when I go,' I told him.

9

The head waiter looked appalled and handed me back the roll of notes. 'That won't be necessary, sir,' he said. 'I did not appreciate you would be paying in cash . . . Sorry to have disturbed . . . Quite unusual . . .' and again he faded away.

I put the roll of notes back in my pocket. I hadn't realised it, but they were all fifties. I must have given the taxi driver a hundred pounds for a fifteen-pound fare. I had thought they were tens or twenties, but then of course the bundle would have been inconveniently large. No wonder the taxi driver had blessed me.

I sat undisturbed and watched the restaurant come to life around me. One or two couples had come in and been seated. Two well-dressed women were sitting at the bar drinking champagne. It seemed like a nice place. I liked the sommelier.

A waiter came up and offered me a small plate and said, 'Compliments of the chef, sir; a morsel of eel pâté on a gooseberry brioche.'

I waved it away. 'Nothing before the foie gras, thank you.'

Then the sommelier came back and together we looked at the bottle, which he reverentially cradled in his hands, turning it so that I could see the ornate red letters declaring the name of the château, and the appellation Pomerol, and the year. Then there was a considerable amount of business with decanters and corkscrews, and the extracting of the cork, which was conducted with a surgeon's care, and the decanting of the wine, which was poured as gently as if it were nitroglycerine. Then the decanter was turned gently in front of the flame of my candle, so that I could admire its lustrous colour. The sommelier's face was lined with care as he carried out these tasks and it was only when the cork had been duly sniffed, and presented for my inspection, and the wine was safely in the decanter, that he relaxed and looked towards me for my approval.

I looked longingly at it. I almost wished I had not com-
plicated matters by ordering another wine to start with. Then I
reflected that the anticipation could only heighten the pleasure
I knew I would feel at the first sip.

The foie gras arrived and with it the sommelier came
again, with the Château Rieussec. He treated it, not with
contempt, but with something less than awe. Although this,
too, was a great wine, it was a minor princeling in the
hierarchy of Bordeaux compared with the imperial pedigree
of the Pétrus.

I ate a few morsels of the foie gras, and sipped at the sweet
white wine.

Because I knew or, at any rate, had hoped that I might be
drinking Pétrus that evening, I had prepared myself as best I
knew how for the event. I had read my wine gazetteer to
remind myself of the provenance of the wine. Pomerol lies
east of Bordeaux, on the northern side of St Emilion. Its wines
are described by Robert Parker, the great wine writer, as
'the burgundies of Bordeaux' because of their 'power and
opulence'. I therefore felt it was appropriate to saturate
myself in the wines of Pomerol that day, while I read about
them and thought about the evening that lay ahead.

After breakfast I drank, very slowly, a bottle of Château La
Fleur de Gay; and with lunch I drank a bottle of Château
Trotanoy 1990, the last bottle of that wine and that year that
I had been able to find in the undercroft. I ate, as usual, very
little: just enough to bring out the flavour of what I was
drinking. I usually get something sent up from the restaurant
around the corner. I lingered over the Trotanoy well into the
afternoon. I thought about opening another bottle, but
decided against it. I came to the restaurant with the tastes of
Pomerol still lingering on my palate: two great wines from
the district which yet, in the wine drinkers' map, were as

foothills to the great peak of Pétrus on whose summit I soon would tread.

It was inevitable that the wine affected me. My balance, which has been deteriorating these last few months, was not good. I have also developed a distasteful tendency to perspire heavily when I am not drinking wine, and I find my hands tremble. As I am no longer inclined to drive, since the accident, it matters less than it might otherwise have done. I have a Screwpull corkscrew and that opens all but the very oldest bottles without trouble, no matter whether my hands are shaking or not. And when I drink wine I find I become very peaceful, very reflective, sometimes even devotional in my moods. When I am not drinking it, I become restless, prone to unhappy memories of events earlier in my life. I walk around my flat in Half Moon Street, which is on the edge of Mayfair, in the West End of London. I pick up books and put them down unread. I go out into Hyde Park and try to blow the memories away in the fresh air. I walk down Piccadilly and look into the shop windows, or prowl among the bookshelves of Hatchards, or stare at the mountains of crystallised fruit in the windows of Fortnum's. The memories won't go away, and so I go back to my flat and bring up a bottle of wine from the small cellar of perhaps a thousand bottles that I keep there, and drink it. My main collection of wine is still in the undercroft at Francis Black's old house in the North of England, which I acquired when I bought his house from his executors when he died. From time to time I go up there to gaze at my wine and make sure everything is all right, and I check that the temperature controls are working, and the security alarms are correctly set. I ship another few cases back to Half Moon Street to keep me going. The quantity of stock never seems to lessen, though — as if, when I am not there, the wooden cases and the racked bottles are secretly multiplying themselves. But I never linger for more than a few hours there: too many ghosts.

When I have opened the wine, rotated it this way and that in the glass, and savoured its aroma, and when I have sipped the first sip, then peacefulness gradually returns.

I finished the foie gras and sipped at the Rieussec. It was a good wine, with a delicious honey flavour, almost too powerful. I knew I would forget its taste instantly with the first glass of Pétrus. They took the plates away and I was left in peace for a moment, to glance about me. This was a restaurant for the rich and famous. It had taken quite an effort on my part to reserve a table, some weeks ago. Now there was scarcely an empty place in the room. The restaurant had filled up. But it was not noisy. There were perhaps only a dozen tables in quite a large room, well apart from each other so that one could neither overhear nor be overheard. I supposed that if I ever read the newspapers, I would recognise some of the people in here. There were three men ordering their dinner at the next table, and one of them was, I am fairly sure, a government minister. But I felt no real curiosity and I am sure I was invisible to them – not smart enough, sitting on my own, an object worth only a moment's glance until the eye moved on to something more rewarding to look at elsewhere in the room.

The lamb arrived underneath a huge silver dish cover, and then one or two people did glance my way, their attention caught by the theatre of the waiters removing the dish cover with a flourish, to show the rack of lamb underneath with its little paper crowns on each cutlet.

The sommelier was at my elbow asking if I would like to taste the wine. I dared not speak, but simply nodded my head in assent. A very little was poured into my glass, and the waiter warmed the bowl with his hands and moved it just enough so that the dark, almost purple liquid lost its meniscus for a moment. Then he handed the glass to me. First I inhaled the scent of the wine and then, when its flavour had filled my nose and lungs, I sipped it.

I knew what to expect: flavours of truffles, spices and sweet fruit. Then those tastes receded and it was like entering another country, a place you have always heard of and longed to go to but never visited. It was an experience almost beyond words, not capable of being captured by the normal wine enthusiast's vocabulary. I sipped the wine and I was so happy, all of a sudden, that a huge smile came over my face. I think I laughed.

The sommelier smiled too. 'Is it wonderful, sir?'

I handed him the glass and he too inhaled it. 'It is wonderful,' I told him.

He smiled again and said, 'There is nothing else on earth like it, monsieur.' Then, with true grace, he poured me a full glass of wine and left me alone to enjoy it. The waiter presented me with two cuts of lamb from the rack, and I ate part of one of them – just enough to allow its taste to complement that of the wine.

I ate morsels of lamb, and sipped from my glass. And in that other country, where the wine took me, was Catherine. Not exactly sitting at the table with me; it was more subtle than that. She was somewhere behind my left shoulder and, although I could not see her, I knew how she looked. Twenty-five years of age, and pretty as a picture, just as she had been for the last two years. I could smell the perfume she wore, and it smelled the same as the wine. Then, above the clatter of the knives and forks and the growing din of conversation from the tables around me, I could hear her humming. She had once been a member of a choir and it was an air from Bach that she was singing. I don't remember which one but I remembered the tune very well, and the pure sound of her voice. I hummed along with her, as I sometimes used to, even though she said I had no ear for music.

The head waiter appeared at my elbow: 'Excuse me sir, but would you mind not humming so loudly? It might disturb the other guests.'

The image of Catherine vanished in a moment, and I felt dislocated inside my head. The wine tasted suddenly flat and insipid. 'Was I humming?' I said, restraining my annoyance at having my tranquil mood disturbed. 'I'm terribly sorry.'

I bent my head over my plate and ate another forkful of lamb, in order that the head waiter would go away.

He bowed his head and said, 'So sorry to disturb you, sir. Most considerate, sir. Thank you so much.'

The sommelier came and poured a little more wine and I noticed I had drunk more than half the bottle. I said to him as he filled my glass, 'I think you said this was the last bottle but one?'

'Yes, monsieur, that is correct. One last bottle and then it is gone. I do not know that there are many bottles of that vintage left in the whole of London now.'

'Then bring it up and decant it, please.'

The sommelier replied, 'Are you certain, monsieur? Two bottles of a wine like this in one evening, for one man. Is it not too much sensation at one time?'

The thing is, I knew he was right. It was, without a doubt, overdoing it. I could not possibly enjoy the second bottle as much as the first. My palate would become dulled and furred with the wine. Moreover it would be the fourth, possibly the fifth bottle of wine I had drunk today, and that was before I found my way home and drank the bottle of Montagny that I always had as a nightcap.

The fact remained that I could not bear the thought of anyone else having that bottle. It had to be mine. It was as simple as that. 'Please bring it, anyway,' I said.

The sommelier bowed but there was doubt in his eyes, and I saw him go and have a conversation with the head waiter. I think they were wondering whether I would make more of a scene if I drank the wine than the scene they knew I would make if they did not bring it up for me.

Then he disappeared and after a few minutes came back with the second bottle of Pétrus, and whilst he went through the same rituals as before, he found time to refill my glass from the first bottle. I noticed some curious glances from around the restaurant. One man, more inquisitive or ill-mannered than the others, arose from the table of three that I had noticed earlier and walked across to me.

'Forgive me for intruding,' he said, 'but I noticed the label on that bottle of wine. Is that Pétrus you're drinking?' Without waiting for an answer he bent over and examined the label, which the sommelier instinctively turned so that he could read it.

'My God. The 1982,' he exclaimed, and then turned and said to me with some admiration, 'I say, you really know how to push the boat out. Well done, old boy. Enjoy yourself!' He went back to his table and there was a little extra buzz to their conversation. I tried hard to ignore their looks and after a while the wine absorbed me again in its powerful and aromatic embrace. I found that I was drinking wine from the second bottle. It was nearly the same, but not quite: once again the sense of being in a different place, but now seeing the landscape of this unknown country from a new vantage point. And Catherine came back, somewhere nearby, and together we sang a few bars of 'Jesu, joy of man's desiring'.

This brought the head waiter back. 'I really must ask you not to sing quite so loudly, sir,' he said. 'It is disturbing the other customers.'

'And I really must ask you not to interrupt me while I am

drinking my wine,' I replied. 'It is impossible to enjoy it properly if I keep being distracted like this, and I feel I have paid a fair price for the goods in question and am entitled to a proper enjoyment of them.'

It sometimes happens that my mannerisms of speech become a little strange under the influence of a lot of wine. I find my language tends to become ornate, almost flowery, and sometimes bends and even breaks under the weight of the complex ideas I wish to express. I stopped humming for a while, and after a moment the head waiter went away again. But by now I was the object of some attention around the restaurant. I think that, by then, everyone in the room knew that I was sitting drinking my way through more than six thousand pounds' worth of expensive wine on my own.

I heard, or I imagined that I heard, snatches of conversation: 'He doesn't look like he could afford a can of Special Brew, let alone one of the most expensive wines in the world.' 'He's probably a hedge-fund manager having a blow out after making a few million quid.' 'Or after losing it, more likely.'

'What an odd-looking creature,' said a woman's voice.

'He's so pale,' said another. 'I hope he's not going to be sick all over the place.'

'*Darling!* I'm trying to enjoy my dinner, thanks very much.'

It was too much. I stood up and turned around to try and catch sight of Catherine, to ask her what to do. My chair fell over backwards. I raised my glass of wine in the direction where I thought Catherine might have been standing a moment or two ago, before I turned around, and sipped it and said, 'Darling, come and try some of this. It's really very good.'

The room moved sideways and I found the head waiter had put his arm around me affectionately. That was very nice of him. I had begun to form the impression he did not really like me.

'Get him a taxi,' I heard him say to someone, as we both slid towards the floor. He was trying to hold me up, I realised, but I was just a bit heavy for him.

'Where do you live?' he asked me. Now he was staring down at me from somewhere far above, and his voice sounded very remote. The great claret was exercising a strong narcotic effect on me. My eyes felt heavy.

'What do we do about the bill? We're down more than six grand if he doesn't pay,' whispered another man nearby. I realised it was the sommelier's voice, and he was no longer French, but from Birmingham.

I reached into my pocket. I didn't want any trouble. It was odd how often these difficulties arose when I ate out. I thrust the bundle of notes in the direction of the voice and managed to say, 'Do take what I owe from these notes. And do remunerate yourselves for the trouble and inconvenience I may be causing you. Please convey my sincere apologies to my fellow guests for any disturbance.'

How much of this I actually managed to speak out loud, I do not know, but the notes were snatched from my hand. I found that if I moved my head a little to the left I could pillow it on the head waiter's shoes. They were black and well polished and surprisingly comfortable to nestle against.

'What's his name?' someone asked.

'Table booked in the name of Wilberforce.'

'Do we know his address?'

'No, he's never been here before.'

'I think we would have remembered if he'd been here before,' said a sarcastic voice.

'Has he got any ID?' asked the first voice. I think it was the head waiter's.

A hand snaked its way into the inside pocket of my suit

jacket and found my wallet. 'Found a card here in the name of Wilberforce, address Half Moon Street.'

Then everything went black.

Two

'You've been out of it for three days,' a voice said. I recognised the voice. It was a kind voice, but also a voice that I associated with someone telling me things for my own good. Confusion swarmed in my head. I opened my eyes and saw a cream ceiling. Well, that meant nothing. After a moment I found the energy to turn my head, and realised I was in a place I knew.

I let my head flop back on the pillow and tried to make sense of my life. I had been away on a trip to South America. There had been trouble in a café in Medellín, in Colombia. I chased away these remarkably convincing images, which flashed on and off deceitfully in my head, and made a mental effort. Then I knew, or thought that I knew, that I was in my own bedroom.

Of course, it might not have been my own bedroom. That might have been another one of those odd memories. Of one thing I now felt sure: the voice was Colin's.

'Colin?' I said faintly.

The voice spoke again from somewhere behind me: 'How are you feeling, dear boy?'

'I don't know,' I said. 'Sleepy. Cold.'

There was a pause and then Colin came into view: tall, fair-haired, blue-eyed and good-looking, as slender as when I had first known him at university twenty years ago, his face set in that expression of detached and reproachful kindness that some doctors acquire.

He handed me a glass of water. 'Sip this,' he told me. 'You must be quite dehydrated. We've had you on a drip but there's no substitute for water.'

I sipped the water. It tasted disgusting but I made myself swallow some. After a while I found I could half-sit up on the pillow. I looked around and, after all, the room was familiar. It was my own bedroom.

'How long have I been asleep?' I asked. Colin pulled up a chair. He was wearing a tweed jacket over a checked shirt, a spotted blue tie and twill trousers. On anyone else these clothes would have looked old-fashioned. On Colin almost anything looked elegant. It was a professional asset, I used to think. He made all his patients feel inadequate and so more inclined to do everything that he told them to do. He had been just another unruly medical-school undergraduate when I had first met him, although even then his clean-cut English-public-schoolboy looks had marked him out as different from the parade of spots, straggly beards and unwashed ringlets that had characterised many of the rest of us.

Then he had managed to find a position in a practice in Pimlico; a couple of years later he had married the daughter of a very wealthy family of London *rentiers* and bought into a private practice in Eaton Place. His patients included most of the ruling families in the Middle East, the Ukraine and Russia. He had taken me on a couple of years ago, for old times' sake.

'You haven't been asleep. You've been in a coma.'

I stared straight ahead of me at a picture on the opposite wall. I found it too much of an effort to turn and look at Colin, after the first glance. My eyes roved up to gaze at the ceiling and somehow, wouldn't stop looking at it.

'A coma?' I replied. 'Isn't that the same thing as being asleep? – only for a long time?'

Colin took my wrist, felt for my pulse and said nothing,

but I knew he would be looking at his watch. After a time he dropped my arm as if it had lost any further interest for him, and asked, 'Do you remember anything about where you were and what you were doing before you woke up just now?'

Instantly the bees started humming in my head. Fragments of experience crowded in at the gates of my memory, clamouring for my attention. I had arrived in Bogotá on the Avianca flight from Medellín. I had had to leave Medellín in a hurry, but I couldn't recall exactly why, in my present state, and somehow I felt thankful that I couldn't. Someone had been following me in Medellín, and the same someone was following me in Bogotá. I went into one of the better hotels and whoever it was did not like to come in after me and I managed to get out of the side entrance and go down a back street. But then a few blocks from the hotel I heard hurrying footsteps behind me, echoing in the street, and that smell I had noticed in Medellín. I hadn't liked the smell. I hadn't liked it at all. I turned, but the street was empty behind me. The pavements gleamed slick with recent rain. I could taste the fear in my mouth. Then I remembered another taste: the spice and caramel of Pétrus; and I remembered how I had been drinking some of the 1982 only a moment or so ago.

'I think I was in a restaurant,' I told Colin. 'Drinking some wine.'

'Yes,' said Colin, 'you were. You were drinking quite a lot of wine, they tell me.'

'It was Pétrus,' I said simply.

Colin said, in a sharper tone of voice, 'Wilberforce, look at me.'

I wanted to look at Colin, and explain to him how good the wine had been, but I found I could not move my gaze from the ceiling. It seemed like too much trouble to move my eyes.

'I'm OK as I am,' I said.

'You're not OK,' replied Colin. I heard his chair scrape as he pushed it back and then he walked around to the front of the bed. Now I had to look at him, or rather the top of his head. My eyes still refused to travel down as far as his face.

'We both know you are in an advanced stage of alcoholic addiction,' said Colin, in his most reasonable voice. 'After all, I've been telling you for some time how it would end, and you haven't really ever tried to deal with this.'

'I have tried,' I said. 'I did the Twelve Steps when you booked me into the Hermitage. I did the detox, and the rehab. I did all those things, but it always seemed such a waste not to drink some of the wine Francis gave me. I'm not an alcoholic. I just love Bordeaux.'

Colin shook his head and looked at his watch again. 'There's a nurse downstairs,' he told me. 'She's called Susan. I've arranged for her to stay here for a few days. She'll look after you and I've told her to make sure you have no alcohol. At the moment a drink – any alcoholic drink – might well kill you. I've got a consultation to go to, and then I'm going back to my office to get the results of some tests we did on you when they brought you home. I'll come back this evening to see how you're getting on, and we'll see what the tests can tell us. Meanwhile, stay in bed, and keep as warm as possible. Nurse Susan will come up shortly to make sure you are all right.'

He gave me his kind and empty smile again, and then left the room. I heard him go down the stairs and then the front door was slammed briskly shut.

I lay in my bed feeling awful. The sense of confusion was beginning to lift but everything seemed to be in a faint haze – not just in my mind: my vision had been affected and the room looked as if a fog had crept in through the windows, blurring and dimming the outlines of everything that I looked at. I shook my head to clear it, but it did not clear. After a while I found that I could move my gaze from the curious, locked position it had assumed, managed to look down at the bed I lay in, and noticed the sticking plaster on the back of my left hand where the drip had gone in. I could hear someone boiling a kettle downstairs. My hearing seemed to have sharpened commensurately with the blurring of my vision.

I felt cold. I could feel the warmth coming from the radiators, yet it did not penetrate. I felt a deep chill, and shivered and pulled the bedclothes closer around me. How long had Colin said I had been asleep for? I tried to remember what I had been doing whenever it was I had fallen asleep. It was ridiculous to use a word like 'coma'. Colin was always trying to intimidate me with medical claptrap of that sort, but it cut no ice with me. And another thing: referring to wine as 'alcohol' was so insensitive and crass I could only imagine he did it to annoy me.

Thinking about wine reminded me again about the Pétrus. How glorious that had been! I tried to remember where, and when, I had drunk it. All that I could recall was that Catherine had been there, and she had sung to me while I sipped the wonderful, heady wine.

Thinking about sipping the wine made me look at the clock on the bedside table, and I saw it was eleven in the morning. By now on any normal day I would be at least halfway through my first bottle. That was another reason it was wrong to describe me as an alcoholic: an alcoholic wouldn't care whether his wine came from a box or a bottle. He wouldn't wait until he had breakfast before he drank; his first drink would *be* breakfast. He would not sip what he drank meditatively, sometimes making tasting notes in a little black leather book bought from Smythsons. That was what I did. My drinking was, I supposed, capable of being described as a form of mania, but no different from collecting butterflies, or birds' eggs, or rare books. Perhaps it was a more expensive mania than some, but it was the same passion: to know, to possess, everything that could be known about, or obtained for, one's collection.

At that moment the person Colin had referred to as 'Nurse Susan' came into my bedroom carrying a cup of tea. I loathe tea. I could smell its hideous bouquet. I could smell, almost taste, the tannin, the unpleasing chalky notes of lactose from the milk she had splashed into it, the sickly undertones of sugar beet from the teaspoonfuls of white sugar she had shovelled into the cup. I felt nauseous.

Nurse Susan was a brisk-looking middle-aged lady in a white uniform. She saw that I was awake and said, 'Now then, how are we?' She spoke with the sharp accents of North-East England, which I remembered from a different era of my life.

I muttered something.

'What you need is a nice hot cup of sweet tea,' she told me firmly. Immediately, the nausea overwhelmed me and I started to retch. Before I could bring anything up, Nurse Susan had miraculously put the cup of tea down on the bedside table and produced from somewhere a plastic bowl and a damp towel. She had the bowl in position as I threw up into it, the beads of sweat starting from my forehead and running down my cheeks. Then she mopped my face with the towel and took the bowl away, returning in a second with a glass of water.

'There now, petal, just drink this. I've put something in it to calm your stomach down.'

I tried to take the glass but my hands were trembling too violently, so she held it to my lips and I managed to take a few sips. At first I thought I was going to be sick again, but I wasn't, and after a while my feelings returned to something like normal.

When I could speak I said, 'Please take the tea away.'

'It would do you a lot of good, petal, if you drank it.'

'I can't stand the smell of it.'

Nurse Susan shook her head doubtfully, but she took the tea away.

As she was about to leave the room I called, 'Nurse?'

She stopped and turned to see what I wanted.

'In the kitchen, in the wine rack, you'll find a bottle of Château Yon Figeac 1996. I hope it is the 1996. Could you open it and bring me a large glass of that, please?'

She shook her head. 'No alcohol. Doctor's orders, Mr Wilberforce. It's very naughty of you to even think of such a thing.' Then she left before I could confront her with the very many compelling arguments as to why Colin had no right to stop me drinking wine in my own flat, why it was my body and I could do as I wanted with it, why I had survived perfectly well on a regime of four or five (or maybe five or six) bottles of wine every day of my life for the last few years, and why she could take herself off and go and be more use elsewhere, if she was not prepared to let me take my preferred medicine in my preferred way.

I heard her go downstairs and, a moment later, the sound of the television in the kitchen.

I love wine. I have not always loved it, but I have made up for the woeful ignorance of the first thirty years of my life by the passion and intensity of my relationship with wine ever since. I need to be more precise: I very much like white burgundy, I am fond of some red burgundies, I have flirted with some excellent and intriguing wines from Tuscany; but I adore Bordeaux. When I say wine, I am speaking of red Bordeaux – or claret, as some of us who drink it still call it. I am speaking of the wine that is made from the grape varieties of Cabernet Sauvignon, Merlot, Cabernet Franc and Petit Verdot. I am speaking of vines planted on the light land of Médoc, on the clay levels of St Emilion and Pomerol, on the iron-rich soils of the *terroir* of Pétrus. I am speaking of wines made from a *triage* – a selection of the best berries – of grapes, which are destemmed by a *fouloir égrappoir* and then pumped into the *cuvée*, where fermentation takes place over many anxious days and nights. Then the grape skins are added back in, and maceration takes place for a further ten or fourteen days, adding colour and body to the wine. Once this process is complete, the wine is removed from the vat to the barrel, where it may reside for a further period of two years or more, before it is finally bottled.

All this is chemistry, technology and then, finally, wizardry. You and I might do it by the book and produce something undrinkable despite using the same equipment and the same methods as the great winemakers; but a Jacques Thienpoint or a Christian Moueix can add magic to the process and suddenly the base grape juice is transmuted into something wonderful, even celestial.

Then, as I lay in bed thinking about wine, the familiar restlessness crept upon me once again. I felt a need to keep twitching my arms and legs, as if I had just taken too much exercise, or else not enough. My hands and feet felt chilled. After a while the whole of my body was covered in a light film of perspiration, as if I was weeping through the pores of my skin.

When I experience those sensations, there is only one thing to do and that is have a glass of wine. My regime is to start with a bottle of youngish Bordeaux, between breakfast and lunch time. I find the slight tartness in a young claret leaves the palate clean and sharpened, as if one has been eating gooseberry fool. Thus I prepare myself for lunch, when the more serious wine-tasting begins. I might very probably follow with a second-growth claret over lunch, followed by another fuller-bodied wine at tea time, and finishing off with some great classic *premier cru* vintage with dinner – though recently I have sometimes risked diluting the final explosion of taste with a few glasses of a white burgundy, as a nightcap.

The question was: how was I to manage to drink a glass of wine with this hired nurse wandering around downstairs? I had no doubt she was probably equally well qualified in the martial arts as she was as a nurse, and she would simply stop me, by force if necessary.

I lay considering the problem for a while, but after a few minutes the twitching, restless feeling in all my limbs became so overwhelming that I felt I had to get out of bed and move about. I swung my legs on to the bedside mat and sat on the edge of the bed, collecting my wits. I felt unsteady at first, but managed to take a few steps in the direction of an armchair, where I stopped for a while, like a swimmer grasping a rock for a moment's rest, before continuing my journey. Then I came to my dressing table, with my wallet and my keys upon it, and my money clip, which was empty. I appeared to have spent over six thousand pounds whenever it was I last went out. It must have been the Pétrus. I picked up the wallet and went on to the window, which I opened. I threw my wallet out. Then I went, at a better speed, to the bedroom door and from there to the head of the stairs.

'Nurse Susan!' I called. 'Come quick!'

The television in the kitchen was flicked off and she was immediately at the kitchen door, looking up the stairs at me. 'You shouldn't be out of your bed, flower,' she told me.

'Never mind that.' I replied. 'I was trying to open the window to let some fresh air in and I had my wallet in my hand and I've stupidly dropped it into the street below. Please go and get it before someone picks it up. It has quite a lot of money in it.' As a matter of fact, there was no money in the wallet and the credit cards were probably either out of date or over the limit.

Nurse Susan hesitated, then said, 'You stay there and I'll go and look,' and walked quickly to the door, snicked up the catch and went out.

The thought of the Yon Figeac gave me strength. In a second I was at the foot of the stairs, and in the next moment I had slammed, bolted and triple-locked the door. The downstairs windows were always locked. There was no other way into the house except a door to a little basement area, which I never used.

I went to the wine rack, took the bottle of wine out, and opened it with a swift motion of my Screwpull corkscrew. I thought I would let it breathe for a few moments before I tried it. The doorbell rang, first briefly, and then more persistently. I ignored the sound and thought about the wine. It was a 1996, after all, and could be drunk now or left for as long as ten years. I had not tried this wine before. There were half a dozen bottles of it left in the undercroft. Francis must have opened the case and drunk some, before he left me the cellar. The doorbell had stopped ringing now and there was a tapping at the kitchen window.

I went to the cupboard and found a large wine glass. As I turned to go back to the table I caught sight of Nurse Susan at the kitchen window. She was leaning over the iron railings that protected it and could just reach the window to tap on it lightly with my wallet. When she saw that I had seen her, she smiled and held up my wallet, and mouthed something at me. I couldn't hear it but I think she was saying something like, 'The door has locked itself. Could you let me in?' She didn't look cross. She looked damp, and I realised it must have started to rain outside. Her expression was pleasant, but a trifle crafty, like Mr Wolf at the window of the Three Pigs' house, asking to be let in.

The door had locked itself. Oh, really. I smiled and waved a hand at her, and poured some of the wine into the glass. I put the wine glass down on the table and watched the purple liquid fill the glass. As I swirled the wine, it clung to the sides of the glass for a moment, promising me a voluptuous taste to follow. I sniffed the bouquet. It was – not Pétrus, but still heaven. After a moment's anticipation more, I reached for the glass, raised it and my eyes to the ceiling, and took a single delicate sip.

For a while I continued to stare at the ceiling. I don't know what it was about ceilings, but whenever I looked at them I found it hard to look away. My eyeballs seemed to roll up in my head and then stay there, unmoving. While I was doing this, the tapping at the windows went on for a while longer. Then, after a pause, the telephone started to ring. That went on for quite a long time too. Then there was silence. I managed after a while to detach my gaze from the kitchen ceiling, and at once noticed that Nurse Susan was no longer at the kitchen windows. It was raining quite heavily outside now, and I assumed she had become discouraged and had gone to fetch Colin. But Colin would be busy. His other patients paid a great deal more than I did for his time, no doubt, and he would not break their appointments except in the gravest emergency. I calculated that I had several hours yet before Colin returned to my flat. When he did, I would let him in and explain to him courteously the terms on which our association would continue.

The other thing I noticed was that, despite having only taken a single first sip from my glass of wine, the glass was quite empty and indeed the bottle was more than half empty. I didn't remember drinking the rest of the first glass, let alone the second glass I must have consumed. That was a shame. I poured a little more into my glass and put the empty bottle into the bin. I took a sip again and rolled the liquid around on my palate, to savour its complex flavours to the full.

Then the glass was empty. I looked at my watch, then looked down at myself and realised that I was still wearing pyjamas and a dressing gown at one in the afternoon. I swayed slightly and steadied myself by holding on to the back of the kitchen chair. After a while I made my way upstairs, showered, shaved and dressed in one of my two good suits, put on a cream shirt and a dark tie, then went downstairs to see about lunch.

There wasn't anything except wine in the fridge, but I found a jar of pâté in the store cupboard, and an old box of Ritz crackers. There wasn't much else, but that would do very well. I wondered if I could give Nurse Susan a shopping list when she came back. Then I went downstairs to the little basement room I used as a cellar. It was not, of course, my main cellar. My principal collection of wine was kept in the huge vaulted undercroft of Francis's old house, Caerlyon, and protected by many bolts and alarms. Here in London I only kept a few bottles, perhaps a thousand, for instant drinking, cellared here for a year at most, and constantly restocked when I went on my frequent devotional visits to the main cellar.

I went downstairs and sat and looked at the racks of wine, wondering what to have with the pâté. Of course my first thought was to take a bottle of Gewürztraminer. But then I thought, as I usually drank claret at lunch, it might be wiser not to change my regime too violently, from a medical point of view. In the end, after much debate with myself, and looking at labels, I selected a Château Palmer 1982.

I looked at my watch: it was nearly three o'clock. I must have been down there for more than an hour. I was wasting time. Colin might be here in a couple of hours: barely time for me to finish my lunch-time wine and start to think about what I would drink before dinner.

I went upstairs and opened the Palmer, decanted it, then poured myself a glass. It was still slightly chilled, but by the second sip was almost at room temperature and quite delicious.

Francis used to say to me, 'The first sip is always the best,' and sometimes he would take no more than half a glass from a bottle before pouring the rest away, having extracted a knowledge of the wine from that brief encounter that was sufficient for his needs. My needs were different. I wanted to inhale the wine, to sip it, to drink it. I would have swum in it if I could have. I know that for Francis one of his greatest pleasures was simply to sit and look at it. His cellars and his shop are different now. The shop, of course, is closed. The till no longer rings its antique ring; customers no longer gather there in the hope of a free tasting, or catching up on the gossip about the shooting and the fishing, or the racing; the candles that were always lit within it have long since guttered and gone out. That was where I first met Ed Simmonds, as he then was, who became my friend for a while. Now he is the Marquess of Hartlepool, and we no longer speak, but not because of his accession to the family title.

That was where, in the days of my apprenticeship in wine, I sat beside Francis as his gaze wandered over the thousands upon thousands of bottles in the racks that lined the walls, the piles of wooden cases of wine that formed islands and towers around the enormous room. He would softly murmur a comment here about some château with a name out of Arthurian legend, and he would speak about the great vintages of his parents' and his grandparents' day. The reflected candlelight would glint on the bottles and occasionally he would get up and pull a bottle from a rack and say, 'Look at that. Cocteau painted the original design for that label,' or 'That château no longer exists. The Germans blew it up in the Second World War. This is probably one of the last bottles of this wine in existence and when you, or I, or some ignorant customer drinks it, its whole history will be snuffed out for ever, as if it had never existed.'

His knowledge was more than encyclopaedic. It was like the knowledge that is acquired by a saint or hermit who has spent all of his life studying the gospels. He knew everything: every grower, every shipper, every vintage, every *terroir*, every *clos*. Even now, after those evenings of listening to him, after devotedly reading all the classic works on wine, even going at one point to evening classes, my knowledge is not to be compared to Francis's. His knowledge of wine was like a great panorama of enormous, snow-capped mountains. My knowledge in comparison was like a molehill at the feet of the foothills of those mountains. When Francis died, the world little knew or cared what knowledge died with him. His wine lives on: the bottles sit in their racks, and the timeless vintages age more slowly than men do. Even so I know that now some of them are dying, leaving the long plateau of their mature years and descending slowly towards a vinegary graveyard. Some bottles are already dead, turned from rich dark red to a thin brown, acetic liquid. When Francis himself lay dying, he warned me that one day the wine would start to die as well.

I can't drink it all, try as I might. It would be a breach of a sacred trust to sell any. In any case, I could not bear to part with a single bottle. I will drink what I can while life remains in me.

'You were a little tough on poor Nurse Susan,' said Colin, sipping his cup of tea. Nurse Susan was at the sink, washing up the plates I had used for lunch. She could have used the dishwasher but she explained she didn't want to waste all that electricity for a few plates.

'Oh, don't mind about me, flower; worse things happen at sea,' said Nurse Susan, turning and grinning at me over her shoulder. I sat drinking the remains of my tea-time bottle.

'I told you not to drink that stuff,' said Colin, 'but I suppose you can't help yourself.'

'Colin,' I told him, 'it's not a matter of "can't help". It's a matter of choice. I choose to drink wine. It is my hobby, as you well know.'

'Yes, well,' said Colin, 'you no doubt have a perfectly good set of reasons for going on doing what you are doing. Addicts always do.'

There was a silence. Colin looked at his watch. He measured out the minutes of his day as carefully as I tried to measure out my glasses of wine.

'About those tests,' he said. I braced myself for the usual lecture. 'Most of it is nothing new,' Colin went on. 'You have all the gastrointestinal problems one would expect. You have acid reflux into the oesophagus, which might tend towards producing cancer in a few years' time, if you don't get it somewhere else first. Your cholesterol level is extremely high, because of free radicals. In layman's terms, your liver is disintegrating and as it does so your cholesterol level goes up, increasing the risk of a stroke or heart attack. I dread to think what the condition of your bowels is.'

'Not great,' I admitted.

'Are you taking any of the tablets I gave you for any of those things?' asked Colin.

'No, they made the wine taste odd, so I threw them away.'

'Then you have a lot of the other symptoms of alcoholism, such as sweating, weight loss, and mental confusion. You're sweating now – rather a lot, as it happens.'

I wanted to stand up and open a window, but it seemed

like too much effort; so I simply said, 'It's very hot in the kitchen.'

'Why are you dressed up in a suit?' asked Colin. 'Are you going to a meeting?'

'No, I just wanted to make an effort.'

Colin drummed his fingers on the table, then moved his chair around and said, 'You're not looking me in the eye.'

'I know,' I said. 'I can't help it. My eyes seem to be wandering a bit since I woke up this morning.'

Colin took a small torch from the leather bag that he always carried, and came and shone it in both of my eyes. He peered into them. I flinched. He went and sat down again and said, 'Do you know how alcohol works?'

There he went again. 'Stop calling it alcohol,' I said. 'This isn't chemistry; this is wine we're talking about.'

'Well, *I'm* talking about chemistry. Actually I want to tell you about brain chemistry. No, just listen for a few minutes, while you can still understand some of what I tell you. The kind of habitual drinking you indulge in is no different in degree from the addiction of a heroin addict. In both cases the brain becomes progressively more damaged, probably irreversibly, by an excessive consumption of a harmful substance. Your ability to produce important neurotransmitters, such as dopamine or serotonin, is being damaged. Dopamine is the neurotransmitter that enables you to feel either pain or pleasure. In your case, your tolerance of pain is growing: you never complain to me about your physical state, which must be becoming more wretched every day. A normal person would be asking to be admitted to hospital if they felt like you must feel.'

'Thanks,' I said.

'Don't be flippant,' admonished Colin. He held up a finger as if to place it against my lips, to seal them, but he lowered it again and said, 'The sad part is that your ability to feel pleasure is disappearing at the same rate, perhaps for ever. The pleasure you think you feel in drinking wine is, on the whole, a delusional construct. Another thing that is happening to you is the destruction of your ability to produce serotonin. That's the happy chemical. If you don't have enough of it, you become depressed, you take more of whatever your poison is to counter that depression, and you get into a loop that eventually kills you, but not before you experience the most utter wretchedness it is possible to feel. That's part of what is going on in your nervous system right now, and you won't do anything to stop it. Maybe you don't want to. I'm not a psychiatrist.'

There was a silence while I tried to take in what Colin had just told me.

'You mean, I'm not very well?'

'Yes,' said Colin gently, and for the first time his smile disappeared and a rare look of concern replaced it; for the first time I felt real worry about what he had been telling me. The worst thing was that I had already forgotten most of what he had just said. 'Yes,' Colin repeated, 'you're not well. In fact you are dying, although whether you will die tonight, or next week, or next year, I can't tell. I imagine we will need to hospitalise you in a year at the latest, based on your present test results. I hope you still have plenty of money and can afford to go private. It would be a fairly grim outlook in the NHS. Victims of self-abuse are low on their priority list just now.'

'Don't worry about my money,' I said: 'I've got endless amounts of the stuff. And don't worry about hospital. I'm drinking the healthiest drink invented by man: red wine. I think I know a thing or two about this as well, you know.'

'Have you ever been to Colombia?' asked Colin.

'What?' I asked, startled by the abrupt change of subject. But as Colin spoke I was somehow in two places at once. In my kitchen, in my home, it was warm and stuffy and Nurse was next door in my sitting room, watching television; Colin was drumming his fingers again, waiting for my reply. At the same moment I was walking quickly along a rain-soaked street in Bogotá. It was always raining in Bogotá – never for too long, but it never stopped for long either. The pavements were slick with rain and the lights of passing cars gleamed on the wet stone. I was heading for the Hotel Bogotá Plaza. I had just flown in on the Avianca flight from Medellín, and I'd had the taxi drop me two blocks from my hotel in case anyone had picked up on me at the airport. Footsteps echoed behind me, and in the silences between their echoes I thought I could smell that awful odour of putrefaction. It was probably nothing.

'Why do you ask?' I said again.

'You talked about it a lot while you were out for the count: about travelling to Bogotá from Medellín, and about people following you. It sounded like a bad script for a bad movie except that you went into a creepy amount of detail.'

'I've never been to Colombia in my entire life – as far as I know,' I said.

'As far as you know,' said Colin. 'I mean, you would know, wouldn't you? You don't travel ten thousand miles to another continent and then forget you've been there – do you?'

'I don't know what I mean,' I said angrily. 'You're confusing me. Why are we talking about Colombia?'

'We're really talking about why *you* were talking about Colombia.'

I gave up and said, 'Look, is there anything else I should know?'

Colin got to his feet and said, 'I'm sending Nurse Susan away now. There doesn't seem any point in having her here if you don't want her.'

'Nothing personal,' I said.

'There's something else wrong with you,' said Colin, abruptly. 'It's not a condition I have ever come across before, and I need to talk to a specialist I know before I can confirm my opinion. I hope I'm wrong.'

'You're being very depressing, Colin,' I told him. I tried to smile but couldn't.

'I'll call again tomorrow if you're in – at about this time?'

'I'm always in,' I said.

Three

When I had told Colin that I had endless amounts of money to pay my medical bills, I was being optimistic about my financial position. I used to have a lot of money, which I made from the sale of the software-development business I had built up. We had been going to take the company public, on the AIM market, but a trade buyer had nipped in at the last minute, offering a reasonable price. I ended up with a small fortune when the sale went through. The company that bought us gave my job as managing director to Andy, my finance director, and I resigned. I wasn't enjoying it any more, in any case. I didn't think I needed the salary, and I felt sure Andy did not want me to stay on. He had not wanted me to sell the company in the first place. So I left.

Some of the money went on buying Caerlyon, Francis's family home, from his executors, including the vast store of wine in the undercroft beneath it. I spent a lot more buying the flat in Half Moon Street in London, for Catherine and me to live in.

In the last few years I seemed to have run through a huge amount of money, passing interesting wine-tasting evenings like the one I had just spent somewhere or other with a bottle or two of Château Pétrus. If you go out twice a week, and spend several thousand pounds on dinner and wine, it adds up after a while. Apart from the spending of my walking-around money of five or ten thousand pounds a week, other expenses were mounting up: Colin's medical bills, for example. In the last two years, when Colin and one or two other members of my rapidly shrinking circle of acquaintances had pestered me, I had found myself splashing out on visits to health farms and drying-out clinics such as the Hermitage. I'd given that up now as a waste of time and money – time and money that could be better spent on Bordeaux.

All of this came to mind the following morning, when I was sitting at my desk in my sitting room, sipping a glass of Château Carbonnieux and reading a letter from my bank manager. It had been on the kitchen table for some days now, but I had learned, after having had the telephone and the electricity cut off a couple of times, that eventually one does have to get around to reading one's post, especially anything in a brown envelope or from a bank.

The letter enquired after my health, and then went on to remark: 'Your current overdraft of £50,327.09 is above the limit of £30,000 that was previously agreed. Unfortunately this means the Bank has had to charge an unauthorised-overdraft interest rate of 7 per cent. Please can you advise us at the earliest possible opportunity of when you will be able to remit funds into the account to reduce borrowings to below the agreed limit?' The letter closed with the friendliest possible good wishes from the odious Mr Rawle, my Personal Banking Relationship Manager. Nevertheless, the tone of menace was unmistakable.

I found a felt-tipped pen and wrote on the letter: 'Please increase overdraft limit to one hundred thousand pounds. Thanks, Wilberforce.' Then I found both an envelope and a stamp in my desk and addressed the letter back to Mr Rawle.

I had forgotten I had started to go into overdraft. I was so used to having my account in credit, and just dipping into it for my weekly walking-around money, that it had seemed impossible I might ever be in debt. Now that griping anxiety came back to me that I remembered from the early days of my business, when we'd had to drive around to collect cheques from our customers and then go straight to the bank to cash them, just to keep on the right side of insolvency.

I opened the next letter, but it was only from some restaurant advising me that, following the recent unfortunate incident when I was dining with them, they regretted that they would be unable to accept any further reservations from me. I couldn't remember anything about it, except that someone – not me – had been wearing very highly polished black shoes. In any case, there was no problem. If I wanted to go back, I would just make the reservation in the name of Francis Black. Then they could go and stand beside his grave and complain all they wanted to.

I returned to the more pressing problem of money, and poured myself another glass of wine to help me think. The only thought that occurred to me was that I had better sell some more shares and transfer the money I raised to the bank. I rang my stockbroker and said, when I got through to him, 'Chris, I need to sell some shares.'

'Good morning, Wilberforce,' he said. 'How are you?'

I had forgotten that Christopher Templeton was quite old-fashioned and one had to go through the 'How's the weather? How are the children?' small talk before one could get down to business. He had originally been an adviser when we were thinking of floating my company on the stock market and, when we didn't, I had given him some of my money to look after to make up for all the professional fees he hadn't earned.

'Never better. How's the family?'

'Oh, very well, thank you. Ivor is in the first eleven now and Maria . . .' and he went on for some minutes with tedious details about his children whom I had once met when he asked me go to Lord's to watch the cricket with him, in that period when I had had, for a while, a social life.

After a while he must have detected a lack of sufficient

enthusiasm in my 'Oh, really?' responses, and said in a brisker tone, 'How much were you wanting to raise, and by when?'

'A hundred thousand would suit me, by the end of this week, if possible.'

'Well, it's Friday today, so that might be difficult.'

'Oh, is it?'

'Just a second, while I get your account details up on the screen.' There was a pause and some tapping noises in the background and then Chris said, in a different tone of voice, 'Wilberforce, you haven't got a hundred thousand pounds with us. I hadn't looked at your account for a while, but I see there have been regular sales and the balance has been reducing for a couple of years now.'

I paused to think. The information was disappointing, but not unexpected. I said, 'Well, what can I raise?'

'It depends on the market. You have some BP, and some Glaxo Smith Kline – both very good quality stocks. You'd probably get about fifty thousand. And then that's the last of it.'

'Please sell them, then.'

Chris said, 'You'll have quite a big capital-gains tax bill on both of those trades.'

I thought that I would worry about that when the time came. I thanked Chris for his help and asked him to close my account when the sale was done. There was some unenthusiastic talk of meeting up for a drink one day, but I don't think Chris really meant it. I know I didn't. Why go out for a drink, and risk drinking some wine bar's ghastly house red, when you can drink real wine in the comfort of your own home?

I went on opening the pile of brown envelopes that had accumulated over the last few days, putting them into two piles: those that had to be paid if I was to continue to enjoy the provision of basic services such as heat and light; and those that could wait until the next demand. Finally I came to one from Her Majesty's Revenue and Customs Capital Taxes Office. I opened it, as I always opened letters from this source, with a certain amount of apprehension. It asked for immediate payment of tax overdue of fifty thousand pounds on share sales last year, plus interest running on the late payment.

I sat at my desk, and again felt chilled and damp with sweat. I had just sold the last shares in a portfolio which had once run well into seven figures and had been intended as my pension fund. According to Colin, I was unlikely ever to live until I reached pensionable age so perhaps that was not a problem after all. But I had hoped to win a few weeks', or even a few months', grace from the conversation I had just had with Chris Templeton. Now it seemed as if the last of my capital would go into my account in five days' time, and leave it again just as fast.

I finished the bottle of wine and sat for a while thinking about my life. The trouble with spending a lot of money, when one didn't have any income, was that it only worked for a time. That time had come. It had been a long while since I had been able to think clearly about my future and I wasn't sure I was able to start now. I decided to go for a walk to clear my head, to post my letters and the paid bills, and to buy something to eat from the shop on the corner of Curzon Street. Then I checked my wallet, the one that Nurse Susan had kindly returned after I threw it out of the window. It contained three out-of-date credit cards and no cash. I knew my money clip had nothing in it. With some apprehension, I realised I was first going to have to walk down to St James's Street to my bank and cash a cheque.

When Francis's executors offered me Caerlyon Hall, I said

yes, as I had promised Francis I would. The main house and grounds had been let on a long lease to the Council, as a Community Outreach Centre. One wing at the back of the house with a couple of bedrooms, a sitting room and a large kitchen had been kept by Francis for his own use, and so had the huge vault beneath the house, which so resembled the crypt of a church that Francis called it 'the undercroft'. I had also promised Francis I would take back the main house from the Council, and make my home there, but that part of the promise I have not, so far, fulfilled. It does not look likely that I will ever live there now. Things have changed. Francis had no right to expect me to take on the burden of his house as well as his cellar. He had no right to extract a promise from me, although he did.

The undercroft itself was a huge Elizabethan vaulted cellar, which went right under the house. It was reached by going into a small stone building next to the stable block and down wide stone stairs to a large antechamber. That was where Francis had spent most of his life – in his 'shop'. The shop area was where Francis displayed the wine he wanted to sell. The undercroft beyond was where he kept the wine he wanted to drink. The undercroft consisted of a central room, about fifty yards long, with chambers opening off it every few yards, like side chapels in a cathedral. In the main vaulted chamber Francis stacked the cased wine he had inherited or accumulated over the last forty years. There were several thousand wooden cases of wine, piled one on top of another, so that the effect was like a nineteenth-century city, a grid of great avenues and lateral side streets between the cases. There was no order, no system. Margaux was piled on top of Pomerol, St Emilion on top of Médoc; 1982s were stacked on top of 1998s and no one except Francis could ever have found anything. I have tried drawing a map of this cellar and, to an extent, I have succeeded. I have an approximate idea of the location, vintage and château of about half the wine I now own. The rest is a mystery to me – an exploration in progress. It might take me the rest of my life to find all the wine I own; it might take me longer than the rest of my life. My map is not complete; it could never be complete, for there is simply too much there to remember.

Francis had an eidetic memory. If he had once seen that he had a case of Château Latour 1979 resting on top of a case of Sauternes, he would remember for ever the position of each and, if you asked him about either of those wines, he could lead you straight to it.

In the side chambers were the special wines, behind locked iron grilles. There were pre-phylloxera Imperial Tokays; Châteaux Yquem from the 1880s; bottles of ancient port; odds and ends, collector's dreams that might have been sold for the most enormous sums at auction. They will never go to auction now. Francis could never part with a bottle of wine he really loved, and neither will I. I thought about it once, but I would never do it. I could not bring myself to do it. Francis was my friend. To sell his wine would be a betrayal. There has been enough betrayal . . .

I remember the first time I went to Caerlyon – such an odd name: a remnant of the Dark Ages, before the Saxon and Dutch settlements. Caerlyon had survived and kept its identity intact, an island in the flood tide of Saxon and then Danish place names that arrived after the Romans left. The present version of the house was early Victorian, I believe, but there had been settlements in that place since the Bronze Age: Roman, medieval, an Elizabethan house. The Victorian house had been built in the days of the Black family's greatest prosperity, when they had mined the rich coal seams that lay under the poor farmland that had sustained them in earlier centuries. That evening I had left my office as usual at about half past seven in the evening. My office, a miracle of black glass and marble, was in almost the last building at the edge of a modern industrial estate, south-west of Newcastle. It was an evening in late May. It was the time when I normally left work in order to get to the local shopping centre to buy a pizza or some other form of instant nourishment before all the shops shut. I would buy whatever pre-cooked meal came to hand, go home, microwave it and eat it, sit in front of a computer for an hour or two and then try to get five or six hours' sleep before heading back to the office around five in the morning.

I still remember what a beautiful evening it was, with the magical light that occurs as spring changes into early summer. The sky was a pale pink, shading to a light green, which hinted of the Aurora. The industrial estate where I worked, a wilderness of aluminium sheds and modern glass-and-brick palaces like my own offices, was eating slowly into the side of a green hill. At the top of the hill, green pasture shaded into brown and rushy fell. For no reason, I turned off the road to the shopping mall and went up a little lane, driving up the side of the hill instead of along its base, towards the pale edge of the evening sky, as if there was a message waiting for me at the top of the escarpment. The offices and the factories below were already shrouded in the gloom of approaching night. I thought that it might be pleasant to see the last of the evening sunlight, as if I had, for a moment, sickened of all those years of neon-lit offices.

At the top of the hill, which I had driven up with some spirit in the Range Rover that I had bought for myself that year – the first (and last) expensive car I ever owned – I pulled in to the side of the road. Beyond me was a different land-scape of small farms and allotments rising up to the great brown slopes of the Pennine moors. Just beyond where I had stopped the car was a little lane, with a brown sign pointing down it, and in white lettering the words 'Caerlyon Hall'. I felt light of heart. I was breaking my routine, and I found that it was refreshing. I made a promise to myself that I would give it another ten minutes, then would turn around to go and buy my pizza and put in my couple of hours working on a new computer program. I turned the car down the lane through a planting of dark trees, and there in front of me was an enormous grey house. The drive gates were locked and barred and a sign said, 'Gateshead County Council: Community Outreach Centre'.

I drove along the lane beside a high stone wall. The lane seemed to head towards the back parts of the house. After a hundred yards I found an opening in the wall that led into a cobbled courtyard, with stables and outbuildings. A large 'A' board was positioned by the side of the road: in gold Palace script on a burgundy-coloured background it announced: 'Francis Black: Fine Bordeaux Wines. Visitors welcome.'

I remember feeling a little like Alice must have felt when she found the table at the bottom of the rabbit hole, with the little bottle labelled 'DRINK ME'. She knew very well that it would be wiser not to drink it, but strange things had already started to happen to her since she'd fallen asleep in the garden that afternoon, and seen the white rabbit and decided to follow him into Wonderland. So she thought, Well, why not? Looking back, now, I feel that the unexpected image that then came into my mind of a dimly remembered book from my childhood, that subconscious association of the burgundy-coloured sign with the bottle that Alice found labelled 'DRINK ME', was one of those irreversible moments in my life. I had other such moments later, but that was the first stage of my journey out of the world I knew. I turned my back on the safe world of pizzas and expensive cars and accountancy and computer-programming, with one innocent, unpremeditated step: the beginning of a journey that left that world behind for ever. So I thought, Well, why not? I pulled the car in to the side of the road, turned off the ignition and got out, feeling the evening sunlight warm upon my cheeks, smelling the sweet and woody smell of heather blowing in from the distant hills; and I sauntered in the general direction of Francis Black and his fine Bordeaux wines.

I walked down Piccadilly and turned into St James's Street. As I passed the steps of one of the three gentlemen's clubs at that end of St James's, Ed Hartlepool, who was once close to me, a member of the circle of friends who adopted me and for a while were almost my family, came out of the door of his club and stood at the top of the steps down to the street, taking in the scenery. I was surprised to see him: Catherine had told me he had been forced to go and live in France as a tax exile and only came back to England for a few weeks a year. He looked the same as when I had last seen him: tall, very thin, in an immaculate navy-blue double-breasted suit, the whole effect set off by a shock of unmanageable curly fair hair starting from the top of his head. He turned to answer a comment from a large person behind him, which obviously amused him, for as he turned his head back in the direction of the street he was smiling. Then he saw me, and his smile vanished immediately. I half-acknowledged him with raised eyebrows: we were only yards apart, and I wondered if he, in his turn, would notice my presence in some way, making it necessary for me to say something to him. He said nothing; he cut me dead, looking at me and through me as if I was made from glass. I had not seen or spoken to Ed since Catherine's funeral. Then, as I had entered the church on my crutches, he had gazed at me with a look of such deadly hatred that it had turned my legs almost to jelly. When I saw his look I had had to steady myself in order to avoid losing my balance. That had been rather an emotional occasion, and I couldn't think now why Ed should have looked at me like that, or spoken to me in the way he did just after the service finished. Everyone knew that Catherine's death hadn't been my fault.

It was unsettling to see Ed again, to think he haunted this street so near to where I lived. I averted my gaze from him and hurried on towards my bank and, as I did, I heard a short, hard laugh behind me. I did not turn my head.

Once in the bank I presented my cheque and, not entirely to my surprise, there was a delay. Then my Personal Relationship Manager, Mr Rawle, came to the counter and said, 'Good afternoon, Mr Wilberforce, good afternoon.'

'Hello, Mr Rawle,' I said. 'Is everything in order?'

'Oh, yes, everything is more or less in order. Perhaps if we could just have a quiet word over at my desk?' He rubbed his hands and looked sideways at me with soft and pleading eyes, like a spaniel in a pinstripe suit.

I followed him over to a screened-off area of the banking parlour and sat opposite him at his desk. I found that my eyes strayed up towards the ceiling, and locked on it, so that Mr Rawle had to talk to my chin.

'Mr Wilberforce, I wonder if you received a letter I sent you, about your account?'

I said yes, I had, and I had taken steps to put funds into my account.

'Oh, excellent news, excellent,' said Mr Rawle, rubbing his hands until I wondered if they might catch fire. 'Might I ask what amount of funds?'

I said, as carelessly as I could, that I had moved fifty thousand across for the time being.

'Are there any other pressing liabilities just at present?' asked Mr Rawle.

A small tax bill. How much? I couldn't exactly remember. I managed to detach my eyes from the ceiling and speak directly to Mr Rawle, rather than to one of his ceiling lights.

Would it be all right if the bank cashed my cheque now, as I had an appointment?

Mr Rawle stood up, and almost bowed, and said, 'A cheque for how much, Mr Wilberforce?'

'Just the usual five thousand pounds,' I said, trying to recapture the old insouciance with which I had asked for such sums of money in the past.

But Mr Rawle shook his head sadly. 'I'm terribly sorry, but until the cheque you spoke of has been cleared and the funds are in your account, I don't have the authority. I can let you have a thousand, I suppose.'

'It's very inconvenient,' I told him.

He bowed again but would not give in. 'I'm so sorry, Mr Wilberforce. I'm so sorry, but there it is.'

It ended with me writing another cheque for one thousand pounds, and then Mr Rawle took it personally to the cashier and stood there while they counted out the fifties – in case they gave me one too many, I suppose. Then he ushered me to the door, and I went back out into the street feeling rather unsettled. There was a humming, like bees in my head again.

I had just arrived in Bogotá on the Avianca flight from Medellín. I had been there for several weeks in unsatisfactory discussions with representatives of FARC, the narco-terrorist group that had recently been taking European hostages in Colombia. The current list included three French tourists, two Brit backpackers, and two employees of BP Colombia. The latter were insured at Lloyd's of London, which is why I was there. The idea was to do a deal on ransom, but for the last few days I had been feeling increasingly uneasy about the negotiations. I had no proof of life. The FARC representative wanted me to trust him. He wouldn't, or couldn't, offer any evidence that any of these people were still alive. That meant either that they had been killed, which I thought was unlikely because that would be a very uncommercial thing for FARC to do; or it might mean the little weasel-faced man who called himself an FARC representative had nothing to do with them at all. He might be from the cartels, or some other group wanting to make money from the situation.

I know that when he proposed a change of venue for our daily conversations, somewhere just outside of the city, I decided that it was likely he and his friends had decided I mightn't be a bad bargaining counter myself. I thought they would probably set up a kidnap attempt of some sort the next day, so I rang London on the satellite phone to explain the position, and we agreed I should head back to Bogotá for a few days and get away from the front line.

There was something else that happened in Medellín, though – something very unsettling; but I couldn't remember what it was. There was a smell, and there was a sense of something or someone always on the edge of my vision.

In the taxi from the airport we stopped at traffic lights; there was a rapping at the taxi window and I almost had heart failure. It was only one of the street children selling cartons of Pall Mall cigarettes, either fake or contraband. We drove up the hill away from the city centre towards the Bogotá Plaza Hotel: the pavements were slick with rain and the headlights of passing traffic made gleaming reflections in them.

Some instinct made me stop the taxi a few hundred metres before we got to the hotel. I wanted to walk; I wanted to see if any other taxi or car behind me stopped, or whether anyone would follow me. It was not far to the hotel; it was a relatively safe part of town and the streets were usually busy.

I got out and paid off the driver, picked up my bag from the back of the taxi, and started to walk up one of the streets that runs parallel to the main avenue, which brings you out in a small park at the back of the hotel.

In fact, the street was deserted, but as I walked along it I heard the hurrying echoes of other footsteps. Startled, I turned around. There was no one behind me. I walked on and then stopped again. In front of me, in the middle of the road, was a manhole cover. I was walking up the middle of the street, avoiding its shadowed edges, when the manhole cover started to rotate. A second later it tipped out of its seat and was pushed aside into the road. Two small and very grimy children, dressed in assorted rags, climbed out. More street children: there were thousands of them said to be living in the rain drains beneath the city. Every now and then the police went looking for them and culled a few, and they vanished into the foul drains, where no one would ever follow them. These two scrambled out into the street. They saw me, decided I was not dangerous and approached with outstretched hands, begging for money. They spoke a few words in a patois of Indian and Spanish that I could not follow, but the meaning was clear.

I was just getting out a banknote to give them when one of them looked behind me and said, '*Quién viene detrás de ese hombre?*' and the other replied, '*No me gusta la pinta que tiene. Vámanos.*'

They both ran off into the dark, without taking the money I was offering. I smelled the smell of mould and rottenness, and I saw the flap of some dark garment in the corner of my eye. As I did so, the meaning of what they had just said arranged itself in my mind: 'Who is that walking behind the man?' 'I don't like the look of it. Let's get out of here.'

I turned about in a hurry and walked straight into the arms of the person who was following me.

The person I had bumped into caught my elbow, and steadied me. 'Whoa,' he said. 'Take it easy!' It was Colin. He did not let go of my elbow, but steered me to the side of the road, and back to the pavement.

I felt dislocated in time and space. I couldn't remember who I was, or where I had just been.

Colin spoke again, and the sound of his voice dispelled some of the confusion. 'What were you thinking of?' he asked, '– *walking* down the middle of the road? There were half a dozen taxis honking their horns behind you. I think they had just about decided to run you over. We had an appointment this afternoon, remember?'

I didn't remember, but I followed Colin gratefully to my own front door in Half Moon Street. My heart was still thumping from the shock of bumping into him. I must have been daydreaming. He helped me find my keys and we let ourselves in. Coming in from the street I realised with a shock that the house smelt bad: stale air, wine lees, a smell of mould coming from somewhere. For the last few weeks I had done without a cleaner. In part it was to save money but also I had done something to upset the agency that sent the cleaners, possibly as a result of forgetting to pay them.

We went into the kitchen; I saw Colin wrinkle his nose and look at the stack of unwashed crockery and glasses beside the sink. 'Don't you ever tidy up?' he asked. He pulled out one of the chairs at the kitchen table, flicked some dust from it with his handkerchief, and then sat down.

'I'm going to have a glass of wine,' I said. 'Would you like one?'

'I'll join you, if it helps,' said Colin. 'Maybe a drink would do you good, for once. You were as white as a sheet when I bumped into you just now. Who did you think I was?'

'Oh, just somebody I didn't want to meet.'

I went to the wine rack and took a bottle of Château Cheval Blanc 1953 from it, opened it and poured a glass each. The wine tasted thin, spiritless. I sniffed it but could smell nothing and said to Colin, 'I'm so sorry. I think this bottle might be corked.'

'Tastes perfectly all right to me,' remarked Colin.

Perfectly all right! The wine I served was never 'all right'. The wines from my cellar were amongst the rarest wines, the finest vintages, that had ever been assembled under one roof. The Cheval Blanc 1953 was over fifty years old now, one of the few clarets of that age that could still be drunk, which had not yet oxidised. It was another wine of which I now had only one or two more bottles left. I took Colin's glass from him and opened a bottle of Fitou. It was the only other red wine in the kitchen that would be close to room temperature – an oddity that I had found in the undercroft that must have been one of Francis's more recent and whimsical additions to his collection. I poured both glasses and the rest of the bottle of Château Cheval Blanc down the sink. Then I refilled our glasses with the second wine. It tasted much the same to me, but I said nothing.

Colin sipped his wine and said, 'Quite a jolly red wine. A bit more taste to it than the first one, though there was nothing much wrong with that.'

I bit my lip, said nothing and waited for Colin to tell me why he was here, because I could not remember.

'I took your test results to a neurologist friend of mine. He's had a look, and I've discussed some of your symptoms with him,' said Colin.

'What symptoms?'

'You have quite acute ocular ataxia, and gaze-evoked nystagmus.'

'Do you want to put that in English?'

'You can't control your eye movements, some of the time. You're doing it now.'

'No, I'm not,' I said, but I could not withdraw my gaze from the ceiling when I spoke.

'Another thing is: you seem to have these periods of mental confusion. I think I interrupted one when we bumped into each other outside, just now. Do you find that you have vivid memories of places you have never been, or people you have never met? Do you sometimes imagine yourself to be someone quite different, Wilberforce?'

'No, I don't,' I said, but we both knew I wasn't telling the truth. There was something on the edge of my memory all the time these days: a rain-slicked street at night that I didn't want to go down, but found myself walking along despite myself. Where was that? It wasn't Newcastle, or even London. It was somewhere warmer and, at the same time, somewhere with thinner air.

'You talked a lot in your sleep about Colombia, when I came in to look at you the other day. Do you remember that?'

'I'm not sure,' I said. 'Maybe I remember something – a dream I must have had.'

Colin sipped at his wine again. My glass was empty. Colin said, 'Go on, pour yourself another drink. You can't do yourself much more harm than you already have.'

I felt fear inside me. Colin wasn't lecturing me any more. He was preparing me for some news I wasn't going to like.

'Wilberforce,' said Colin gently, as I poured myself a second glass of Fitou, 'we think you have a condition called Wernicke's encephalopathy.'

'Werner's what?'

'Not Werner's – Wernicke's. It is a by-product of excessive alcohol intake. It causes a failure of thiamine production in your liver.' Colin folded his arms and looked at me, as if to say: You see what you've done?

'Oh dear,' I said, because I seemed expected to say something. 'What does that do?' I didn't really want to know, but I knew Colin would not leave until he had told me.

'Your liver produces thiamine, which is converted into a chemical called thiamine pyrophosphate. It's a crucial component in nerve-impulse transmission. If you have Wernicke's encephalopathy, which we think you have in a well-developed form, your liver stops producing thiamine. You may develop some quite distressing symptoms.' He paused, but I said nothing.

'You will experience sensations of hypothermia. Your taste and sense of smell will be impaired. You'll start to lose control of eye movement. Those are the early stages, and well developed in your case. The later stages include mental confusion, retrograde amnesia, and a strange side effect called Korsakoff's psychosis. In Korsakoff's psychosis, the patient starts to suffer from severe confabulation: the confusion of invented memory with real memory. Eventually, he loses any ability to distinguish his real-life experiences from his invented ones. In the final stages, just before coma and death, he may slip entirely into the delusional world he has constructed.' Colin stopped speaking.

'What delusional world?'

'It might be constructed around a film you once saw, a magazine article you read a dozen years ago, a chance remark someone once made to you. Stuff that the brain has dumped, and is sitting in some remote archive of your memory, suddenly fires through into your consciousness. Your brain is losing its ability to distinguish those false memories from real ones.'

I sat at the kitchen table, poured myself a last glass of wine and regarded Colin with horror. Supposing I forgot the real world, forgot about my wine, forgot about Francis, or even forgot about Catherine. Then I would cease to exist. I might go on living, but I would no longer have an existence.

What would happen to all the wine?

'Is it treatable?' I asked Colin.

'In most cases, it's treatable if caught early enough. But it gets harder to reverse the changes in body chemistry in its later stages, though not impossible. The odds in your case are not as good as I would like.'

Would they sell the wine when I died? Would it simply be forgotten about, or would the undercroft be broken into by vandals once it became known I was no longer returning to Caerlyon. I had a dark vision of bottles of Château Margaux being traded on street corners on Tyneside, in exchange for drugs.

'How is it treated?' I asked again.

'The treatment involves an intensive course of intramuscular injections of thiamine. But there's no point even starting with all that unless you stop drinking.'

'And if I don't stop?'

Colin tipped the last drop of wine down his throat, and stood up. 'I must go,' he said. 'Think about it, and I'll come and see you at the same time on Monday. I'm away for the weekend in Hampshire.' He pulled his wallet from his coat pocket and extracted a card, then underlined a number with his pen. 'That's my number in the country. Call me there if you have an emergency.'

What sort of emergency? I wondered. I repeated my earlier question. 'And if I don't stop drinking?'

'If you don't stop drinking, the confabulation gets stronger. The false memories take over your life. You slip more frequently into coma; while you are in coma your body temperature will drop and in one of those episodes you'll simply die. Think about what you want to do, Wilberforce, and we'll talk again on Monday.'

I sat staring at the table. In some ways it didn't sound a bad way to go. But what would happen to my wine?

Four

I awoke the next morning feeling cold. I got out of bed and checked to see if the central heating was on. There was a faint warmth coming from the radiator; perhaps it wasn't working properly. Or perhaps I wasn't. I went downstairs. There was a brown envelope on the doormat, which I opened and read. It was from the electricity company and announced that, as my direct-debit payment had been refused by the bank, supplies would be interrupted unless immediate payment of the outstanding amount could be made.

I went into the kitchen and looked in the fridge for something for breakfast. There was the same in the fridge that there had been yesterday and the day before: nothing. Of course, one had to shop if one wanted to find things in the fridge. Somehow I had not got around to shopping for food, even though the shop on the corner was open at all sorts of hours. I thought I would go there later, when I got up. I did not really want to go out in the street, though, in case I met someone I didn't want to meet.

I looked at my watch and saw that it was half past ten. I must have slept for more than twelve hours. I yawned. The kitchen was rather depressing to be in. The plates never seemed to get washed and the whole place smelled rather stale. I cleared some dirty wine glasses from the table and took them as far as the sink. I took two empty bottles and pushed them into the bottle bin, which was full. Someone ought to empty that, I thought. There seemed little point in having breakfast this late. I decided I would open a bottle of wine and take a glass up to bed, and get up later. I opened a bottle of red wine from the Murrumbridge Irrigation Area of New South Wales that I had found in the basement, and took it upstairs with a glass. I climbed back into bed, poured the wine and put the bottle on my bedside table. I stared at the label for a moment and wondered why Francis, a lover of Bordeaux, had allowed this stranger into his cellar. I decided it must have been part of a parcel of wines he had picked up at auction somewhere.

As I sipped the wine, which was young, I considered my affairs. It was clear I was going to have to find some money. I supposed I could sell the flat, which must be worth quite a lot; but then where would I live? I had taken out some fairly large loans against the security of the flat some time last year, in order to pay off an overdraft at the bank. Still, it was worth looking into, when I got the time. Then there was Catherine's jewellery, which her family kept asking me to return. I supposed I could sell that. It was my property really, and she didn't need it. That might at least pay off a few bills while I sorted myself out.

Sorting myself out was a silent conversation I had with myself every now and then. Sometimes it progressed as far as writing a number of proposed actions down on a sheet of paper, for example:

1 Talk to bank about second mortgage being increased
2 Consider working as an IT consultant to bring in some income
3 Get out and meet people
4 Do not drink at breakfast or before the middle of the day
5 Go for at least an hour's walk in Hyde Park every day

There were several such sheets of paper in and on my desk at present, for the simple reason that the waste-paper basket was so full there was no point trying to throw them away.

I supposed the wine at Caerlyon was worth quite a lot – at least a million pounds. It was a comfort to me that it was still there, that it would always be there. I wondered whom I should leave it to. It sounded from what Colin was saying as if I ought to make another will. I had made one when Catherine and I married, and in it I had left everything for life to her, and then afterwards to the children that we never had. It was probably a good idea to have another look at that. To whom would I leave the wine?

The thought was discomforting. There was no one. No one except Francis understood wine and cared for it as I did. He was dead, and Colin was trying to convince me that I was dying. Trying? He was making a good job of it.

What was it that he had said I had? Werner's philosophy? That wasn't it, but it was like it. Whatever the condition was called, it didn't sound very appealing: falling into an endless sleep, haunted by dreams of a life I had never had, my own memories pushed into far corners of my mind from where they could never escape, eternal prisoners in nightmare oubliettes.

I found I was perspiring heavily, and my pyjamas and the sheets were damp. I climbed out of bed and went and looked at myself in the mirror. I was tall and once had black hair and a pale face and blue eyes. My hair was now streaked with grey and plastered to the top of my head, shining with sweat. My face was no longer pale but dead white, decorated with a few patches of rough red skin, and covered in a sheen of perspiration. Catherine had once told me, in the first effusions of our love, that she found me physically attractive. I do not remember that I looked different from anyone else. No one except my foster-mother had ever commented on my physical appearance until Catherine did. My foster-mother had told me I had been a beautiful baby, but she had spoken as if all those charms were in the past.

If I had been attractive either as a baby or as the man whom Catherine married, I was very far from being so now. My skin was the colour of old newspaper. There were dark circles under my eyes and their whites were no longer the brilliant white they had once been, but a yellowish-grey colour, the colour of milk gone bad. I looked nearer to seventy than thirty-seven.

Not too bad, considering everything. I decided to get up and have a shower.

In my sitting room, on the mantelpiece, are two photographs. One is in colour and is of Francis Black, standing with one arm around Catherine and the other around Ed Simmonds. Ed, a few years younger than he is now, is wearing tweed plus fours and an old khaki jersey. His face is almost split in two in an urchin grin that makes him look much younger than thirty, which is about the age he was when I took that photograph. His unruly, tightly curled blond hair is sticking out all over the place, mostly upwards. He looks more like the Artful Dodger in *Oliver Twist* than the future Marquess of Hartlepool, heir to twenty thousand acres and Hartlepool Hall. He is enjoying himself enormously, and it shows. In the middle stands Francis, exactly like Francis always looks: silvery grey hair still streaked with black brushed straight back from his high forehead; an aquiline nose jutting from his face, deep laughter lines on either side. Francis is not smiling, though. I don't remember him ever smiling much, but his thin mouth has that familiar, ironic expression that he adopted for the company of younger friends such as Ed and me. Francis is wearing a sleeveless Fair Isle jumper over an open-necked, check shirt, and baggy tweed trousers. His complexion is tanned – surprising for someone who spent a lot of his life in a wine cellar. The adoring Campbell, his spaniel, is at his master's feet, looking upwards with a rolling eye.

Then there is Catherine: at least a head shorter than the other two, she stands slightly at an angle to the others, with Francis's arm draped loosely over her shoulder. She is laughing, I think at some joke of Francis's, as I was taking the picture. Her thick blonde hair is wind-blown. Her usually pale face has colour in it, from the open air and the exercise of walking over heather. Her grey eyes are looking at me, the person taking the photograph. She is looking at me and, I believe, thinking about me perhaps for the first time as someone distinct and separate from most of Ed's circle of friends. I always think she has the elegant, slightly drawn and fragile look of a film actress from the 1940s or 50s: a younger Celia Johnson in *Brief Encounter*.

Behind the three figures are rolling hills purple with heather, and above the heather the sky in the photograph is so white from a thin, bright overcast that the three people in the foreground have an etched, almost three-dimensional clarity, as if they might step out of the picture frame at any moment.

The other photograph is in black and white, taken of Catherine dolled up for her coming-out dance. I think it was on an inside page of *Country Life*. She looks very young: she was probably only eighteen when it was taken. In this photograph her hair is carefully swept back, falling to her shoulders. She must have worn it a lot longer in those days. Her face is poised, reflective, the hint of a smile at the corners of her mouth. It is a studio photograph and it has an incongruous quality for me, as if she has been caught trying on her mother's ball gown, her mother's jewellery, and her mother's make-up.

I remember the day I took the photograph on the moor. Ed Simmonds had asked Francis and me to come and shoot grouse with him, on his moor at Blubberwick. Francis hadn't shot, but had brought his spaniel, Campbell, to pick up behind the line. Catherine had been with Ed then, and she had spent most of the day standing with him. I didn't know anything about shooting grouse, and I only shot for one drive, with a minder standing with me. When the brown birds rocketed over the horizon and whizzed through the line of butts I was too surprised to shoot, at first. At last one unlucky bird tumbled in the air and sped past me, to bounce in the heather behind the butt. Others followed. It was incredibly exciting to be out in the heather, shooting grouse. I remember that at lunch Catherine came and sat on the grass next to me, as we made a picnic by a small burn. For the first time, I became very conscious of Catherine's nearness to me, her perfume, and the sound of her voice. That was when I first started to think about Catherine as somebody other than Ed's friend.

She gave me the portrait photo just before we married. 'This was taken when I still had my looks,' she told me. She was smiling as she said it, her eyes dancing, inviting a compliment. She looked a thousand times more beautiful than in the photograph. I told her so.

'You really do love me, don't you?' she said breathlessly, for I had folded her into a tight embrace.

'Of course I do.'

'It's hard to tell, because you never talk much.'

I let go of her and said, 'I've just been all work and no play for so many years, I've forgotten how.'

Catherine picked the photograph up from the table where I had put it down and studied it. 'It's funny,' she said: 'when that was taken all I was thinking about was parties, and you were already sitting behind a computer writing programs. You've never really had any fun in your life at all, have you?'

'No, but that's about to change.'

That was when we were still undecided about where to live after we married, before we made the decision to come and live in London.

I decided I would get dressed, go out and buy something to eat. It seemed a long time since I had eaten, and I felt a little dizzy from lack of food. The wine I had drunk lingered on my palate and in my brain, and when I stepped into the street I nearly fell over, misjudging the distance from my doorstep to the pavement. I walked down to Curzon Street, went into the shop on the corner and started to look along the shelves for something to eat that wouldn't be too much trouble.

I was just reaching for a box of oatcakes when an advertisement caught my eye, a white poster on the wall on which was printed, in heavy black type: 'TNMWWTTW'. It occurred to me that it was not the first time I had seen those letters. They were familiar to me, in some way, but I could not recall why. Perhaps I had seen the advertisement before. It must be one of those ridiculous teaser campaigns, designed to mystify, intended to make you think, What's all that about, then? so that when the name of the product or service being advertised was finally explained, it would be such a relief you would immediately go and buy some out of sheer gratitude.

'TNMWWTTW'. It grated on me that I could not make the connection. The letters stood for something, but what? It looked like a mnemonic. Then I thought it was a mnemonic, and one that I knew, if I could only call it to the front of my mind.

'Can I help you, sir?' asked somebody nearby. But I could not take my gaze from the poster. I gestured in its direction.

I was beginning to feel distinctly odd, but I managed to ask, 'What is that advertisement for?'

'What advertisement is that, sir?'

I waved my hand at the poster. I could not take my gaze from it. The letters grew larger, blurred and swam, turning into huge dots dancing across my vision. I felt sick and faint, as if all the blood had left my head in a rush. The room darkened and moved about. I heard a shout and then knew nothing more about it.

When I awoke, I was lying on something hard and a voice was saying, 'Can you remember who you are?'

It was a good question: I could not. Then a name came into my head and I whispered, 'Is it Wilberforce?'

A sponge was applied to my face, dabbing at a crust of what felt like dried blood, which appeared to have grown on it.

'Yes, Mr Wilberforce, that's right.'

'Where am I?'

'You're in the A & E department at the Chelsea and Westminster Hospital. You had a fall.'

I didn't want to be in a hospital. I wanted to be at home, being looked after by my own doctor. The trouble was, I couldn't remember who he was: his name was on the tip of my tongue, but I couldn't get the word out, I couldn't remember exactly what it was – as if I wanted to say 'Pimlico' but could only think of Pershore.

'Is there anyone we ought to contact to tell them you're here?' asked the voice, coming into view for the first time. It was a young Indian doctor.

'Francis Black,' I told him.

There was someone else in the room, sitting behind me, gently sponging my face. Now she spoke. 'Can you remember his phone number, dear?'

'I'm afraid not.' Then I remembered Francis had died of cancer three years ago. 'I'm sorry, he's dead, anyway.'

'We found you at an address in Mayfair. Can you remember how you got there? Can you remember where you live?'

'I live in Bogotá.'

Why in God's name had I said that?

The Indian doctor said, 'In Bogotá? In Colombia? You're a long way from home then.'

The two voices conferred above my head, and one of them said something about 'concussion' and 'retrograde amnesia'.

'Don't worry just now, dear,' said the woman's voice. 'You're still a bit muzzy from your fall, aren't you? We'll take you to a nice quiet room on your own and you can get some sleep, and then we might do some tests and try to find out what went wrong with you.'

I was wheeled out of the theatre on the gurney and along a corridor. Gentle hands lifted me into a bed, and then I fell asleep.

When I awoke, I saw that a drip had been attached to my hand, once again, and another plaster near my elbow suggested someone had been helping themselves to my blood. I stared around the room, which was painted a restful green colour, and wondered how I had got here. I had been shopping, hadn't I? A nurse came into the room holding a clipboard, and looked at me with a rather severe expression.

'And how are we feeling?' she asked.

'About the same as ever,' I told her. She glanced at a clipboard and said, 'Do you feel well enough to answer a few questions, Mr Wilberforce?'

'I'll do my best.'

'We checked your blood pressure and did a blood sample when you were admitted. Your cholesterol was raised and the sample indicated a high level of alcohol in your blood. Had you been drinking recently?'

'Only in moderation.'

The nurse looked at her clipboard again. 'That isn't consistent with your blood-sample level. How many units of alcohol do you drink in a week?'

I could not remember what a unit was, and said so.

'A glass of wine is about one and a half units.'

'Oh.' I have always been quick with numbers. When I was growing up, counting in my head or calculating prime numbers had been one of my greatest pleasures. That was how I had once become a very good software developer and programmer. I worked it out in my head and said, 'I suppose I drink around 260 units a week. Unless I go out. Then I might drink a bit more than that. But I don't go out very often.'

The nurse put down her clipboard on my bed and stared at me. 'You mean twenty-six, surely?'

'Well, if you assume the average glass holds 125 millilitres and a bottle of wine is 750 millilitres, then you can get five glasses from every bottle. If each glass is 1.5, that's 7.5 units per bottle, and if I drink five bottles a day then that's 260 units per week, you see. I'm sorry if my arithmetic's gone wrong somewhere. My brain is still not working properly.'

I could see the nurse doing some mental arithmetic of her own, as her lips moved silently. She said, 'You're a very sick man, Mr Wilberforce. I don't know that there's any point in any further questions.' She left me alone.

I began to wonder whether I could not discharge myself and get a taxi home. The only snag was, I could not remember where home was. I could remember some details of what it looked like. I could, for example, remember my bedroom ceiling. I was fairly convinced that my home was in London, too, rather than Bogotá. When I had been in Bogotá, I had stayed in a hotel the name of which also escaped me for the moment. Someone else came into the bedroom, and at first I assumed it was a doctor, because he was holding a large board in front of him of the kind used by opticians for sight tests, so that all I could see was the hands gripping the board, which obscured the doctor's face and most of his body. More tests. I hoped this was not going to go on all afternoon.

'Can you read the letters?' asked my visitor, in a hoarse whisper, and with the words came an exhalation of something mouldy, something rotten. But the voice sounded familiar. It reminded me of Francis.

'How nice of you to look in on me. How did you know I was in here?'

But my visitor made no acknowledgement of my greeting. He simply repeated, 'Can you read the letters?'

I looked at the board. It read:

TNMWWTTW
TNMWWTTW
TNMWWTTW
TNMWWTTW
TNMWWTTW
TNMWWTTW
TNMWWTTW

'Can you read the letters, Wilberforce?' whispered my visitor. His fingers, holding the board, were long and very bony, and the fingernails were uncared for, almost talons.

'Yes, I can,' I said shortly, holding my breath. Whoever he was, the smell of body odour was sweet and corrupt.

'Then tell me what they say?'

'Ten Naughty Mice Went Walking Towards The Wensleydale,' I told him. There! I knew it was a mnemonic. I knew it would come back to me. But what was it a mnemonic for?

A movement distracted me and I turned from my visitor and his sight-test board to see someone else, this time definitely a doctor, come into the room. When I turned back to look at the sight-test board to see if it would give me any further clues it, and the person holding it, had gone. So had that foul smell, thank God.

The doctor came up to me and asked how I was.

'Feeling better,' I said. 'I'd quite like to go home soon.'

'Oh, I think we'd better keep you in overnight, just to see how things go. Now, if you don't mind, I'd just like to check your vision is OK.'

'What, again? Someone's just been giving me a sight test. I could read all the letters.'

'Someone? I'm the only doctor on this ward this evening. Do you mean a nurse?'

'Ten Naughty Mice Went Walking Towards The Wensleydale,' I said proudly. 'I could read all the letters, even the ones right at the bottom of the board.'

'What sight board are you talking about?'

'Didn't you see him? He must still have been in the room when you came in just now.'

The young doctor ran his hand through his hair, and then said, 'I'm afraid you must be mistaken, Mr Wilberforce. There's no other doctor on duty on this ward tonight, there was no one in the room when I came in, and there could have been no one, because the ward cannot be entered except by people who have the code number for the key pad. The main door is kept locked at all times. It may be you are experiencing some slight after-effects from your concussion, you know. Let me shine this torch into the back of your eyes for a minute.'

He looked into my eyes, then made a dissatisfied noise and left without any further explanation. Time passed and I lay in my bed halfway between waking and sleeping, my face beginning to hurt quite a lot as whatever painkillers I had been given wore off. At odd intervals in the middle of the night I was awakened by a nurse coming in wheeling a trolley offering treats such as spaghetti hoops and jam sponge in custard. Despite the fact that I had not eaten for so long I could not bring myself to take anything, and sent them away. How long was it since I had had a glass of wine? I lay on my bed and tried to remember all the wines produced in the Bordeaux region of Pessac-Léognan and Graves. In the darkness I murmured to myself: 'Haut-Brion. La Mission Haut-Brion. Carbonnieux. Smith-Haute-Lafitte, Château Chasse de Frites . . . and . . . and Malartic-Lagravière . . . and . . . and . . . Haut-Brion – no, I've done that one . . . and Pape Clement, of course . . . and . . .'

As I tried to remember other names, my body became damp with perspiration, and my arms and legs twitched restlessly. I had some Château Carbonnieux in Half Moon Street. Half Moon Street! That was where I lived. I could not at present say what number it was, but the door was painted a dark blue. Now I had remembered where I lived, why should I not check myself out and get a taxi to take me home? There must be some money in my pockets. Hadn't I intended to go shopping?

I rang the night bell, and after a few moments the night-duty sister put her head around the door and said, 'Is everything all right? Can I get you something?'

'I want to go home,' I told her.

'At four in the morning? I don't think that's a very good idea, Mr Wilberforce. Much better you stay here until the day doctor has been in and had a look at you and we find out a bit more about what's wrong with you.'

'I know what's wrong with me,' I told her. 'I've got my own doctor.'

'Who's that, dear?'

I tried to remember, and this time the name came. 'Colin Holman – Dr Colin Holman. I've an appointment with him. What day is it today?'

'It's *very* early on Monday morning.'

'Then I must go home,' I told her. 'My appointment is later today. I must go home. It's very important.'

'And what does he say is wrong with you, dear?' asked the night sister.

'He thinks I'm dying of too much drink,' I told her, 'although I only drink wine, and then always the same amount, of very good quality Bordeaux. I never drink spirits, of course, and I never drink excessively.'

Two hours later I had managed to make them bring me my clothes, found my money and my flat keys, signed several forms to allow the hospital to release me, and managed to find a taxi to take me home.

The taxi driver looked in the driving mirror when I climbed into the back of the cab. 'Blimey, you've been in the wars, mate,' he said cheerfully.

I caught a brief glimpse of my face which was livid purple on the side I had fallen down on, with bandages taped over where I had cut myself. 'I've been in Bogotá,' I told him.

'Really? Must be rough over there, then,' he said.

I sat in my kitchen at home, relieved beyond measure to be back within my own four walls. I still felt distinctly unwell, and very empty, but somehow another trip to the shop, which would be open by now, did not appeal just at present. Perhaps I could ask Colin to get in a few things when he came to see me later in the day.

Meanwhile, it had been a very long time since I had drunk a glass of wine. With, I admit, trembling hands I found the last bottle of Château Carbonnieux and opened it. An alcoholic, which I am not and never have been, would not have sat and let it breathe for half an hour, and let it come up towards room temperature. He would not have poured it lovingly into the large bowl of a tasting glass, to ensure the bouquet could develop properly. Nor would he have checked the glass first for any mustiness. So often a musty glass can destroy the taste of the wine in it. I could smell nothing on the glass, although a smell of mould did seem to linger about the house. I decided I ought to see about getting someone in to open the windows.

An alcoholic would not have rolled the purple liquid gently around in the glass, to capture the aroma of the wine, and then taken a single sip, allowing the complex chemicals of the wine to release themselves upon his tongue. He would not have made the effort to characterise the tastes from the wine in the approved wine taster's vocabulary: sweet black cherries, toasty oak in the background.

The day passed pleasantly enough in this manner. I still felt odd – a thundery feeling in my blood as if somewhere not far away a storm was brewing. I put that down to the trauma of having fallen over and, worse still, having spent nearly two days in hospital. I was looking forward to seeing Colin, though not particularly because I wanted to hear what he had to say. It would be the usual stuff, and perhaps more about this odd Werner's condition. No, Colin could be very boring when he got on to all that medical stuff, though I suppose, as he was a doctor, I couldn't really expect anything more. The truth was, I felt lonely. Looking at those photographs of Catherine and Ed before I had gone out shopping, I had suddenly remembered how nice it had been to have friends. It had been, in fact, wonderful to have friends. That had been really the only period of my life when I had ever had any.

I thought about those days when I still lived in the North of England, before circumstances had made me sever my links (except for the wine) with all that part of my life. I remembered the exciting, heady days when I had been building up my company: at first in the spare room of my dismal flat; then in some rented space in the corner of an old warehouse; finally in the glass-and-marble palace it had occupied when I sold it. I had no friends then, apart from my business partner Andy. I needed none. I had no time for a social life. I was, if nothing else, content in those days.

I thought about the months and years of my friendship with Francis, of the people I had met through him: Ed Simmonds, Eck Chetwode-Talbot, Annabel Gazebee, and Catherine. I know I was really happy then.

I was still happy now, wasn't I? Only I was happy in a different way from before. My life had been changed by what had happened coming south from Caerlyon. I knew I was happy: it just felt different from what I had thought of as happiness before. I was a little lonely sometimes, too. It would have been nice to be able, on occasions, to talk about my wine to people who really understood. From time to time I came across a wine waiter who showed some awareness of the depth of my knowledge and experience, but on the whole, these days, drinking wine had become a solitary occupation. It was a pity Colin was not more interested. Perhaps if I offered to leave my wine to him he might become more enthusiastic. I wondered what he would say if I told him I'd put him in my will.

The thought put a smile on my face. I looked at my watch, which was scratched on the face but still seemed to be working. Colin would be here soon.

I thought I heard the door bell ring and went through to let him in. There was no one there. I put the catch up so that it would not slam shut on me, and stepped into the street to look for him.

The evening was damp with rain and the headlights of passing cars gleamed in the wet black pavements. I had just got into El Dorado airport in Bogotá on the Avianca flight from Medellín.

Five

I had just flown into El Dorado airport in Bogotá, on the Avianca flight from Medellín. From there I had taken a taxi uptown, asking the driver to take me to the Hotel Bogotá Plaza. Then, some instinct made me decide not to take the taxi all the way to the front of the hotel. Instead I asked the driver to drop me off at the corner of the Avenida 100 and Calle 27, by the big Toyota dealership. I paid off the driver and took my travelling bag from the back seat. The air was damp and thin, and spitting with a fine rain. I stood by the side of Avenida 100 for a moment, but no other taxis stopped in the vicinity. I didn't think the person who was following me used taxis.

As I walked along Calle 27, towards the side street that would lead me to the back entrance of my hotel, my eye was caught by a flashing neon sign, one of the animated kind where a computer programs thousands of different miniature bulbs to switch on and off, creating changing patterns and colours. It showed an Indian boy raising a brightly coloured bottle of Coca-Cola to his lips, followed by the slogan '*Disfrute Coca-Cola*', which scrolled across the screen.

Then the image vanished and letters started moving endlessly across the screen from left to right: *TNMWWTTW* . . . *TNMWWTTW* . . . *TNMWWTTW* . . . My bag in my hand, the fine, warm drizzle moistening my face like tears, I stared up at the sign, trying to recall its meaning.

Then I smiled to myself. *TNMWWTTW* . . . *Ten*

Naughty Mice Went Walking Towards The Wensleydale . . . That was it, that was the mnemonic I had been having such difficulty recalling. I remember someone asking me in a hoarse voice to read it to him.

TNMWWTTW . . . The Night My Wife Went Through The Windscreen.

This was terrific. I could remember everything. The warm rain ran down my cheeks and I savoured its salt taste. The night my wife went through the windscreen. The night Catherine died in that car crash. Knowing I would try and forget and bury the memory for ever, I had tagged it with a mnemonic and archived it somewhere in the back of my brain. It is so rewarding when, one's memory having become a little rusty in certain regions of one's life, some mysterious lubricant starts it working again.

The night that Catherine had died: I remembered it very well now, standing there halfway down Calle 27, in uptown Bogotá. I remembered the flashing blue lights, the chirruping of the police and paramedic radios, the clatter of the air ambulance settling down on to the grass beside the road, before starting its fruitless journey carrying Catherine, already dying or dead, to the hospital. I remembered lying on a stretcher in the rain, with a policeman rousing me, asking questions. It had been raining that night too, just like this night, half a world away, feeling bruised and shaken but somehow unhurt, watching Catherine's body being loaded on its stretcher into the helicopter, and thinking, 'Thank God it wasn't me.'

My right arm was beginning to ache from holding the bag. I shifted it to my left arm and walked on.

Then I saw a manhole cover in front of me start to rotate. It was pushed aside from beneath and, after a pause, two street children climbed out and looked about them. They were clothed in rags and very dirty. One of them saw me and

75

turned as if poised for flight, but then they must have decided I was not dangerous, for they advanced on me, speaking their incomprehensible patois of Indian and Spanish in wheedling voices. They wanted money, of course, and so I put my bag down and reached into my coat pocket for some small-denomination notes or change.

Just as I brought a fistful of coins out from my pocket, one of the children looked behind me and stiffened like a hare. They were looking behind me, and in that moment of stillness before they spoke again, I could distinctly smell that odour again, the odour of mould and decay. The children exclaimed something and ran off, frightened by whatever it was that was coming down the street behind me. I watched them go. Then I looked up to the sky to see if I could still see the stars. Once, long ago, the night sky had been full of them. Now I could not see any at all. A dark and rainy sky pressed down on me.

I could put it off no longer. I did not want to turn about, but turn I must.

He stood not far away, beneath the illuminated sign that still scrolled the letters *TNMWWTTW . . . TNMWWTTW* . . . across it, as if drawing attention to this important message from his sponsors. He was, as I had glimpsed him in the hospital and a thousand times in my dreams, dressed as he always had been, in a cardigan out at the elbows, and faded corduroy trousers and a check shirt. His hair was brushed back from his face, but it was no longer silver and black as I remembered it, but clung to his skull like wispy strands of cotton. He was so thin – so dreadfully thin. His face was half hidden from me by shadows, but what I could see of his face was comfortless. In the blackness I fancied eyes gleamed at the back of their sockets, and fleshless lips were drawn back from his teeth, as he smiled at me. His hoarse voice whispered, 'Wilberforce . . .' as if he were sighing with

76

despair, for the days past, when we had been living friends, for all the wine that had turned to vinegar in the undercroft. His voice was the echo of all the saddest memories of my life, all the love I thought I had found and then lost. It was the voice I remembered so well from when Francis Black spoke to me as he lay dying on his bed, a voice familiar to me, a voice that had murmured in my ear many times as I lay asleep.

One bony hand was half extended towards me, beckoning. Then I knew that, after all, it was not Francis who was following me. I was following him. I was seeking him out in death as I had sought him when he was alive. Whether he put his arms around me and took me to my grave tonight, or whether it would be the next night, or the night after, I could not say. It would be soon, and that was all that mattered. I could see my destiny very clearly now, as Francis stood beneath the flickering illuminated sign. He held out his arms towards me. It was an image that recalled how he had stood long ago, in the undercroft, spreading his arms wide, as if to encompass the treasure store of wine around him that he was offering me. It was a beguiling gesture, promising much, offering nothing. He would put his arms around me very soon now.

2004

One

Catherine gave me a photograph of herself, just before we were married. 'This was taken when I still had my looks,' she told me. She was smiling as she said it, her eyes dancing, inviting a compliment.

She looked a thousand times more beautiful than in the photograph. I told her so.

'You really do love me, don't you?' she said breathlessly, for I had folded her into a tight embrace.

'Of course I do.'

'It's hard to tell, because you never talk much.'

I let go of her and said, 'I've just been all work and no play for so many years, I've forgotten how.'

Catherine picked the photograph up from the table where I had put it down and studied it. 'It's funny,' she said: 'when that was taken all I was thinking about was parties, and you were already sitting behind a computer writing programs. You've never really had any fun in your life at all, have you?'

'No, but that's about to change.'

'Yes, it will be a relief to be finally married, won't it? Then people will stop making such a fuss about Ed, and we can just get on with our lives.'

There had been a great deal of ill feeling when Catherine had told Ed Simmonds that she wasn't going to marry him after all. I was glad I had not been present when the conversation took place, at Hartlepool Hall. Catherine had stood up to the combined forces of her parents and Ed with a great deal of courage and determination. I admired her for it.

Her parents weren't on speaking terms with me any longer, and neither was Ed. The general view was that I had gone behind Ed's back and betrayed the trust of a friend. I didn't look at it like that at all. It was just something that had happened. After all, Ed wasn't perfect himself. I knew for a fact he'd spoken unkind words about me behind my back in the past.

In those days Catherine and I were very happy together, making plans, then changing them and, as Catherine had wanted, having fun. She had said there hadn't been much fun in my life; I'm not sure she had known much fun either since she had become engaged to Ed Simmonds.

We went on holiday not long after Catherine told her parents she wasn't going to marry Ed, just to give everyone time to get used to the idea, and to take ourselves out of the way for a while. We went to India for three weeks. It was all arranged by Catherine. I wouldn't have had any idea where to go, or how to get there. I was happy just to write the cheques and leave the organisation to Catherine.

'It will be a sort of practice honeymoon,' she told me.

But people didn't get used to the idea of her broken engagement with Ed. Catherine's parents told her they would disinherit her if she married me; they certainly had no intention of coming to the wedding.

To my surprise, my foster-mother Mary showed some resistance to the idea as well: 'She sounds very nice dear,' she said, when I told her that Catherine and I were to be married. 'But I don't think I can come to the wedding. It really isn't fair to the poor young man she was engaged to.'

'But you didn't know the poor young man,' I said to her in exasperation. 'What does it matter? Catherine's going to marry me. She hasn't run away from him; she never married him; she's just changed her mind.'

'Well, I don't really think people should change their mind,' said Mary. I gave up. Why should I care what my foster-mother thought? I couldn't recall her ever showing much interest in *my* thoughts and feelings.

The only person who didn't throw us over was Eck Chetwode-Talbot, Francis's godson. Eck had left the army quite a few years ago, but he still carried himself as if he was on parade: very upright and brisk in his movements. He came to Caerlyon for a drink soon after the news broke. Catherine was upstairs in Francis's flat and I was in what had been the shop, which I now used as an office.

'Where's Catherine?' he asked, as he settled into a chair. I opened a bottle of white wine, handed him a glass and said, 'She's upstairs, getting changed. We've been moving my furniture in from my flat.'

'And you're both well? No sign of Simmonds sending around a death squad? How are the Plenders taking it all?'

'We're not on speaking terms, I'm afraid. I'm glad you're still speaking to us. You're about the only one who is.'

Eck laughed. 'I think the whole thing's absolutely marvellous. There was a distinct shortage of gossip until Catherine ran off with you. Now everybody has something to talk about. In fact, they won't talk about anything else. And if the Plenders won't speak to you, it's a win double. You get the daughter without having to take the mother-in-law on board as well. You don't know how lucky you are.'

I shook my head. I disliked the idea that 'they' were all talking about Catherine and me. 'Eck,' I asked, 'are you going to drop us as well?'

'Not at all. Why should I? I was very fond of old Francis and I know for a fact that he longed for you and Catherine to get together. A sort of paternal thing with him, I think. He quite liked Ed for his father's sake. He used to see a bit of Simon Hartlepool when Simon still saw people. But he adored Catherine. All the people Francis really liked were our age. He never seemed to want to mix with his own generation. Anyway, I'm sure he never wanted Catherine to get married to Ed.'

'I know,' I agreed; 'he said that to me once or twice.'

'That's the trouble with being a bachelor,' Eck went on: 'you develop an excess of unsatisfied paternal instinct. You adopt the young. Then you start to want to rearrange their lives. In Francis's case, he adopted Catherine first, and then you, for quite different reasons, I should think.'

'Did he adopt you?' I asked.

'God, no. Francis saw through me from day one. He never minded having me around, but one complete waster can always spot another.'

Just then Catherine came into the shop, looking fresh and pretty. Eck stood up and kissed her and then asked, 'So when's the great day?'

'Next month. There's no reason to wait any longer,' Catherine told him.

'I quite agree,' said Eck. 'The sooner you get married the sooner everyone will get used to the idea and stop making such a fuss.'

'Are they making a fuss?' asked Catherine. 'I know my parents are. I haven't talked to anyone else for a while.'

'I was telling Wilberforce: no one talks of anything else, wherever I go.'

Catherine shuddered and said, 'How awful: I hate the idea of being talked about. Eck, there's something we want to ask you.'

Eck smiled. I suspect he knew what was coming.

After a glance at me, Catherine said, 'Will you come to our wedding? Before you say yes, I should warn you: you'll be the only guest.'

'Of course I will,' said Eck. 'I'd give you away, except you're not mine to give, so I'd better be Wilberforce's best man.'

'You are sweet to agree,' said Catherine, and hugged Eck. Eck looked pleased, and as we all raised our glasses in a toast, I knew that he was also thinking what a good story it would make, and how many lunches and dinners he would be asked to, so that people could hear him make a joke of Catherine and me getting married, with Eck casting himself in the roles of father of the bride, best man, and witness.

After our wedding, we decided to go and live in London. There was too much history for us in the North: Catherine hardly dared go out for fear of meeting someone she knew, and being snubbed. Now I had sold the business and separated myself from Andy and all the others I had once worked with, there was nothing to keep me there either. A fresh beginning seemed like a good idea, to both of us.

We found a flat in Half Moon Street, in Mayfair. It cost an enormous amount of money, but I didn't mind. It was ideal: two bedrooms, a kitchen, a small sitting room and, best of all, a basement that could be adapted to store some wine. Catherine was appalled when I told her how much it would cost to buy it and do it up, but I told her that the money from the sale of my business had to be put into something: why not property? I sold my flat in Newcastle and we moved south a month or two after we were married. It was a happy time. We settled into the new flat and started to do it up. It was just off Piccadilly and near almost everywhere we wanted to be near to.

We went to the theatre and the cinema, or a concert, or the opera, as Catherine loved music. We ate in a restaurant almost every other night. Catherine took up singing again, going one night a week to choir practice. I went to an evening class in wine-tasting once a week.

In the daytime I sat in my office making plans for the new software consultancy I was going to set up, and Catherine busied herself buying things for the flat, having chairs and sofas covered and arranging for curtains to be made. She had already decided the spare bedroom was going to be a nursery when the time came.

We had lunches – sometimes quite long lunches. I would open a bottle of wine or two, and we would sit and talk, and sip the wine, although Catherine never really drank her share, and then either I would go back to my desk, or we would go into Green Park if it was a sunny day, or walk down to Knightsbridge to look at the shops; or sometimes we would just go upstairs and go to bed together.

One morning I went out to the bank to arrange some money transfer or other, and came back to find Catherine sitting in the kitchen, crying. I went up to her and put my arms around her and asked, 'What's the matter?'

'I rang my mother up, to see how she was.'

'And how was she?'

Catherine wiped the tears from her cheeks with an angry gesture. 'When she knew it was me, she put the phone down.'

It was only the occasional shadow such as that that interrupted our happiness. We made new friends to replace those that had separated themselves from us since our marriage. I bumped into an old university friend, Colin Holman, who had become a successful doctor in private practice. Catherine rediscovered a few married ex-school friends who had settled in London, and we began to go out to dinner from time to time, or have the occasional dinner party in our new flat. Our life was busy enough, our new-found friends, if they had heard about Catherine's broken engagement with Ed Simmonds, cared nothing about that, and our past lives became, at least for me, a dim memory.

One morning, after dining at the flat of one of our new

friends, Catherine said to me, as we sat drinking tea in the kitchen at breakfast, 'Darling, I think you were quite tight at dinner last night. You talked a great deal about wine. I'm not sure everyone's quite as interested in the subject as you are, darling.'

'I'm sorry,' I said. 'I didn't think I'd had too much to drink, because I didn't really like what they were serving. It was far too young, absolutely stiff with tannin.'

Catherine stirred her tea and said, 'Yes, darling, I'm sure you're right. But don't you think you're drinking just a little too often at the moment?'

I was surprised by her remark. 'Am I? Don't confuse tasting with drinking, darling. It is one of my great interests in life. That's why I agreed to buy Caerlyon and the wine from Francis.'

'I know that, darling. Don't be grumpy. I was only saying.'

I thought it was an odd remark for her to make, and after a moment I drank my cup of tea and said, 'I'm going next door; I've got bills to pay.'

At lunch that day we opened two bottles of wine, a good white burgundy with the small starter Catherine had prepared, and then a bottle of Bordeaux with the poached eggs and salad. Catherine matched me glass for glass, as if to apologise for her remark at breakfast and show me that she had not meant it; afterwards we stepped out into the bright sunshine, went to Hatchards and bought a pile of great, glossy recipe books for the new kitchen and Robert Parker's definitive work on the wines of Bordeaux, for me.

It was about six months after we were married that we had our first real row.

Catherine had gone out to have lunch with a girlfriend, and I sat at home and decided it would be interesting to compare a 1989 and a 1990 Château Talbot. I opened both bottles and let them breathe for an hour and come up to room temperature, and then poured out a little of each into two glasses. For me, the 1990 was almost thin, whilst the 1989, if not a great wine, had far more power and finish. It was a fascinating contrast of tastes, similar and yet dissimilar.

When Catherine arrived home, I was scribbling some tasting notes in my book. 'Nice lunch, darling?' I asked her.

'Yes,' she replied, and bent to kiss me. Then she said, 'Darling, you do rather reek of wine.' She looked at the two empty bottles, which I had placed on the sink, and said, 'Have you drunk all that yourself? Now, today?'

'Tasting, darling, not drinking,' I reminded her. She said nothing, but looked at me, and then looked at the two empty bottles, and then back at me. She bit her lip for a second, and then left the kitchen and went upstairs.

I said nothing. I wasn't going to be lectured about drinking wine. It was the great enthusiasm of my life: I was learning something new every time I opened a bottle. I finished writing up my tasting notes and then went next door to the sitting room, and sat down at the desk I kept my papers in. When Catherine came downstairs, I pretended to be engrossed in the business plan I was writing for my new software consultancy. As a matter of fact, I had been writing the plan for some months now.

'How's your new business idea coming on?' said Catherine, sitting down next to me.

'It's coming on,' I said.

'You never seem to go and see anybody about it. I thought that's how you got business – by going and seeing people.'

'I'm not quite at that stage,' I told her. 'I'm still working on the basic concept.'

Catherine was silent for a moment, and I marked a page with my pen. Then she said, 'It would be good for you if you went back to work, in a way.'

'That's the idea,' I told her, 'but there's no rush. When

you've worked non-stop for most of your life, a few months off is no bad thing.'

'But don't you get out of touch, darling? I mean, if you don't go and see people, how can you know what's going on, or what sort of things they might need? Aren't people simply going to forget all about you?'

I said, 'I think my reputation as one of the best software developers in the country might last more than six months.' I was starting to get angry, because there was truth in what Catherine was saying. People would forget me; most people forgot all about me five minutes after meeting me. They remembered Andy; they remembered the name of the company, except that now it wasn't called Wilberforce Software Solutions any more, but Bayleaf UK, after the giant American software business that had bought it.

'Well, even so, aren't you getting bored just sitting around the house all day? I mean, most men of your age do something. It can't be good just sitting around drinking all the time.'

I turned and looked at Catherine. 'Are you getting bored with me? Is that what you're saying?' I asked her.

She looked shocked, and said defensively, 'No, darling. But I don't like it when you drink so much. You need something else in your life.'

I could feel real anger running through me now, like a virus multiplying itself at raging speed. Where had it come from? I felt that if Catherine said another word about my drinking too much, I would hit her. Instead I jumped up, and the pages of my business plan went flying all over the room. Catherine started, and put her hand to her mouth in alarm.

I said, 'I'm tired of this conversation. I don't like being lectured. In case you hadn't noticed, we're living in my flat, bought with my money, earned by my hard work, in one of the best streets in London. I'm entitled to do what I like, I should think.' Then I left the flat, slamming the front door, and walked about twice around Hyde Park before I felt able to return home.

When I came back, I went up to Catherine, who was sitting in a chair in the sitting room, reading a novel, and I kissed her on the cheek. 'I'm sorry,' I told her. 'I didn't mean to be cross.'

'I tidied up your papers,' she said. 'I hope I've put them back in the right order.'

'I saw,' I said. 'Thank you, darling.'

She was very quiet all that evening, but the next day it was as if there had been no row, and everything was as it always had been between us. Except that it wasn't as it always had been. It was as if a fine crack had appeared in a once perfect porcelain bowl. The damage had been mended and could not be seen. But the bowl, which had been unblemished before, was cracked now.

For a few weeks I made a conscious effort to taste less wine at lunch time, at least when Catherine was there. I set up one or two meetings and went to them, and talked to a couple of people whom I thought might back my new business venture. But my heart wasn't in it: I couldn't persuade myself I really wanted to do this, and I don't think I convinced them.

'Keep in touch,' they said, but they didn't mean it.

Then I hit upon a different idea: instead of having to go through the effort of setting up meetings which I didn't want to go to, and where I could never think of what to say, I thought I would tell Catherine I was having lunch with one or other of my old customers, and then just go and have lunch somewhere by myself.

The drawback in this plan was that it was not always possible to find somewhere with a reasonable wine list. I resented paying over the odds for wines that I would hardly bother to open at home. But I decided I had to be realistic; it was better to spend a bit of money to have a glass of decent wine, even if I knew I was being robbed. This worked well. I found, to my surprise, a few wine lists which were really quite interesting even if expensive, with wines that sometimes were new even to me.

At first Catherine was very pleased with me. 'You see,' she would say as I rolled back into the flat cheerfully after another of my solitary, but satisfactory lunches. 'It makes all the difference getting out and meeting people. You're in a much better mood now you're getting out and about.'

'Yes,' I said, 'you were absolutely right about that, darling.'

'And what do they think of your new idea?'

'Oh, I think they'll go for it.'

'That's brilliant!' said Catherine, jumping up from the sofa and giving me a hug. She sniffed. 'What have you been eating?'

'Peppermints,' I said, bringing a bag of them out of my pocket. 'Want one?'

I suppose this new plan became too much of a good thing, after a while. Catherine didn't say anything, but her initial enthusiasm about my getting out and meeting people began to wear off. It might have lasted a bit longer except that one day I decided to have lunch in a restaurant in Walton Street that had become rather a favourite of mine. I ordered a starter and drank a bottle of a good white Rhône wine with that. I was just in the act of tasting the glass of Bordeaux that the sommelier had poured for me, before the next course arrived, when Catherine came into the restaurant with Sarah, one of her girl friends. I might have known it was a mistake to eat somewhere so close to Sloane Street. I knew Catherine was shopping and having lunch with someone that day.

She saw me and I saw her at the same instant. I began to

prepare the words I would say to her when she came over. But she didn't come over. She turned away. Sarah hadn't seen me. She had only met me once or twice and quite possibly wouldn't have recognised me anyway. I wouldn't have known her, had she not been with Catherine.

I finished my lunch as quickly as I reasonably could, and paid my bill. Catherine had been given a table at the back of the restaurant. I could not see her, and made no effort to look for her. I walked slowly home, went to my desk, pulled out my wretched business plan and made a few more notes in its margins. When Catherine came back to the flat half an hour later, I was still at it.

I heard her come in and shut the door. Then she went into the kitchen and I heard the kettle boiling. After a moment, I went to the door of the kitchen and looked in. She was sitting at the table with a mug of tea, smoking a cigarette, something she hardly ever did. She did not smile, or say anything, when she saw me.

'That was a funny coincidence,' I said. 'My date stood me up. He had to go to a meeting and rang me on the mobile after I'd sat down. So I thought I'd just have lunch anyway. Ha ha.'

Catherine said nothing for a moment. Then she said, 'You looked so damned . . . furtive.'

'I'm sorry?'

Catherine stared at me. She had avoided looking at me before, but now she stared at me in the same way Andy once had, when I had told him I was selling the business without consulting him; the way Ed Simmonds had when I had admitted I'd been seeing Catherine without his knowledge. It was a weary, contemptuous expression. She said, 'You haven't been having business lunches with anyone, have you? I was pretty sure it was all a lie, but now I know what you've become.'

I didn't ask her what she thought I had become. I didn't want to hear her tell me I was a drunkard, because I knew it would make me angry. My face felt rigid and frozen.

'My *God*!' said Catherine. 'If Sarah had seen you, or recognised you. Sitting there red-faced with a bottle of wine, on your own. I would have died.'

'I think I'll get on with my work,' I told her, 'if you've nothing else to say.'

Catherine didn't reply. She sat smoking her cigarette, with the same distant expression on her face. I went back to my desk. A few minutes later I heard the front door shut, as she went out again.

Later that evening she returned. I was sitting in the kitchen, watching television, drinking a glass of wine. 'Where have you been?' I asked.

'Out.'

'Do you want something to eat?' I asked. 'We could go to Shepherds Market and find somewhere?'

'I'm not hungry,' said Catherine.

'Neither am I, really.'

She took her coat off and hung it up and went upstairs. A few minutes later she came down again, and sat opposite me. 'Pour me some wine,' she commanded.

'Of course,' I said. 'What would you like? I've got some Bordeaux open, or there's a bottle of—'

'Just whatever's open,' she said, so I poured her a glass and refilled my own.

She sipped it, without showing much appreciation, and then said, 'Wilberforce, what's happening to us?'

'How do you mean?'

She sipped some more, looking at me searchingly. 'This isn't what I thought being married would be like. I should have got to know you better first, shouldn't I?'

'What more is there to know?' I said. 'I haven't changed.'

'Ah,' said Catherine. 'Perhaps you're right. Maybe there isn't anything to know about you. It's just that I thought there was. But maybe there isn't. Maybe you're completely empty inside. Is that why you have to fill yourself up with wine every day?'

'I don't know,' I said. I wasn't angry now. It suddenly seemed to me to be very important that I understood what Catherine was trying to tell me, but somehow her words made no more sense than if she had been speaking in Mandarin. 'I'm not a drunkard, as you seem to think. Since I inherited the undercroft, I've become very interested in wine.'

'You didn't inherit anything,' said Catherine. 'You're not Francis's family. You're not anybody's family, as far as I know. You bought the wine when you bought Caerlyon, Wilberforce. I think you told me that one way or another it cost you a million pounds. That's not the same as inheriting, is it?'

'No, I just meant that I think of it as an inheritance.'

Catherine pushed her glass across to me. 'Pour me some more. I'd better keep up with your drinking, if we're to stay together.'

I filled her glass without replying.

Catherine said, 'If I'd married Ed Simmonds, I might have been bored to death. He might have screwed around. I'm sure he would have done, just like his father. But at least I'd have known what I was getting into. With you, it's like living with someone who's dead but doesn't know it.'

I stared at her. I simply couldn't understand what she meant. 'I'm not dead, Catherine. I'm a very fit thirty-five-year-old, everything considered.'

She laughed. 'Poor Wilberforce,' she said. 'You've no idea how to be a human being at all, have you? That's why I thought I fell for you. I thought you were different. That's

94

why I left Ed. Different? I'm not even sure what species you are.'

The next morning, though, everything was all right between us again. In a way.

TWO

We had just returned from a few days' shopping in Paris. It was a sunny afternoon in early October, a warm autumn day with that radiance of light that comes just before the dark season. Catherine was unloading endless carrier bags from our taxi whilst I brought the suitcases in. As I put the cases down in the hall I heard the phone ringing. I went into the kitchen and picked it up.

'Hello?' I said.

'Wilberforce, it's Helen Plender here,' said Catherine's mother. 'Have you been away? I've been ringing and ringing.'

'We thought we'd take a few days' break in Paris,' I told her. Helen Plender spoke as if she had never hung up the phone on her daughter every time Catherine had rung her over the months since we had been married. I would never have known from her conversational tone that she had refused to attend her only daughter's wedding because her daughter was marrying someone of whom she did not approve.

'How nice,' said Helen Plender. 'Is Catherine there?'

She did not ask me how I was, or what I was doing, or whether the sun had shone for us in Paris. I put my hand over the phone and mouthed at Catherine, 'It's your mother.'

'My mother!' Catherine came and took the phone from me.

I went outside and paid off the taxi driver. When I came back in, Catherine was busy listening to whatever her mother had to say to her. It sounded like a one-sided conversation. I took the cases upstairs and began to unpack.

We had been taking a break in Paris so that Catherine could buy some new clothes. As far as I could see they were exactly the same sort of clothes as she could have bought in London; but it had become important to us to go away from time to time. Although Catherine and I had patched up our relationship after she had caught me out in my harmless fiction about going out to business lunches, our lives together were not as easy as they had been. The great thing about going to Paris, as far as I was concerned, was that no one, not even Catherine, could disapprove of my drinking wine. If you can't drink Bordeaux in Paris without exciting comment, where can you drink it? That was my view, and provided I took a generous view of Catherine's shopping, she was prepared to allow that I might have my bottle or two at lunch and my bottle or two in the evening. There were, after all, wines on restaurant lists in Paris that I had never even heard of before, let alone tasted. Some of them were delightful.

I finished unpacking and went down to the kitchen to see how Catherine was getting on. She had just hung up.

'Well?' I asked.

'It was quite extraordinary. She was all sweetness and light. It was quite as if we had never quarrelled.'

'That's good, isn't it?'

Catherine said, 'It's too good to be true. She asked about the flat, what colours I had done it up in. She asked what I was doing, whether there was any sign of children. She even asked what you were up to.'

I said, 'What did you tell her?'

'I said you were putting together a new business and she said, she hoped I wasn't going to be left too much on my own.' Catherine smiled to herself when she said that, somewhat grimly.

I went to the fridge, found a bottle of St Veran, opened it and poured a glass for myself.

'Want a glass?' I asked Catherine.

'A bit later, perhaps,' she said. She was still thinking about her mother's call. 'You know,' said Catherine, 'Mummy asked me all the questions that mothers are supposed to ask. It's extraordinary. She won't speak to me for six months and then she expects to pick up exactly where we stopped the day I told her I wasn't going to marry Ed – as if she hadn't said the awful things she said to me that day, the awful names she called me; the words she used about you.'

Catherine had never talked to me about what had happened that day. Whenever I had asked her about it, she had just shaken her head and wouldn't answer. Now she stood in the middle of the kitchen, in a patch of afternoon sunlight, biting her lip, deep in thought.

Suddenly she burst into tears. 'How can she act as if nothing ever happened? How can she?'

I poured Catherine a glass of wine and refilled my own glass. She took it and came and sat opposite me at the table, and we drank our wine.

Catherine said, 'You don't know how horrible it feels to be cut off by your own family, because you've never really had a family of your own.'

'I suppose that's true,' I said.

'And now she expects I'll drop everything and go up and see her, because she's decided that I've been punished enough.'

'*Are* you going to go and see her?' I asked.

'I don't know,' said Catherine. 'I don't know what I'll do.'

Later that evening we went out to dinner, as there was nothing to eat at home. Night had fallen, and people seemed to be hurrying everywhere: late office workers scurrying home, couples on their way to the theatre or the cinema. As we walked arm in arm down Piccadilly past the Ritz Hotel, a man in a covert coat who was walking briskly in the direction of Hyde Park Corner stopped us. It turned out to be Eck.

'Ah, the young married couple,' he exclaimed; 'how nice to bump into you like this!' He and Catherine kissed each other on the cheek, and Eck patted me on the arm. 'How are you, old boy,' he said. 'Is she looking after you?'

It was ages since we had seen him. Just after we had moved into our flat in Half Moon Street he had looked us up on one of his rare visits to London. We had sat on packing cases in the kitchen, because there were no chairs, and Eck and I had drunk a lot of Bordeaux from Caerlyon, and we had laughed a lot; or at least, Eck had laughed a lot.

'Yes, of course,' I said. 'Eck, where are you off to? Why don't you come and have dinner with us? We were just on our way to find somewhere to eat.'

'I can't,' said Eck, 'I'm on my way to the Cavalry Club, to have a drink with a man who is proposing to sell me the hind leg of a racehorse which has come last in its past three outings. The good news is that I expect my share of the animal to be cheap. Then I'm getting a late train down to Hampshire. My cousin Harriet has become engaged to a rather nice soldier called Bob Matthews, and there's going to be a party to celebrate.'

'Oh, Eck,' said Catherine. 'What a pity. We could have had a gossip.'

'Well, come up north,' said Eck. 'We're all still there. You won't need a passport.'

'Well, if we do, will you come and have dinner with us in the flat at Caerlyon?' asked Catherine.

Eck promised and hurried away. Catherine and I walked on.

'Oh, it *was* nice to see someone from home,' said Catherine. 'Dear old Eck. You can never get hold of him. He's so social. He's always busy doing something.'

We found our way to a restaurant, sat down and ordered dinner. Catherine was in a better mood: seeing Eck had lightened her heart. She didn't speak much, though. I could see she was still thinking about her mother.

'You want to go and see your mother, don't you?' I asked, after she had crumbled her bread roll into small pieces on her plate.

'I think I ought to. She is my mother, after all. I know she behaved terribly badly – to both of us; but that doesn't mean I should behave badly to her in return. She's not getting any younger and my father is ten years older than she is. Who knows how long they'll be around?'

The potted shrimps arrived.

'Well, I need to visit Caerlyon soon anyway,' I said. 'I need to check the cellar is in good order and probably bring back a few more cases of wine to London. I'd like to have a few more different wines and vintages down in London to choose from.'

Catherine looked up and I saw she realised that some sort of a deal was being offered.

'I might not come and see your parents on this first visit,' I said. 'I think it would be best if you went over to Coalheugh for the day whilst I check Caerlyon and perhaps go and see my own mother.'

So a plan was made, and the next morning Catherine rang her mother, and fixed a date.

It was the beginning of December when we went up there. We drove up in my Range Rover because I wanted to stack a few cases of wine in the boot to bring back. We had telephoned the agent who looked after the property for us to get someone in and switch on the heating, and make up beds and air the flat before we arrived. Catherine brought some expensive scented candles from Jo Malone to give her mother as a peace offering. I bought a new toaster from Tesco to give as a present to my foster-mother.

We drove up the A1, and as we approached Newcastle Catherine sat straighter in her seat: she seemed divided between a sense of apprehension and a longing to see her home again. I, too, was filled with longing, to see Caerlyon and the undercroft again. It was months since I had been there.

We made an early start and arrived at Caerlyon before lunch: it was intended that Catherine should go and lunch at Coalheugh and come back to Caerlyon later in the afternoon. We had managed to persuade Eck and Annabel Gazebee to come for supper that night. My job was to go and buy some more or less instant food from the shopping centre down in the valley, so that Catherine didn't have to cook.

When we arrived Catherine said, 'It all looks a bit sad and lonely here, now.'

Grass was growing amongst the cobbles in the courtyard and dead leaves had blown here and there. The paintwork on the shop door was peeling. Everything had an abandoned and desolate look. The agent was supposed to keep an eye on the place and there was meant to be someone coming in and weeding and sweeping up leaves, but if he had ever been, there was little evidence of it. We took our cases inside and then I called a taxi to come and collect Catherine. Within half an hour of her arrival Catherine was on her way to see her mother. Just before she left, she asked, 'What are you going to do now?'

'I must just check the undercroft is all right,' I said, 'and then I'm going to drive into Newcastle to see Mary. I'll do the food shopping on the way back.'

'I should think I'll be back about four,' said Catherine. Then she was gone.

I watched her drive away, then let myself into the shop and unset the alarm on the undercroft. I had longed to see the place again. Sometimes I would wake up at night, in London, imagining that there might have been a break-in and that the cellar had been vandalised; or that an unknown pipe had burst and there had been a flood. I had sometimes tried to picture the undercroft in my mind, but as the weeks and months had gone by, the images of the stacked cases and bottles of wine had gone dim, had assumed the uncertain quality of a half-remembered dream. There was always a slight feeling of dread when I returned to the place, as if it might have changed, or diminished, in my absence.

I went downstairs, flicking the lights on as I went past the switch. The undercroft sprang into being before me, in all its glittering mystery. It was as if it had been suspended in another dimension and had now reappeared, like some enormous craft coming from beyond space and time, with its miraculous cargo. I stood in awe as I saw again the thousands of cases in their columns and islands, the gleaming racks of bottles along the sides of the cellar.

I walked along the gangways, from shadow to light and back to shadow again. Occasionally I stopped to examine the stencilled words on a case, or picked a bottle from a rack and examined the label. It was like coming home: it was being amongst my own friends; my own family. Château Trois Chardons; Château Sociando-Mallet; Château Vieux Robin; Château Ducru-Beaucaillou. I murmured the names softly to myself, and turned the labels this way and that.

'Francis,' I said, 'I have never drunk a bottle of your Canon La Gaffelière. Isn't that extraordinary? You never produced one for me ever, and yet I'm sure we've talked about it. I must have walked past this bottle twenty times without noticing it.'

Francis was dead and did not reply, but the lights flickered for a moment and I knew that he approved my choice. I took the bottle back upstairs to drink before dinner. Then I decided that I would have a taste of it now, in case it disappointed later. I sat in the shop sipping the wine. Francis would have sat opposite me, in the old days, in the chair behind his desk. He would have told me stories about the wine we were drinking, the family that grew it, the place where it grew.

'This is delicious,' I said aloud. 'I wish you could taste it, Francis.'

He was almost real to me. I could picture him in my memory: the black hair streaked with silver brushed straight back from his forehead, the arched eyebrows over deep-set brown eyes, the beak of a nose; the look of gentle irony he always wore. He would have sat in the chair, one long leg crossed over the other, in his faded corduroy trousers and battered old suede loafers, and he would have said, as he once had said, 'Drink this, in remembrance of me.'

I started, for the words had been spoken out loud, and for a moment I thought I did see Francis sitting in front of me. But it was my voice that had spoken.

I refilled my glass and looked at my watch. I needed to get going, if I was to see my mother and give her the toaster and then buy the food for supper before Catherine returned. Then I looked at the label of the bottle again.

'Nineteen seventy-one,' I said to myself. 'I wonder if he's got any of this from 1987?' I thought I might just have a quick look downstairs in case. The best thing was, not to see my mother and just go and do the shopping. Then I would have plenty of time. We could always go and drop off the toaster tomorrow, before we went south.

I was still sitting in the shop, finishing off a second bottle of La Gaffelière that I had found, when Catherine came back.

'I wondered if I'd find you here,' she said. She did not look especially angry, or disappointed. She was very pale.

'How did it go?'

Catherine sat down in Francis's chair opposite me. I

thought for a moment that I should tell her not to, but decided that, in the circumstances, it would not be tactful.

'I don't suppose you went and bought any food?' she asked.

I shook my head.

'Or saw your mother?'

'No. I'm afraid I've been sitting here looking over the wine, trying to decide what to take back to London with us, and I simply forgot all about the time.'

Catherine said nothing.

'That's what Francis always used to say, do you remember?' I asked her. 'He used to say, "This place steals your time."'

I laughed, but Catherine did not laugh with me. She did not even smile. Her chin was resting on the heel of her hand; her elbow was on the desk in front of me, and she was staring at me.

'It's true what Eck says about you, isn't it?'

I didn't like the sound of this. 'What does Eck say about me?'

Catherine ignored my question. She said, 'About quarter of an hour after I arrived at Coalheugh to see my parents, guess who suddenly turned up for a drink?'

'Who? Eck?' I felt confused.

'No, Ed. He turned up and said something like, "Oh, it's you. I thought I'd just pop in to see if I could extract a gin and tonic from your parents. I had no idea you were going to be here." We all know Ed has gone to live in France as a tax exile since his father died. He doesn't "pop in" anywhere in England. He might even have flown back especially just to "pop in" at my parents' house today. If they handed out Oscars for bad acting, Ed would win one every time.'

'I don't understand,' I said. 'Why was Ed there?'

'Keep quiet, and I'll tell you. The whole thing was a set-up.

104

Ed didn't stay for long, of course. He was very nice, very sweet – asked how I was, asked about the flat. He even remembered to ask about you. He didn't say much about himself – just gave a general impression of a man who was pining for his lost love, and then he went.'

Catherine stopped talking for a moment, and I could see she was thinking about Ed. I began to feel a pulse beating in my neck. I didn't speak.

'Of course, as soon as Ed left, my father vanished out of the room and I was left with Mummy. I asked her what the hell was going on.'

Suddenly I didn't want to hear the end of this story. I looked at my watch and said, 'Shouldn't I be going to get the food for dinner?'

'No one's coming to dinner. I rang up Eck and Annabel and cancelled. Let me finish. You need to hear this. Mummy said, "Of course we know all about your husband's drink problem from Eck. Eck said he came to see you once for dinner and your husband was as tight as a tick. He said you'd confessed to him that – what's his name? – Wilberforce – he doesn't even appear to have a Christian name – had a serious drink problem." '

'Did you say that to Eck?' I asked.

'Not that night, another time. He rings up, sometimes, just for a chat and to see how I am. I should have known better than to say anything to Eck. You might as well go to the top of Durham Cathedral with a loud hailer and tell your secrets to the world.'

The pulse in my neck was beating faster now. I said, 'You've been talking to Eck about me on the phone?'

'Well, Wilberforce, it can get quite lonely living with a man who gets drunk after breakfast and drunker still by dinner. Anyway, listen to the rest of it. You'll love it. It's so like Mummy.' Catherine paused, and laughed without pleasure.

'Mummy said, "We've always thought there was something very odd about that man you married. We all make mistakes, you know. Ed's still there for you. You could see that, couldn't you? He'd take you back like a shot if the chance arose." '

She stopped talking, and for a long time we sat quietly. I didn't feel like finishing the wine in my glass.

After a while I said, 'Let me see if I've got this straight. You went to see your parents, Ed turned up, then when'd he'd gone your mother told you to dump me, because I'm a drunk – get divorced, I suppose, and then marry Ed after all. Is that about it?'

'Well summed up, Wilberforce,' replied Catherine.

I stood up. I said, 'I'm going to go and see your mother and have a word with her.'

Catherine held up the car keys. 'You left these in the ignition. I'm not going to let you drive anywhere. You're drunk, again. We're going to go back to London. I can't stand this place: it gives me the creeps. There's no reason to be here. Get our bags from the house and put them in the car. I'm going to drive us back. I don't want to be within a hundred miles of my mother for a minute longer, if I can help it.'

I said, 'We can't go yet.'

'If you don't do as I say,' said Catherine slowly, 'then, you know what – disgusted as I was by my mother's scheming, I might just drive back to Coalheugh instead and follow her advice. It's very difficult to live with you, Wilberforce. I'm trying my best to keep us together, because that's what I promised to do when we were married. It can be hard to remember that sometimes.'

There was nothing more to say, after that. The pulse still beat in my neck. I felt anger rising inside me. I didn't want to leave the undercroft so soon. I felt as if everyone I knew was turning against me, betraying me: even Eck; even Catherine.

All the same, Catherine's demeanour made me feel that it was better to do as she asked. I put the bags into the back of the Range Rover and set the alarms on the undercroft and on the flat. Then we got into the car; Catherine switched on the engine, flicked on the headlights, and we drove out of the courtyard into the lane.

It was when we were going down the little, winding lane that led down the side of the hill to the valley below, that I remembered. 'Stop,' I said to Catherine. 'Turn back. I've forgotten something.'

She slowed down for a moment, but did not stop. 'What have you forgotten?'

'I've got to go and choose some cases of wine to bring back. That was the whole point in my coming here.'

Catherine did not stop. Instead she speeded up again and said, 'There's no way I'm going back to that place, Wilberforce. There's no way you are going back to it. It's destroying you, can't you see? It's destroying me.'

'But you promised!' I shouted. The pulse in my neck was going like a hammer. They all did this to me in the end: all those who should have loved me betrayed me. Now Catherine was going to break her promise and prevent me bringing back my wine. I reached across for the wheel, to try to make her turn around.

'Don't,' said Catherine, pushing me away. 'You're drunk, Wilberforce; you're behaving like a madman.'

'I'm not a drunk,' I screamed, 'I just like tasting wine.' I reached across her again and grabbed the steering wheel, to turn us around. The Range Rover veered across the road, across a wide grass verge and went over a small bank. I was conscious of the branches of trees brushing past. There was the sound of breaking glass, and a scream, suddenly cut off. Then I banged my head and everything went black.

*

When I awoke, there was a throbbing in my head. I was lying on a stretcher on the grass by the roadside. Blue lights from two police cars flashed constantly, and I could hear the chirrup of police radios. I shut my eyes because the blue lights hurt, and groaned.

Someone said, 'This one's coming round,' and another voice nearby said, 'Can you hear me, sir?'

'Yes,' I said. It hurt to talk. My ribs felt bruised and my head ached. My face was wet with the fine drizzle that was falling. I opened my eyes and saw, in the light of headlamps, a policeman was bending over to talk to me.

'They're taking the lady to the hospital,' he said.

'Catherine? Is she all right?'

I tried to sit up but an arm from behind me restrained me and the first voice said, 'Just take it easy, sir; don't try and move until we've had a chance to have a proper look at you. There's an ambulance on its way.'

There was a clatter of rotor blades above and a bright light shone down on us. I saw the giant black shape of a helicopter settling on to the grass, and then two paramedics scrambling up the bank with a stretcher: on it, a limp figure covered in blankets. The figure did not move. The stretcher was loaded on to the helicopter in an instant, and the machine took off again, almost before I had time to realise what had happened. Then I heard sirens from the valley below.

The policeman said, 'That'll be the ambulance coming for you now, sir.'

They took me to a different hospital from Catherine. There was nothing much wrong with me. I had suffered a couple of cracked ribs, a badly bruised knee and a few scratches and contusions. They took Catherine to another hospital in the city, which specialised in head injuries.

When I arrived at the hospital I was X-rayed and then

checked over by a doctor. I kept asking, 'Where's Catherine? What's happened to Catherine? Is she going to be all right?'

Nobody could, or would, tell me anything. They put me in a room on my own and I lay on the bed remembering trying to take the wheel, remembering the car swerving and then the terrible sensation of falling through the air, whilst the branches of trees brushed past. But I couldn't remember what had happened to Catherine. If only she hadn't been so stubborn. If only she had turned around, as I had asked, none of this would have happened.

'Mr Wilberforce?'

I looked up. The policeman I had seen when I was lying by the road had come into the room, together with a nurse.

'Might I ask you a few questions?'

'Where's Catherine?' I said.

'Is Catherine your partner?' asked the policeman.

'She's my wife.'

'Ah,' he said, and made a note. 'So you are her next of kin, then?'

'Of course.'

He closed his notebook and assumed a serious expression. 'I'm sorry to have to tell you, Mr Wilberforce: Mrs Wilberforce was dead on arrival at the Royal Victoria Infirmary, about an hour ago. I'm afraid Mrs Wilberforce doesn't appear to have been wearing a seat belt. She went through the windscreen when the car crashed, and she suffered serious head injuries. I've only just been informed. They had some trouble in tracing you to this hospital; the paperwork hadn't caught up with you.'

I lay back on the bed, tears welling up in my eyes. 'Oh, Catherine,' I said out loud. If only you had let me go back for the wine, I said to myself. If only you hadn't broken your promise. Then none of this would have happened. 'I know this is probably not a good time to talk,' said the policeman, 'but I need to have a few details of the accident.'

I wiped my eyes and sat up on the bed. 'Let's get it over with,' I said, 'and then I want to be left alone.'

'Of course,' said the policeman. 'Nurse, could you possibly get them to bring us both a nice cup of tea, and we'll fill in these forms as quickly as we can. Now, sir, just tell me in your own words exactly what happened.'

'Catherine,' I said. 'Catherine was driving.'

Three

I was discharged from hospital the following morning and given a set of crutches to use until the swelling on my knee went down. The police had been to see me several times during my brief stay. A more senior officer had joined the first policeman, bringing photographs of tyre marks, showing where the Range Rover had suddenly turned at almost right angles to the direction of the road, before swerving across the grass verge and plunging down the bank. This officer wanted to understand why the Range Rover had veered across the road so suddenly, but I couldn't help him.

'Catherine was upset after going to see her parents,' I told them. 'She was probably driving a bit faster than usual.'

'And you were driving all the way back down to London the same day you had driven up. Was that wise?'

'Like I said, Catherine was quite upset after going to see her parents. She wanted us to go back home to London, instead of staying the night at Caerlyon as we had planned.'

'So why didn't you offer to drive?' the policeman asked me.

'I'd had a couple of glasses of wine. I wasn't expecting that we would return to London so soon. It was a sudden decision of my wife's.'

He laid some photographs of tyre marks beside me on the bedside table. They meant nothing to me. My head ached. I could remember the car falling through trees. I wanted to see Catherine and find out how she was. Then I remembered they had told me she was dead.

'It's very noticeable when a vehicle changes direction as abruptly as that. It wasn't icy that night. The roads were a bit damp and we can see where the turn became a skid. But what started the turn? We really need to know before we can close the file for the coroner.'

'All I know is that we were on our way to London. I said I'd had a couple of glasses of wine. I was probably dozing. I don't know. The last thing I remember is branches brushing against the window, and then I banged my head.'

For a while I really couldn't recollect any more of what had taken place. It hadn't been my fault – I knew that much. Catherine had promised that, if we came up North together, I would be able to bring back a few cases of wine. Then she had gone back on her promise, and then whatever had happened had happened. Now, my poor Catherine was dead. It just showed how quickly things could go wrong if you didn't stick to a plan.

At last the police stopped asking me questions. I made an arrangement to go and formally identify Catherine's body later that day, but for now I could leave.

I took a taxi back to Caerlyon. I had been given the contents of the Range Rover before I left the hospital, including the keys to the flat at Caerlyon, the undercroft and the London flat. Everything was surprisingly intact. The only two casualties of the crash were Catherine herself and the car, which was a write-off for insurance purposes. When I returned to the flat at Caerlyon, I opened it up and brought the bags in. I unpacked mine again and was starting to unpack Catherine's when I realised there was no point. So I sat on the bed with my head in my hands, feeling numb. It was very cold. I don't know how long I sat there, but after a while I became conscious that the phone was ringing, and had been for some while. I got up from the bed and went and answered it.

'Wilberforce, are you all right?' asked Eck.

'Yes, I think so.'

'I'm so dreadfully sorry about Catherine,' he said.

'Yes, it is very sad, isn't it?'

'Can you face seeing me if I come over?'

I thought about this and said, 'I'm not really feeling very sociable at the moment.'

Eck made a sound like clearing his throat and said, 'No, of course not. But the Plenders have asked me to come and talk to you about the arrangements.'

'What arrangements?'

'For Catherine's funeral,' Eck told me. So I told him that of course he could come, and he offered to drive me afterwards to the hospital to identify Catherine.

'You'd be better off having company for that visit,' Eck told me. 'It won't be easy for you.'

About an hour later, he arrived. Whenever Eck arrived anywhere, it was as if someone had opened a door on a windy day. He brought with him laughter, activity, vitality; but when Eck came to my flat this time, he crept in like a ghost. There were dark rings under his eyes and he looked as if he might have been crying. Of course, Eck had known Catherine since they were both small children. All the same I felt jealous that he had been grieving for her, whilst I had simply been sitting on my bed with my head in my hands, empty of all thought or feeling.

We talked for a while about the arrangements for Catherine's funeral. Eck was going to take care of matters for the Plenders, and he just wanted me to agree to the proposals, which were that the funeral should be held as soon as possible, it should be as small as possible and as simple a service as possible. I agreed to it all, and then offered Eck a glass of wine. For the first time ever, he refused.

'I'm not really in the mood,' he said. 'But you have one. You probably need one.'

This reminded me of what Catherine had told me the night before, about Eck telling her parents that I drank too much. 'No,' I said. 'I don't feel like drinking anything.'

Eck raised an eyebrow, but said nothing.

'Shall we go to the hospital now?' I asked.

'Before we do,' said Eck, turning away from me and fiddling with something on the kitchen table, 'can you just tell me something?'

'If I can.'

He had picked up Catherine's handbag without thinking. He saw me looking at him and put the handbag down on the table again. 'How on earth did the car come off the road like that? Catherine was a very good driver. The police said it almost did a right-angled turn. How did that happen?'

I shook my head. 'I can't remember what happened,' I told him. 'I banged my head fairly early on. Catherine was driving. Only she could tell us what happened, but she's dead now.'

Eck looked at me, waiting for me to say something more. When I did not, he gave a slight shake of his head and then said, 'Well, we might as well get it over with.'

Then he drove me to the hospital where Catherine waited for us. We drove there in silence. Eck seemed to have nothing more to say to me after his last brief question, and my answer. At the hospital they were efficient, and helpful. The registrar came out to meet us and took us to the room where Catherine was laid out waiting for me, wrapped in a winding sheet and stored in a mortuary cabinet. When we came into the mortuary the air was chill. A porter slid a box out from the cabinet, on to an autopsy table. Inside the box was Catherine.

'The head injuries were quite bad,' said the registrar. 'You will probably find this rather distressing. Take your time. There's a chair here if you want to sit down.' Then the registrar removed the sheet that covered Catherine's head.

Eck turned his face away and walked across the room, as far away from Catherine as he could get without leaving the mortuary.

'That's not Catherine,' I said.

'What do you mean?' asked the registrar. 'Isn't that Mrs Wilberforce?'

I shook my head. 'It is her, I know. It's just not how I want to remember her.'

'Those injuries were caused when she went through the windscreen,' said the registrar. 'I'm very sorry.' He quickly covered up Catherine's head again.

The night my wife went through the windscreen, I thought.

So I went to another funeral, but this time it was for Catherine, not Francis. I was still obliged to use my crutches when the day of the funeral came. I sat in a pew near the front of the church, on my own. The Plenders were huddled together with friends and relations on the other side of the aisle. I do not remember much of the service. There were few mourners: the Plenders had restricted the funeral to immediate family and close friends. I saw Teddy Shildon, Eck, Annabel Gazebee and Ed Hartlepool. When Ed saw me hobbling in, he turned his head to stare at me. The hatred in his look was like a blow. I was feeling awful, anyway. Since the night Catherine had gone through the windscreen I had not drunk a drop of wine. I longed to drink a glass or two; I longed to go down into the undercroft to find solace amongst its store. But some feeling prevented me: I wanted Catherine to know that I was not an alcoholic; that I could drink wine, or leave it alone. Now, deprived of the sustenance that the undercroft could offer I felt a nervous excitement within me that prevented me from concentrating on anything. I could hardly take in the fact that I was attending my own wife's funeral.

When someone in their sixties is gathered in, as Francis had been the year before, the feeling is – or the feeling had been, at his funeral – that, untimely though his death was, he had probably managed to have his fair share of the good things that were going. I remember at Francis's service people put their heart into the hymns, wanting to give their friend the best of send-offs. After the burial service, everyone had stood about telling jokes about Francis and his wine collection, sharing affectionate memories of him. This was different. There was an irreducible bleakness about Catherine's service. There was the fact: she was just over twenty-five, and she was dead. Catherine had been taken from me before we had really begun our lives together. I felt oppressed and angry. It was so unfair.

The prayers and the hymns proceeded, but there were not enough people in the church to give the singing any substance. The words of the service and the music of the hymns fell listlessly on my ears. The very air in the church seemed thin and dead, attenuating every sound. Then the service was over, and the pall-bearers took the coffin out. We straggled outside after them, towards the grave. There was a space around me. Nobody talked to me, or even looked at me.

Outside it was a cold December day. A fine drizzle fell from a grey sky. The mourners stood beside the grave as the priest read the last words of the service and this time, unlike at Francis's funeral, none of them stopped afterwards to talk, or reminisce about Catherine, or about anything else. Everyone fled the churchyard as soon as they could. No one stopped to say any last word to me. It was as if I was invisible.

I was starting to make my way back to the other side of the church, where a taxi was waiting for me, when Ed Hartlepool walked up to me. He was wearing a black overcoat over a dark pin-striped suit, a white shirt and a black tie. His face was as white as his shirt, his eyes red-rimmed. His fair hair, always unruly, made him look as if he had been struck by lightning. His cheeks bore the tracks of dried tears. I had seen him briefly when I had entered the church, but he had only looked at me and not spoken. Now he strode up to me and stared me full in the face. His eyes glittered; his normally cheerful, open face looked gaunt and much older. He said, 'You killed her, Wilberforce. I know the police aren't going to do anything about it, but Catherine would never have driven off the road like that. I don't know what you did, but you killed her.'

I stared at him in astonishment. 'Ed, that's so unfair. Catherine was driving. It wasn't my fault.'

He was quivering with anger, and grief. 'It's lucky for you that you are on crutches,' he said. Then he turned on his heel and left.

The vicar came up to me, looking concerned, and asked me if I was all right. I thanked him and he said, 'So sorry for your loss, Mr Wilberforce. She was a very special girl.'

I managed to make my way around the church and down the path to the road where my taxi waited. The Plenders had said they did not feel up to asking anyone back to their house. There was to be no wake, no gathering of any kind. Catherine had been killed in a car accident, she had been buried, and now everyone was driving away. When I came close to where my taxi was parked, I saw that the Plenders were still standing by their car, and when they saw me, Helen Plender came up. I wondered if, at last, she would say something, or in some way acknowledge our shared grief.

She stood in front of me, her face more aged than I remembered it, bitter and birdlike. She said, 'Mr Wilberforce?'

'Mrs Plender,' I said, 'I'm glad to have this chance of saying how deeply sorry I am—'

She cut me off. 'I haven't come to hear how sorry you are. Nothing you could ever say will make the slightest difference to how I feel about you. I came to ask you if you would be kind enough to return my daughter's jewellery, as soon as possible. They are all valuable family pieces, and should be returned to us immediately.' Then she turned to go back to the car.

I lost my temper. I shouted after her, 'It was your fault, Mrs Plender! If you hadn't quarrelled with Catherine, she would never have wanted to go straight back to London. None of this needed to happen. It was your fault, not mine!'

The upright black-covered figure paused and quivered for a moment, but Helen Plender did not turn her head or reply.

Then the vicar was beside me, his arm around me as I started to try and swing on my crutches after Catherine's mother. 'Please, Mr Wilberforce. Remember where you are, and what we have just done. We must respect the dead, and their living relations. Let me help you to your taxi.'

I allowed him to shepherd me back to the waiting car, and help me inside it. 'Thank you, vicar,' I said. I couldn't think what else I ought to say. 'Thank you for a lovely service.'

Then the taxi took me back to Caerlyon.

I remained a day or two longer at Caerlyon after the funeral, until I felt mobile enough to travel. Then I took the train back to London. When I returned to the flat in Half Moon Street, a sense of loss caught up with me at last. I don't know how it was, but I was convinced that when I turned the key in the latch, and put the bags down in the hall, I would hear Catherine's voice from upstairs, calling, 'Is that you, darling? Where on earth have you been?' And I would reply, 'What do you mean, where on earth have I been? Where on earth have *you* been?'

Catherine was not anywhere on earth; her remains were in

the earth, but she herself was gone. I stood in the hallway and, my senses sharpened by grief, it seemed to me I could smell her perfume in the air and hear the rustle of her last movements a fortnight ago, as she had gone about the flat packing up her things for the journey north. In truth, the flat was silent. No one was there now but me. No one would ever be there now but me. I went into the kitchen and sat there for a long time, listening to the dripping of a tap. It must have been dripping like that since we went away. I could not find the energy to stand up and go and turn it off.

It would have been better if I could have wept, but for some reason I remained dry-eyed. The tears would not come.

I went to the wine rack next to the sink, picked up a bottle of Bordeaux and looked at it without much interest. It was a Château Sociando-Mallet 1986. It should be just about ready to drink. I opened it, took a glass from the cupboard and polished it. Then I put the glass down on the table and sat and waited while I gave the wine time to breathe. I said to myself, in a voice very like Catherine's, 'Did I die for this? Does my death mean nothing has changed? Are you just going to climb straight back inside a bottle?'

I sat there, staring at the glass and the bottle, and did not move. The day wore on, but I did not reach for the bottle or leave my chair. I sat looking at the wine and wondering about its taste, and wondering if I should at least pour out an inch into the glass and swirl it enough to release its fragrance. But I did not move.

At five o'clock I went to the phone and rang my doctor friend, Colin Holman. It took a while to get through to him, but I waited whilst he finished speaking to a patient. When he came on the line his voice was friendly, jolly and professional.

'Hello, Wilberforce. How are you?'

'I'm fine,' I said.

'And how's your lovely wife?'

'She's dead, unfortunately.'

There was a silence and then Colin said in a different tone, 'Oh my God, Wilberforce. How terrible! What happened?'

'A car crash,' I told him, without going into further details.

'What a ghastly thing to happen,' said Colin. 'I can't believe it. And what about you? Were you hurt?'

'I was very lucky,' I told him. 'Just a few cuts, a bruised knee, and a cracked rib.'

'Is there anything I can do to help?' asked Colin.

'As a matter of fact, Colin,' I told him, 'there is. I'm about to start drinking again. I've been trying not to all day. It's not that I'm a serious drinker. I just love wine. But I'm worried that if I start again now, I will forget to stop.'

'Are you drinking at the moment?' asked Colin.

'No,' I said. 'Not yet.'

'Then don't start,' he told me. 'I've two more appointments but I can be free in an hour. I imagine you're at the flat?'

'Yes.'

'Stay there. Don't have a drink. Don't go out. I'll be with you as soon as possible.'

'Thank you, Colin,' I said, with a sense of relief. 'You're a real friend. I'll wait for you; take as much time as you like – I'm not going to go anywhere.'

'And don't have a drink,' he repeated.

'No, I won't,' I promised. We hung up.

Colin had not been a close friend at university, but now I was in trouble, he was there for me. Why weren't there more people like that in the world? Where was Eck? Where was Ed Hartlepool? Where were any of them – when I really needed someone? It was funny how people turned out.

The other thing was, Colin was an extremely good doctor. If there was anything wrong with me, he would sort it out. I had nothing to worry about. If I had been drinking a little more than I should have been – and now I admitted to myself that there were times when my enthusiasm for good Bordeaux had perhaps been excessive – Colin would find a cure for it all. There must be some pills you could give people. I would be able to drink just the right amount of wine, and never too much. Colin would fix that for me. I had no need to worry about it any longer.

I thought that Catherine would understand now if, finally, I poured myself a glass of wine. Colin would be here soon, and he would sort me out. The Sociando-Mallet had been open for several hours now: it would be beginning to slowly oxidise and die. I wondered if it would be noticeable. I poured myself a glass and tasted it, but the wine was good.

The wine was very good.

Four

By the time Colin arrived at the flat I had drunk the bottle of Sociando-Mallet, another bottle of a Margaux, and I had just started on a third bottle, of a St Emilion. There was nothing much he could do for me that night except help me to bed. He left a note for me asking me to call on him at his consulting rooms near Belgrave Square when I awoke. I found the note when I came downstairs the next morning. There was no food in the flat, so I drank a glass of white wine and went to call on Colin.

The waiting room where Colin worked was done up like a drawing room, with stiff, uncomfortable chairs, and rows of this month's glossy magazines laid out on a low glass table. I picked up a copy of *Country Life* and turned its pages without reading anything, while I waited for Colin to find a gap between his other patients' appointments.

When I went in to see him, he was sitting behind a large partner's desk with a thin brown folder open in front of him. He waved at me to sit down in the chair opposite.

'Morning, old boy,' he said. 'How do you feel?'

Colin himself looked healthy, and much younger than the reflection of myself I had seen in the mirror that morning. 'I'm fine,' I assured him.

'You were into your third bottle by the time I arrived. Do you often drink that much wine, that quickly?'

'No,' I said. Then, because I thought it was important to be accurate if Colin were to help me, I added, 'I mean, yes, I do sometimes drink a few bottles, but I usually take more time to appreciate it.'

'I see,' said Colin, and made a note.

'I was a bit stressed out yesterday,' I explained.

'Quite. I quite understand. All the same, three bottles is a lot of wine for a single person in a single day, let alone in a couple of hours.'

'I suppose it is,' I agreed. 'I've never really thought of it like that.'

'I'm going to take you on as a patient,' said Colin. 'That is, if you want me to help you.'

'That's very kind of you,' I replied.

'I'm very expensive.'

'That doesn't matter,' I said. 'I'm very grateful.' I was grateful. It would be so nice to have someone taking an interest in me, now I was on my own again.

'There might be more expense on the way,' Colin warned me, 'because I think the first thing you ought to do is check yourself into The Hermitage. I'll make all the arrangements, but you need to understand what we are trying to achieve. You need to want to do it.'

'I'll do anything that you suggest,' I told him. 'What happens at The Hermitage?'

Colin stood up and stretched, then walked around the desk and sat down again in a chair on the same side of the desk as me. 'I'm not a specialist in the treatment of addictive behaviour,' he explained.

'I'm not addictive,' I protested. 'That's people who smoke dope, or use syringes. Drinking a little wine isn't addictive.'

'I'm afraid I think that it is,' said Colin, 'and if you want me to help you, you must be ready to listen to me and then take my advice. Otherwise, we will risk wasting each other's time.'

'Of course,' I said. The thought that Colin might drop me before he had really begun to help me frightened me.

'Wilberforce,' said Colin, 'the causes of addiction can be both familial and genetic. Often it is both. Did anyone in your family drink?'

'I don't know who my real parents were,' I said. 'My foster parents never did.'

'It is a disease,' Colin explained, 'and in the end it is a disease of one's own sense of self. Until you can understand that, and truly accept that you need help that only someone, or something external to you can change the way you are, you will never be cured.

'The Hermitage offer special programmes for people, like you, who have got into the habit of drinking too much, or who have become addicted to drugs of one sort or another. They have a programme called the Twelve Steps, which is based on the work of Alcoholics Anonymous. They have a good record of helping people. I recommend you enter yourself into one of their programmes. It would mean going down to their place in Gloucestershire for a few weeks to give it a try.'

'Of course; if that's what you suggest, I'll do it.'

'It's far from being cheap,' Colin said, 'but, if you can afford it, I can't think of a better way to tackle this. Wilberforce, you've got to want to do it. Otherwise it's a lot of money down the drain.'

'I'll do it,' I told him.

The Hermitage was a large country house, set in rolling wooded countryside. When the taxi brought me down the drive, it reminded me at first glance of Hartlepool Hall; but Hartlepool Hall didn't have modern wings, and brick-built staff houses, or a car park. I went into the hall, and it was like checking in at a country-house hotel. There were cut flowers everywhere; a smiling, elegant woman took down my details and made a print of my credit card; then a porter took my suitcase and showed me to my room.

It was an elegant room. It was faultlessly decorated: a pale-green carpet, green floral curtains tied up with velvet cords, a large double bed with a cream bedspread, and a door into a large bathroom. A bay window looked out on to a wooded valley with a stream running down it.

I was just unpacking my clothes when there was a knock at the door. I went and opened it and saw a man, younger than myself, with hair cut very short, wearing a short-sleeved khaki shirt and blue jeans. Although it was January and there were still patches of frost in the valley where the sun had not been able to reach, the temperature inside the house was very warm.

'Hello,' said the young man. His eyes glinted cheerfully behind round, horn-rimmed spectacles. 'I'm Eric.'

'Hello,' I said. 'I'm Wilberforce.'

We shook hands. I wondered what he wanted.

He said, 'We're going to be spending some time together, and I just wanted to introduce myself. Have you had lunch?'

'Not yet.'

'There's a canteen, but for now I'm going to suggest you and I have a light lunch together, to give ourselves time to get to know one another before you meet some of our other guests. If I call back in ten minutes, would that suit you?'

'Very well, thanks.'

Quarter of an hour later we were sitting in a small room in one of the modern wings I had noticed. The room was sparsely furnished. There was a sideboard with a sink unit built in, a table, two chairs, and a whiteboard. A small fridge stood in one corner. On the table in the centre of the room there were two places laid, and two plates of smoked salmon and lettuce. A jug of water sat in the middle of the table.

Eric said, 'Ah, smoked salmon! My favourite.'

We ate the food. It tasted of nothing. Eric poured me a glass of water and watched me drink it. It tasted of metal and effluent. He said, 'You'd rather be drinking wine, I expect.'

'No,' I lied.

'You see,' began Eric and then stopped. He said, 'What can I call you? I can't call you Wilberforce.'

'Everyone else does,' I said.

Eric shook his head: 'It sounds so formal, using your surname. We're not formal here. We can't be. You and I need to become really good friends. Do you mind if I call you Will instead?'

'If you want to.'

'Great, Will. If you're comfortable with that, then I am. I'm going to tell you a little bit about myself. We will be working hard together, and you need to know about me, and to trust me, Will. I was an alcoholic once.'

I gazed at him. It was quite possible: at any rate, there seemed no reason to disbelieve him.

'You'd never guess it to look at me now,' he said with pride. I did not reply. Eric went on, 'You know, I was drinking a bottle of whisky a day. A day! Can you believe it?'

I didn't know what to say, but Eric wasn't waiting for my responses. He wanted to talk about his life as an alcoholic.

'Yes, a bottle a day. I was a wreck. I lost my job. My wife left me. But I couldn't stop drinking. Then, one day, some friends took me to a group at our local church, which helped people like me. And they got me to take the first step.'

Eric got to his feet, picked up a marker pen and wrote on the white board: 'Step One: We must admit we are powerless over alcohol. We must admit we cannot manage our lives.'

He sat down again, and jerked his thumb at the scrawl on the board, which I could barely read. He said, 'That's the first step, Will. Just now I admitted to you I was once an alcoholic. My own life started to change from the day I finally found the courage to admit it to myself. That's our process here. We need to admit we've got a problem. After that, there will be more steps that we will have to take together. The first step is the biggest and most important. After that, we will take them one at a time. That's how we live our lives here: one step at a time. But with my help, and God's help, you're going to find the strength to walk this road with me and at the end you will be cured, just as I am.'

'Did your wife come back to you in the end?' I asked.

Eric looked a little put out. 'No,' he said. 'But that's another story.' He rose to his feet again, went across to the fridge and took out a can of Diet Coke. 'Want some?'

I shook my head. He popped the can, upended it and took a long pull on it. A trickle of Coke ran down his chin and the side of his neck, which he wiped away with his finger. Then he put the can down beside the sink and came and sat down again.

'So, Will, my question today is: do you think you've got a problem? Let's look at some of the issues around that, shall we?'

'I do like drinking wine,' I admitted. 'I mean, I can drink it, or not drink it, as I please. But I do enjoy it. I'm very interested in it.'

'Wine is a good drink,' said Eric, 'in moderation. Our Lord drank wine. And how much wine do you drink, Will?'

'I like to try different wines. I enjoy comparing the tastes. I keep notes. It's a great interest of mine.'

'Will, you're not really answering my question,' said Eric. 'How much do you drink each day?'

'Oh, it can vary,' I said, 'but I suppose three or four bottles a day.'

'A day!' exclaimed Eric. 'Four bottles a day!' He got to his feet again, and went to the sink, finishing off his can of Diet Coke. He came back and sat down again.

'Will, I want to say something. You've got a big problem. But you've also got a big heart. It took courage to do what you have just done: to admit that you are powerless to stop drinking wine. That's great.' He went and wrote on the whiteboard: 'W. drinks four bottles of wine a day.'

He returned and said, 'That's a lot of wine. That's nearly fifteen hundred bottles of wine a year.'

'I collect wine. I have quite a lot of it.'

'Really?' said Eric. 'And what do you call quite a lot?'

'I have a hundred thousand bottles in my cellars – maybe a bit more.'

Eric said, 'Will, we're not going to get this done if you're going to be flippant. This is very serious stuff we're doing here. This is about your life. This is about changing the rest of your life. So in this room we tell the truth, the whole truth, and nothing but the truth.'

'I am telling the truth,' I said. 'Why wouldn't I?'

Eric looked at me sadly. I had disappointed him in some way. He went and wrote again on the whiteboard: 'I have a hundred thousand bottles of wine.'

He came back and said, 'You dream about wine, don't you, Will? You dream about that wonderful wine cellar, where there's always more wine, where you can always go and find another bottle.'

'Yes,' I said. 'Except that it's not imaginary.'

'I used to dream that I had my own off-licence,' said Eric wistfully. 'I dreamed I had shelves and shelves of whisky: Bell's, Famous Grouse, J & B, and Johnny Walker Black Label. I dreamed I could go there whenever I wanted to get more whisky. It was such a dreadful feeling when I awoke, to find that the whisky wasn't there after all. I used to curl up in a ball on my bed, and cry like a baby.'

'Yes, that must have been very hard for you,' I said with sympathy. 'But I'm very lucky: I really do have a lot of wine,'

I said. It seemed important that Eric should understand this point. 'I drink a lot of wine. I've told you that. But that's because it's my hobby. I inherited some wine from a friend. He built up a fantastic collection. As far as I know, it is one of the largest collections of Bordeaux in private hands in this country.'

Eric smiled. 'OK, Will, you have a hundred thousand bottles of wine. You probably have a million bottles of wine, in your wonderful, secret cellar. OK. But do you own the wine, or does it own you?'

The afternoon continued in this vein. Eric drank more Diet Coke. I longed for a glass of wine, but I knew I had to go without for a while. After an hour or two of conversation with Eric, which was becoming tedious, I decided it would be better, for Eric's sake and mine, if I pretended that the undercroft did not exist.

Eric was very pleased with me when I admitted that point to him. He said, 'I'm so proud of you, Will, for owning up to that. It's like you're telling me you understand the need for truth. If you can be honest with me, you can be honest with yourself. You're close to taking the first step.'

I ate alone in my room that night. Eric said it was too soon for me to meet the other guests, but tomorrow I could join in a group discussion. When I had finished eating the tasteless food, I went and lay on my bed and thought about Catherine. Would she have approved of me being here? I thought she would have been very proud of me. For some reason a memory came into my mind of Catherine and me sitting together at a metal table on the pavement outside a bar, somewhere near our hotel in the Faubourg St Honoré, on our last visit to Paris together. It was a sunny day, warm for late October, and we were both drinking white wine.

Catherine said, 'I hope we can always have happy times together like this, Wilberforce.'

'What could stop us?' I said.

'Because sometimes I worry about you drinking too much. It's not that I mind you drinking a bit. You've earned the right to enjoy yourself, God knows, and I'd be the last person to get in the way of that. But I do worry sometimes. It makes you look ill. You look so much nicer, when you aren't drinking.'

'You mustn't worry,' I said, 'I'll be all right. And you look very good to me at all times.'

'Darling,' she said, smiling. Then she added, 'I only mean, if it's between the wine and me, I hope you'll choose me.'

I raised my glass to her, and she raised hers in reply and I said, 'I've already chosen you.'

I remember how we sat smiling at each other in the autumn sunshine, while we finished our wine together.

Then, as I lay on my bed and remembered how she looked that day, and the sound of her voice, at long last the tears came. I mourned for Catherine for the first time since her death. I couldn't remember what had happened, or why she had been taken from me; but I understood at last the full reality of my loss. She had been taken from me, and now I had to sort out my life. I lay on the bed and stared at the ceiling for a long while, before finally making the effort to undress and get inside the bed. Before I went to sleep, I said, 'I choose you, Catherine. Not the wine.'

The next morning Eric came to take me down to breakfast. All meals were served in a smart self-service canteen. A dozen other tables were occupied by people either sitting alone or in groups of two or three. There was not much conversation. Eric and I collected some coffee and toast, and went and sat together.

'Great bunch of guys here,' said Eric. 'There's Dave, who's a methadone addict – really nice guy: he's a florist. Pete, who's sitting with him, is coming off a whisky habit. I can relate to Pete, ha ha.'

I could see nothing out of the ordinary about either Dave or Pete: two quiet, middle-aged men having a cup of coffee together.

Eric looked around him. 'That girl over there – she's Wilhelmina from Utrecht.' I looked across and saw a tall, pale girl with spectacles, and long, straight red hair, sitting alone at a table. 'She got drunk the other day on two glasses of white-wine spritzer, and checked herself in here. I don't know what we can do for her. She's rather weird. That large man at the service counter – that's Mick. Everybody here calls him "Big Mick". He's a tax accountant from the City, with a telephone-number salary, he tells me. He also has a drugs-and-violence problem: he's a crack addict. But he's a very, very sweet man so long as he's not high. He has his own special plastic cutlery. We don't like him around knives. But don't worry about him: he's more likely to damage himself than anyone else.'

Big Mick was about six foot three and eighteen stone, balding and heavily muscled. He wore a blue tracksuit and was helping himself to a generous cooked breakfast. I decided I would avoid Big Mick.

After breakfast there was a group meeting in a large conference room. Eric and another caseworker called Angela managed the session. The rest of us sat in a semicircle of chairs around the table where Eric and Angela sat. Angela spoke first. She said, 'It's important at these sessions that we listen as well as talk. You must tell the truth about yourself if you can, and be prepared to listen to others tell you the truth about yourself. Eric will facilitate our session this morning.'

Eric stood up, a tin of Diet Coke in one hand, and said, 'People, I'd like to introduce you to Will here. Will's going to tell us why he's here in just a moment, and then I'm hoping some of you will share your own experiences with him. I want Will to know that he's not alone. I want him to hear how all of you have struggled, and stumbled, but have taken one step and then the next on the road to recovery. Are you happy to talk to us about yourself, Will?'

I nodded, and everyone looked at me expectantly. There was a silence.

'Oh, I see,' I said. 'You want me to say something now?'

Angela said, 'Yes please, Will. We truly want to share your problems with you, and work with you to achieve the right outcomes.'

'Amen!' said Big Mick.

I said, 'Oh, well, there's not a lot to say really. I drink wine. I love wine, in fact I collect wine. I'm very interested in it.'

I stopped and Eric looked at me, and then prompted me by saying, 'But one day . . . ?'

'Oh, yes, and then for various reasons I decided I ought to come here because I was probably drinking a bit more than I should be.'

'Will was on four bottles of wine a day before he came here,' said Eric, with dramatic emphasis on the word 'four'.

'The Lord protect you!' said Big Mick.

'Thanks very much,' I said. 'Anyway, one day my wife was killed in a car crash so I thought I'd better get a grip on my life and I went to see a friend; he's a doctor, a very nice chap called Colin whom I was at university with, and anyway Colin said he thought I might be drinking too much, and so I said well, what can I do about it? and he said—'

'Slow down, slow down, Will,' said Angela.

'How awful,' said Wilhelmina. 'Your poor wife was killed.' She started to weep silently and took out a large handkerchief and blew her nose.

'Was you driving?' asked Dave.

'No, my wife was driving; it was an accident.' I felt

exhausted, talking about myself in front of all these complete strangers.

Big Mick said, 'I smoked crack and I was possessed by demons and beat my partner, so that she left me. But then the Lord spoke to me and told me to check myself in here and now I am cured. Praise the Lord!'

'Well, very nearly cured, Mick,' said Angela.

Wilhelmina had finished weeping and now she, too, had something to say. 'I was overcome by drinking some wine and I was at a party and I kissed a man and we went away and he did, oh, such things to me, and because of the wine I let him. Now I am a poor sinner without hope, and all because I drank too much wine.'

'You just had a good time,' said Dave. 'I wouldn't let it get you down.'

The morning passed away with further reminiscences of this kind and then we broke for lunch. I sat with Big Mick, who seemed to have taken a shine to me.

'He's not a bad bloke, your Eric,' said Big Mick confidentially to me. We were sitting together at a table eating pasta and salad. Eric was talking earnestly to Angela at another table.

'No,' I said. 'I'm sure his heart's in the right place.'

'Yes, and he was a bit of a piss artist in his own right, once upon a time,' said Big Mick. 'It wouldn't take much for Eric to be sucking on a bottle of whisky again – know what I mean? Anyway, tell me what you do in the real world?'

'I used to be a software developer. In fact, I used to own a software company until recently.'

'Really,' said Big Mick. 'I know all about that. I'm a tax accountant. I specialise in corporate stuff, sheltering high earners and private equity types from paying more tax than they need to. What was your company called?'

'Wilberforce Software Solutions,' I told him. 'But I sold it to Bayleaf, and it's Bayleaf UK now.'

'Great business,' said Big Mick. 'Those are excellent software packages. I use them myself. I'm really pleased to meet you.' He reached across the table and took my hand and shook it.

For a while we sat and talked happily about tax computations, and the deficiencies of Inland Revenue software.

Later, when we were on our own together, Eric said to me, 'I was so pleased to see you getting on so well with Big Mick. Not everyone can adapt to him. I expect you were talking about religion, were you?'

'In a way,' I agreed.

Eric and I continued our daily sessions together, and every day there would be a group session as well where we traded experiences. Some of the members of the group went; others arrived. When it was Big Mick's time to depart he gave me his business card and said, 'Get in touch some time, if they ever let you out of here. We could maybe work on some ideas for new software packages together, now that I'm cured.'

'Are you cured?' I asked.

Big Mick winked and said, 'One step at a time, Wilberforce. One step at a time.'

I did try to get in touch with him a few months later, but when I rang the number on his card I was told that he'd left the office. I kept asking questions and in the end I found out that he had been shot dead by his crack dealer in a disagreement about money.

Eric continued to work on my case. We spent an unproductive morning talking about God.

'Are you OK about God, Will?'

'In what way, exactly?'

'I mean we believe that it helps in this process if you can

put your trust in a Higher Power. For me, that's God. But, Will, if you don't want to talk about God, that's cool too.'

'I don't think it would be especially helpful,' I said.

Eric looked at me with pity mingled with regret. 'I think that's the wrong judgement, Will, but, hey, it's your judgement. Maybe we'll talk about this again.'

The next day was more difficult. Eric went to the whiteboard and wrote: 'A list of all the persons I have harmed.' Then he turned to me and said, 'This one isn't an option, Will. If you want to get better, you need to understand that your illness may have caused harm to other people. You might have made them sad; you might have hurt them, like Big Mick did; you might have stolen from them, lied to them, or deceived them in other ways.'

Eric looked at me expectantly. I looked back at him. As I so often found with Eric, I had no real idea what he was talking about. I said nothing, so Eric wrote on the whiteboard: 'Mrs Wilberforce'. Then he smudged it out and wrote, 'Mrs Will'.

'Catherine,' I corrected him. 'But I didn't harm her. It was an accident.'

'Don't tell me she sat and watched you drink and wasn't hurt by it in some way,' said Eric.

'I know what Catherine suffered because of me,' I said. 'Yes, Eric. I may have caused her unnecessary worry.'

'Was there anybody else?' asked Eric. 'There usually is.'

Ed Hartlepool. Eck. Catherine's parents. My foster-mother. My foster-father.

'No,' I said. 'I can't think of anyone.'

'Yes, you can,' said Eric. 'There is someone.'

'Catherine left Ed of her own accord,' I said. 'It was nothing to do with me, or drink, or anything.'

'That's interesting,' said Eric. 'We'll come back to that later. But I wasn't thinking about your friend. I was thinking about you. It's you who has been the most harmed by drink.'

I supposed that was true, when I thought about it. I had harmed myself. My life was not better than it had been before I discovered wine; it was worse, immeasurably worse. The day I had first entered the shop at Caerlyon had led me into a new world. I had discovered friendship; I had discovered a kind of happiness that I had never known before. I had discovered I could love somebody, when I met Catherine. I had discovered wine, when I met Francis. Wine had brought pleasures of a different sort. In the secret garden I had entered that evening long ago, it was the fruit in the garden that turned, in the end, to ashes in my mouth. Wine had brought its own labyrinth of experience with it, in which one might twist and turn for ever, forgetting where the entrance to the labyrinth was, forgetting how to leave. If I had not gained the things I had gained – the friendship and the love – I would never have had to experience the loss that I now felt.

I put my forearms on the table, rested my head on them and closed my eyes. I wished I couldn't hear Eric's nasal voice, full of triumph, as he said, 'Now we're getting somewhere. Now we're making real progress.'

I finished my course at The Hermitage three weeks later. Eric had arranged an 'exit interview' for me with Angela.

'I'm too close to it, Will,' he told me. 'We've had our ups and downs, but we've worked together as a team and I feel terrifically close to you as a result. I think you're a really great human being, Will – just a bit of personal development required for you to be able to return to the outside world and lead a full and meaningful life.'

'Yes,' I said.

'Don't let me down, Will. Don't leave here and throw all our hard work away. There are demons lurking in the thickets, Will, who will whisper to you to turn aside from the straight and narrow path you must tread. Take this pamphlet.

I know you don't believe in God, but He believes in you, and He can help you. It's all written down in here. I refer you to page nine specifically.'

'Thanks, Eric,' I said. I took the pamphlet without looking at it.

'Hugs,' he said, and before I could escape he put his arms around me and squeezed me in a tight embrace. He smelt faintly of perspiration and disinfectant.

'Thanks, Eric,' I said again.

'God be with you,' said Eric with a sob. He turned away, and I left the room.

The exit interview with Angela was different. She was a tall, cool, severe-looking woman with short-cut straw-coloured hair, a determined mouth and firm chin. She said, when I went to see her for my final meeting, 'Mr Wilberforce. Come in and sit down. How do you feel about things, now you've spent some time with us?'

'Much better,' I said.

'I'm in two minds about your case, Mr Wilberforce,' she said. 'Eric's given you an excellent report. He says the two of you have bonded well together. But Eric works with his emotional intelligence. He gets very involved. It makes him a good caseworker, don't you think?'

'Very good,' I agreed.

'I'm more of an observer, however,' said Angela, 'and what I have observed in you is a great ability to mask your feelings. I don't really know what you're thinking. I'm not sure what your level of buy-in has been to what we do here. I think you are walking along the edge of a cliff, which you could still fall over. I am not sure you have understood or accepted everything that we have told you, or shown you. What do you think?'

'I feel it has done me some good,' I said slowly. 'I don't want a drink right now.'

'Hang on to that feeling,' said Angela. 'I think we have achieved something together. But I believe in clear outcomes to cases. I don't think we've got one with you. I think you've made progress, but I don't know whether you can change your behaviour altogether.'

'I feel I've made progress, too,' I said. It was true.

'Come back and see us in six months,' suggested Angela, 'and then we'll see how much progress you have made.'

'Thanks, I will,' I promised. But I wasn't sure if I wanted to see Eric again.

'That's a deal, then,' said Angela. 'We'll keep in touch with your doctor, in any case.' She stood up, and we shook hands.

Half an hour later I was sitting in a taxi and on my way back to the station; then home to London. And when I got there, what then?

Five

I came back from The Hermitage determined to change my life. It wasn't the fact that Eric had altered the way I thought about myself with his constant nasal twang, preaching to me about the Twelve Steps. It was the experience of being at the mercy of people like him, which made me so keen to avoid any return journey to The Hermitage, or anywhere else like it. I had a feeling there were places a lot worse than The Hermitage that I might end up in.

I had thought a great deal, too, about being found drunk on the floor of the flat by Colin – the circumstance which had led to my agreeing to go The Hermitage. I knew there would be a lot more nights and days like that, when I had drunk too much. The thought of ending up like some emaciated, magenta-faced, incontinent drunkard lying in a doorway terrified me. I felt clearer-sighted than I ever had about my fondness for drinking wine. Whatever the reasons I had had for drinking in the early days, when I had first begun to know Francis and he had first initiated me into the mysteries of wine, they had long since been overtaken by changes in my body chemistry.

I knew now that Colin was right, and that Eric was right. I was becoming an addict: an alcoholic. I knew enough about life to realise how it would all end, if I ever strayed from the straight and narrow path, as Eric had described it. Things were going to have to change.

I sat down at my desk on the day I returned and made a list

of the actions I would take – the actions that would signal the beginning of a new life:

1 Drink no wine
2 Look for a job
3 Sell the flat and move somewhere smaller and cheaper
4 Get out and meet people

I tore the piece of paper from the pad and went and pinned it up on the cork pinboard that Catherine had put on the wall above the phone. On the board was a note in her neat, sloping hand: '*Get chicken drumsticks. Buy bin liners. Call home.*' I removed the note and threw it away. I didn't want to be reminded of her every time I looked at the telephone. Catherine had been right, too. Above all, Catherine had been right. She had understood clearly what was happening: she had seen the alchemy of the wine from the undercroft at work, and she had tried to tell me. And I had quarrelled with her because I did not like to hear the truth.

I pinned my Action List on the board. Then I went and retrieved Catherine's note from the bin, smoothed out the wrinkled paper and put it away in a drawer.

Then I went back to the Action List and wrote, in big letters: 'SELL CAERLYON. SELL THE WINE.'

As soon as I had written those words I felt a profound sense of relief. That was what I would do. In a stroke I would free myself from the weight of temptation that sat on my shoulders even now and achieve some stability in my life. I was becoming ill and becoming poor at the same time. I had spent a lot of the proceeds from the sale of my company in buying Caerlyon, and more of it on buying the flat in Half Moon Street. What I had left did not produce a sufficient income to cover my needs, and I was steadily using up my capital; not all that slowly, either. Selling Caerlyon would put me in a position where it would not matter whether I worked or not for the next ten years. I was going to get a job if I could, anyway. What else would I do with my time?

Next day I rang the agent who looked after Caerlyon for me in my absence. He received my instructions with considerable surprise.

'Sell Caerlyon? You must be joking.'

'I'm not joking. What good is it to me? I never go there. I'm never going to go back and live there after what happened, am I?'

The agent was conciliatory. Thoughts, no doubt, of the commission he might earn from such a sale occurred to him. He said, 'Well, if you are sure, we would be delighted to act for you. It might take a while, with the Council as a sitting tenant in the main house. On the other hand, it's a good covenant.'

'Well, see what you can do,' I told him. 'Let me know what you think it might fetch.'

'We'll do a valuation,' he said, 'and what would your plans be for relocating the wine? There's quite a lot of it, isn't there? Do you want us to look for some suitable storage facilities for you? I don't suppose you can fit it all into your London flat.'

'Sell the wine too,' I told him.

This surprised him even more. 'I always thought you were very keen on Mr Black's wine collection,' he said.

'I was,' I told him, 'but I'm afraid it's got to go when I sell the house. Francis always told me his family used to buy wine from Christie's. Try and get someone from their wine department to come and value it for me.'

When I put the phone down I felt more at peace than I had done for a long while. I couldn't believe I had been so decisive. I felt Catherine would have been very proud of me. I went out and walked around Green Park in the cold March sunlight. I felt like a different man.

As I walked, I wondered what Francis would think when he found out I had sold the wine. I knew he was dead, but I found it hard to locate him amongst the things that were past in my life. Francis might be disappointed if he knew I had sold the wine. He had entrusted it to me, together with his house. I was to have lived in his house and looked after the wine in the undercroft, the collection of which he considered to have been the one great achievement of his life. He might regard the sale of his wine as a betrayal of his trust. He might be right, too: it was a betrayal. It was also the only chance of my survival. I knew that while the wine was still there, I would for ever return to its call.

The next day I wrote letters to ten different software companies, asking if they would be interested in employing me as a consultant. I hoped my reputation was still strong enough to ensure I received some expressions of interest. Then I sat at my desk thinking about how pleased Catherine would be if I got a job, and gave up drinking at the same time. I never used to drink. It was a habit I had developed after first meeting Francis.

I filled the day with activity. I tidied up the flat, which had become somewhat forlorn and dusty. A cleaner came in once a week but, unsupervised, her efforts were superficial in their effect. I parcelled up Catherine's jewellery, in response to a letter requesting its return from a solicitor acting for her parents. I moved all her clothes out of her bedroom, and her make-up, and hung everything up in the wardrobe in the spare bedroom, or stored it away in boxes.

It was only in the evening that it became more difficult for me. Now, when the day's activity was done, it would have been very nice to drink a glass of wine. I felt the desire to open a bottle growing in me, like an itch, like an ache, like a burning need. I walked from one room to another and talked to Catherine, to stop myself thinking about having a drink.

'I think our marriage is better than it's ever been,' I said to her, 'don't you? If I can just keep going without a drink for a few weeks I know I will be all right again. I'm not really an alcoholic, but you were right to keep warning me. I understand that now.' I was at the desk now, and the air in the little sitting room seemed to me to be fragrant with the Chanel No. 5, which Catherine used to wear. I felt she was with me. 'Within a month, or two months at the latest,' I told her, 'I'll have a job doing contract software development somewhere. I'm not going to be too ambitious at first. I just want to get back into the habit of work, and make sure I'm earning a living and not living off capital. Later, maybe, I'll go back to the idea of starting a new business.'

Catherine nodded in agreement. I wished she'd speak, but even though she did not, she seemed content with what I was saying. I felt that our lives were in harmony again, as they had been in the first days of our marriage. It was such a shame that she was dead.

I went to bed early that night. At first I felt the peacefulness that had come upon me as I had talked to Catherine, wandering about the flat, feeling her presence everywhere on the edge of my vision, feeling a draught fluttering across the back of my neck like the touch of cool fingers. Then restlessness set in. I began to examine my own behaviour and I thought, for a while, lying there in the dark, that I might be losing my mind. Did everyone else who had lost a wife go around talking to her as if she was still alive? I didn't know.

Sleep came in the end. I fell into edgy dreams, with a vivid strangeness to them. In my dream, I smelled something rotten, and I saw a half-familiar shape out of the corner of my eye. I was in a strange city, in a country I did not know, and there was something following me down the street that I did not want to catch up with me.

The next morning I went downstairs and saw that

someone had written on the notepad on the desk: '*TNMWWTTW*'. The letters were not written in my usual handwriting. They were scored into the paper, almost through the paper and into the wood of the desk beneath, with a furious energy. I didn't remember writing them. I did not know what they meant. I sat and looked at them for a long time. I thought I ought to try and remember them, in case I saw them again, in case they had some significance which for the time being escaped me. So I tried to think of a mnemonic to remember them by. It was difficult, but in the end I came up with '*Ten Naughty Mice Went Walking Towards The Wensleydale*'.

Then I went into the kitchen and unwrapped Catherine's jewellery, which I had rolled up in tissue paper before posting it back to her parents. I laid the pieces out on the table. There was a pair of sapphire-and-diamond earrings, and a matching three-stranded sapphire-and-diamond necklace. The stones were a deep blue. There was a heavy gold bracelet and a signet ring, a three-stranded pearl necklace, several diamond rings, an emerald-and-diamond necklace, and various less important pieces.

I could remember her wearing most of them. I thought I could picture each occasion when she had worn the sapphire necklace, which was not very often, for it was a very grand piece of jewellery. I decided that I would not post them for a day or two yet, to give myself another chance to look at them before they went. They were a part of my memory of Catherine, and once they went, her ghost, always present in my mind, would become thinner and less substantial. I wasn't ready to lose any more of her just yet. I scooped up the jewellery and wrapped each piece in the tissue paper it had been wrapped in, then took it to my desk and locked all of it in a drawer.

The next day I received a letter from one of the software

companies I had written to. It was full of enthusiastic praise for the programs I had developed at my old company, and said that the writer would get back in touch with me at the earliest possible moment, if anything came up that he thought would be of interest. There was no suggestion that we should meet.

Over the next few days I received several more letters in a similar vein. None of them had any immediate requirement for my services. One of them went as far as suggesting lunch some time, but did not give a date. Another said they were fully staffed up at present, but might be looking for more people next year. They were the most positive replies I received. The rest were polite, but unhelpful. Only one person rang me up: the managing director of a former competitor.

'Yes, it's a young man's game now,' he said. 'Some of our programmers aren't much more than teenagers. It's like tennis players: you're over the hill by the time you're thirty. But keep in touch, Wilberforce; you never know, something might turn up.'

I also received a phone call from Christie's. Ben Someone rang to say he had been to value the wine at Caerlyon.

'Oh yes?' I said. 'What do you think? It's quite a collection, isn't it?' Ben said, 'Yes, well, it's quite a mixture. Rather difficult to value, in a way.' He sounded hesitant.

I said, 'I would have thought it was quite easy. I always thought he bought most of his wine at auction from you.'

'No,' said Ben. 'Your agent said you thought that, but he wasn't a recent customer. It's an odd mixture. There are a few cases of quite good stuff, all from the sixties and seventies. After that the recent additions to the collection seem more like odds and ends. Did the cellar change hands in the 1980s? There isn't really much of any value later than that date.'

Francis had inherited the cellar from his parents when he was in his early forties, some time in the mid-eighties.

'Yes,' I said. 'That's when Francis Black began adding to his father's collection of wine.'

Ben Ingledew said, 'Well, the later stuff is quite a strange mixture. It almost looks like what we'd expect to get offered to us from bankruptcies or house clearances. You know: a little bit of this and a little bit of that. Some odd choices in there too: Australian and Bulgarian reds that frankly should have been drunk within a year, if at all.'

I became irritated. I had no idea what the man was talking about. I said, 'I believe that Francis in his day was one of the great experts and one of the greatest collectors specialising in the wines of Bordeaux.'

Ben Ingledew said, 'Well, I am sure he knew a great deal about it. There certainly are a few remnants of some very good wines in the cellar, but nearly all the cases have been opened, and a lot of it seems to have been drunk. I mean, we found a couple of bottles of 1974 Pétrus, for example. There's a couple of cases of 1978 Trotanoy. There are six bottles of 1953 Cheval Blanc. But we would have been looking for some of the newer vintages and some of the classic first growths that you'd expect to find in a modern collection of wine. There are hardly any *premiers grands crus classés*. There's no Le Pin, or Le Dôme, or Latour. There's no Angélus or Palmer or Ausone. There aren't even very many decent third- or fourth-growth wines. On the other hand there are quite a few things that probably wouldn't be stocked in the better super-markets. I'm not saying it's all bad news. There are several cases of quite good stuff, and a few exceptional bottles, which must have been laid down a very long time ago . . .' His voice trailed away in embarrassment.

They had obviously sent some young trainee to value the wine – someone who didn't really know what he was talking about. I felt annoyed.

'So, what do you think it is worth, then?' I asked.

'Well, there's about five hundred cases of wine in wooden boxes, and about a thousand bottles of wine in the racks. Say seven thousand bottles altogether.'

I interrupted him: 'There's at least a hundred thousand bottles in that cellar.'

'Oh,' said Ben. 'Well, I must have missed something. I'll send you the inventory in the post. There must be another cellar somewhere, is there? Because we certainly inventoried everything in – what do you call it? – the undercellar?'

'The undercroft,' I told him.

'Anyway, not counting anything else you keep elsewhere, we would recommend that you put a reserve on what we have listed of about thirty, if you send it to auction.'

'Thirty?'

'Thirty thousand,' said Ben, 'and if we are lucky it could get up to fifty on the day.'

'Thirty thousand?' I repeated. 'That collection of wine must be worth more than a million pounds!'

'Well,' said Ben, 'we can't get it to add up to that sort of figure. Or anything like it. As I say, we'll send you the inventory with our values against each lot of wine. The trouble is, we don't really know its provenance, or how it was stored before it got to your cellar. Quite a few of the cased wines in wooden cases, and most of the wine in those little side chambers, we expect may have started to go over by now. A lot of it should have been drunk or sold and the money reinvested in something younger. And those bottles which are of that sort of age aren't always special enough to command a rarity value. Mind you, there are some very interesting bottles of wine there. I don't want to be too depressing about it.'

'I really can't understand', I said, 'how you can put such a low figure on such a marvellous collection of wine. I've been told it is one of the greatest collections in private hands in this country.'

Ben said, so politely that I could imagine him smiling to himself as he spoke on the phone, 'Well, I couldn't really say, Mr Wilberforce. But I would say that if you were to pay more than fifty thousand for what we've seen, you'd be paying over the odds.'

'I see,' I said. This boy was an idiot. I had wasted my time involving him. Why had they sent someone who so obviously had been in the job less than a week?

'Let us know if you want us to put it into auction,' said Ben, 'and let me know, when you see the inventory, if I have missed something.'

We hung up. Now I was going to have to trail all the way up to Caerlyon to check the wine off against his inventory. Fifty thousand pounds! I had paid a million for that wine, and I knew then that it was cheap at the price. I rang up the agent and complained.

'Well,' said my agent, 'I don't know about that. Ben Ingledew is a Master of Wine, you know. I'd be very surprised if he's got it wrong. But when you get his valuation, you'd better come up and check. He's obviously missed something.'

A couple of days later I took the train up to Newcastle and then a taxi to Caerlyon. The daffodils were out, covering the neglected lawns of the old house. The courtyard was covered in moss. Someone had thrown a brick at the shop window, but it had bounced off the wire grille I had arranged to be put up, and the pane was only cracked. The visitor had had more success with the house. Both kitchen windows were starred, where someone had thrown something at them. I unlocked the door and went in, expecting to find that the place had been trashed. But it was untouched, unvisited, unloved. All that had changed was that there was a pile of letters to 'The Occupier' on the door mat.

I put my bags down in the kitchen and turned on the

heating. Then I took the keys to the undercroft from the tin where I kept them hidden and went next door. The shop was dusty and abandoned, but there were footprints in the dust and the desk had been cleared, evidence of the valuer's visit. I went down the stairs to the undercroft, and flicked the light switch on.

For a moment, Ben Ingledew's words seemed to have affected my vision. What, after all, was in this cellar but a few piles of wooden cases, a few thousand dusty bottles of ageing wine? I stood halfway down the stairs, looking into the great stone chamber, and it seemed forlorn, a collection of odds and ends, a dumping ground for the unsold stock of a dozen pubs and restaurants.

Then it came into focus again, and I saw the cellar as it really was: a magician's cavern, full of potency and brilliance. The lights sparkled on the endless bottles lining the sides of the great vaulted space. The small piles of awkwardly stacked wooden cases of wine became columns and towers of wooden boxes, an underground reconstruction of Manhattan, along which one could walk down avenues of Pomerol, Margaux, St Emilion, St Julien.

I looked at the inventory in my hand. There was far more wine down here than they had listed – I knew that. I wasn't going to bother to count it all. I could see it in front of me. The man had got it badly wrong, that was all.

I wandered along the racks on the south wall of the cellar and checked the inventory. According to the list, which I had looked through on the train on the way up, there should be some bottles of Château Talbot 1979 somewhere here. I found the last two and thought, Well, at least Mr Ben so-called-master-of-wine Ingledew has got something right. I decided to take them upstairs to the shop.

I put the bottles on the desk. I wasn't sure why I had moved them from the rack. Then I sat down in my chair, opposite the chair where Francis had sat, and thought. I could feel no sense of Francis now. That sense had become fainter every time I had returned here. The first time I had been back to the undercroft I had felt as if he was telling me what to do, guiding me in everything. I could almost see him. Out of good manners, I never sat in his chair in case he still wanted to use it. He had gone, though – gone for good – and all the decisions were up to me now.

The first decision I had to make was whether I should sell the wine at auction. I was certainly not going to put it into auction at the reserve price that Christie's had suggested. A cheque for thirty thousand pounds in return for an investment of a million pounds made a year or two ago – it simply did not bear thinking about.

I decided I would leave it for a few months and then get someone else to look at it. It was probably going up in value just sitting there.

That solved another problem. While the wine remained unsold, there was no point in selling Caerlyon. I would only have to move the wine somewhere else and, if anything was likely to affect its value, moving it would. Although I knew I really needed to sell Caerlyon sooner rather than later, six months either way wasn't going to make any difference. I decided I would tell the agent to revalue the wine and the house six months from now, using different valuers, and see what the result was compared with the estimates now.

I sat and looked at the two bottles of Château Talbot. Without really thinking about it – thinking more about whether I could find any of Francis's old invoices for the wine he had bought, which might indicate how much he had paid for it and where it had been bought from – I went over to the desk and opened one of the bottles. It was automatic; I just felt the wine should be allowed to breathe.

From downstairs I felt the familiar radio waves vibrating in my blood, singing to me. I heard the whispered names of the wine recited from somewhere in my memory: Bellevue-Mondotte, Yon-Figeac, Chapelle de la Mission. Each name was like a poem that evoked sunny days, the laughter of friends, the love of one's wife and family. I remembered Catherine saying to me, not so long ago, after she had died: 'You must choose one of us. You must choose me, or you must choose the wine.'

She had said something similar a month or two before, when she was still alive and we had been in Paris together. Then I had told her, 'I've already chosen you.' But life isn't as simple as that. Choices are never as straightforward as one would like. In the real world there is more complexity than one can imagine. Compromise is necessary, from time to time.

I poured myself a glass of Château Talbot, and swirled the wine around the glass to release its bouquet. It was old, but it was still going to be drinkable. I raised the glass and took a sip. I said out loud, 'I choose you, Catherine, and I choose the wine as well.'

2003

One

That winter I fell into the habit at least twice a week of leaving the office much earlier than in the old days, and driving out of the industrial estate, up the side of the valley to Caerlyon. Now I left the office at six, not eight. Very often when I left there would still be a dozen cars in the parking slots in front of the building: programmers working late, working the way I used to work. I didn't feel guilty. I had worked like that for nearly fifteen years. I had worked like that because, if I had not, the business would have been overrun by one or other of its dozens of competitors. Clients would not have stayed with us, because what we did was meet deadlines – always, no matter what the costs to our personal lives and the few hours we allowed ourselves away from the office. I worked like that because I had nothing special to go home to.

Sometimes, if I saw Andy's car in the slot next to mine, I did feel uneasy. Andy was the first person I ever employed, as a part-time accountant. He worked for me a couple of hours a week in the first years of the business. He was my age: we were both twenty-two when we first met. He was an audit manager in a local firm of accountants. Like me he had left school at sixteen, and at twenty-two he was already qualified and earning what most people of our age would have regarded as an excellent salary. But he was hungry for more. After the second year I asked him if he could give me a day a week. After the third year I asked him to join me in the business, because by then I realised he was a lot more than someone who could add up. He was much better with people than I was. He didn't mind taking customers out to dinner, or to St James's Park to watch football. I did. I resented the time I spent away from my computer; I hated having to drink pints of beer (and in those early days I did not much like wine either), and then face the prospect of returning to the office at ten in the evening. I dreaded the thought of having to finish a proposal for a client, feeling muzzy in the head and tired, and struggling to find the right words or add up the right numbers. Andy took that problem away from me. He was the person who was best with the customers; he encouraged me to start hiring more staff; he was the person who made sure we had proper employment contracts and paid our people enough to make them want to stay with us. He dealt with pay reviews, he dealt with all the regulations and compliance, and above all he watched the money. He watched the cash to the last penny and he counted up the profits. He wined and dined our bankers every three or four months and took them to watch Newcastle United. When things became tough – for example when we lost a few tens of thousands as a result of a bad debt, which happened a few times in the early years – those evenings with the bankers paid off. They stood by us. They believed in Andy and understood him. They didn't understand me, but so long as Andy was there to explain things to them, they backed us through good times and bad.

Asking Andy to join me was one of the best decisions I ever made. To tell the truth, I didn't give it five minutes' conscious thought at the time. I think the idea had been developing in the back of my mind for a long while, and when I said to him, 'Andy, why don't you come and work with me full time?' and he said, 'What took you so long to ask?' it seemed like the most natural thing in all the world that I should risk everything hiring someone I probably couldn't afford to pay. I doubted I could match what he was already earning, and I wondered that he should risk everything working for a business that was only three years old and barely profitable. But Andy was a risk-taker, even though he was an accountant. He could see even then, perhaps more clearly than I could, what the potential of Wilberforce Software Solutions was. We shook hands, and Andy grinned at me. He was short, about five foot eight, with tight curly black hair and a face that crinkled in deceptively friendly ways. Sharp brown eyes that fixed themselves unwaveringly on whomever he was talking to were the clue to his character: tenacious, aggressive and manipulative.

When I let go of Andy's hand, feeling pleased but uncertain what to do next, he said to me, 'Let's go to the pub and sort this out.'

'I need to get back to the office,' I pleaded. We were standing in the reception area of Andy's firm of accountants.

'No, you don't. You need to come to the pub with me; we need to sort this out, and then you need to have a few drinks. It will do you good, and you've got a partner now. Relax, Wilberforce.'

We went to the pub, and Andy told me he would work for me for a year at half his present salary in exchange for twenty per cent of the equity. After that, the business could either afford to pay both of us what we were worth, or he would go back to his old job, which he felt sure his partners would keep open for him. I don't know if that last part was true. I just agreed with everything he said. Then we had a few drinks, as promised, and that night, instead of going back to the office and working until midnight, I went home and slept eight hours for the first time in years, feeling more relaxed than I had been for a very long time.

At last I had someone to talk to; someone to kick ideas around with; someone who would mind the shop if I had to travel to see clients. I could even contemplate having a day or two off, though I don't remember that I took much advantage of that. But the best part of it was knowing there was someone who would watch my back; someone who would say, 'Don't worry about that, Wilberforce, I'll take care of it,' and mean it. Better than all of that, in those moments of elation when we won a major contract, Andy and I would stand in the middle of the office grinning at each other, and we would shout at each other, 'Yes!! They've gone for it!' That was better than anything I had ever felt when I was on my own; and within a year the business had accelerated and lifted off, and we could have afforded to pay ourselves almost anything we cared to. Andy stayed; a year later he was my finance director and we were running a multi-million-pound business.

Now we had sales of more than ten million pounds a year and annual growth of twenty per cent. We employed a hundred people, and Andy was talking about floating the business on the stock market and raising money to acquire some of those competitors who had frightened me to death a few years ago. Andy's appetite for making money, and more money, was limitless. His tolerance for long hours of work grew, whereas mine did not. What I loved was writing the programs for our software, and solving problems for our major customers. The cascade of money that all this effort generated had at first seemed a wonder; now it seemed like a distraction, wondering what to do with it all. I had other interests in my life now. I had new friends, new interests. I wanted time to explore these new worlds, to get to know these new people.

So when I left work before Andy, and knew that he was still in the office, talking on the phone, or closing off the month-end accounts, or writing a huge spreadsheet to model the next deal, I felt uneasy that I was somehow letting him down.

I would look up and see that his office light was still on, as were half a dozen others: Andy's team didn't like to leave work before its boss. I would hesitate, almost turn and head back to put in another hour of work. Then some sweet scent from the hills to the west would reach me, or reach me in my imagination, and I would get into the Range Rover, head away from the office and find the little road that wound up the side of the valley away from the great conurbation, up towards the upland fells upon the edge of which was Caerlyon.

That evening I had promised to go to a wine-tasting that Francis had invited me to. I didn't really need any special invitation: I often called in on him, expected or not, and he always seemed pleased when I did. Last time I had been in his shop he had said, 'Make an effort to look in on Thursday night, Wilberforce. I'm giving a wine-tasting. There won't be anything particularly worth drinking, but I need to make an effort to sell a few cases to be able to pay my bills. There will be a lot of people guzzling cheap wine and talking at the tops of their voices for a couple of hours. It would be a comfort to me if you could be there, and when we get rid of them we'll share a bottle of something decent. For God's sake don't risk drinking any of the wine I've opened for tasting.'

I had wondered, when I accepted, if Ed and Catherine would be there.

I felt the now familiar sense of release as I drove up the little winding road to the head of the valley, leaving the lights of the modern world behind. It was February, and there was still a glimmer of wintry light on the horizon. As I approached the large, rambling, grey-stone house on the edge of the moors, the sense of liberation that I always felt, as I drove up that winding road, turned to something closer to elation. Caerlyon had become a secret world that I had been given the key to enter. I told no one about it – not my foster-parents; not even Andy. It was a world I did not want to share: Francis; Francis's friends, some of whom were now my friends; Francis's wine.

When I turned into the narrow lane that led to the back courtyard of the house where Francis had his shop, and where the main entrance to the undercroft was, I realised I wasn't going to be able to park anywhere near the house. The courtyard was already full of parked cars, and there were two or three pulled up on the grass verge of the lane. I parked the Range Rover behind an old Bentley and walked down the lane past an Aston Martin, a Ferrari, then past the cars of those of Francis's friends who had plenty of land and not much cash: a very old Subaru with a roll of wire netting in the back; what looked like the very first ever model of the Land Rover Discovery, so covered in mud as to be almost unrecognisable; a Morris Traveller with wooden coachwork, which was the pride and joy of one of Francis's grander friends, the Earl of Shildon.

Inside the shop there was a buzz of talk, and a crowd of men in dark suits or tweeds, and one or two women. I saw Catherine instantly, but could not spot Ed in the crowd. At the centre of the gathering was a long wooden trestle table with open bottles of wine, with numbers on the bottles and tasting notes on the table in front of them; rows of glasses; basins for spitting the wine out into; and plates of bits of cheese.

'Well done, dear boy,' murmured Francis in my ear. I turned and greeted him. He was thinner than ever and it made him look taller. He was wearing a cardigan over an open-necked check shirt, and corduroy trousers. His clothes seemed to hang from him more than usual. Although he was the only man in the room apart from me not wearing a tie, he still looked more elegant and self-assured than anyone else there. His normally tanned face looked pale. The last few times I had seen Francis he had not looked especially well.

'Are you all right?' I asked him, bending down to fondle the ears of Campbell, his golden cocker spaniel.

'I'm as well as can be expected, with this crowd milling around. You'd better have a drink of something, otherwise it will look odd. People will begin to suspect the truth about the wine. Try number 27; it's a harmless Sauvignon. And remember, you are expected to stay on when they all go.'

He led me to the trestle table, poured me a glass of white wine, and then was collared by the Earl of Shildon who said, 'Now then, Francis, what's this bloody awful muck you're serving us? Did you get it at a house-clearance sale?'

I turned away and looked for someone I knew. Eck was standing nearby. 'Eck' was short for Hector Chetwode-Talbot, an ex-Guards officer who, as far as I could tell, did absolutely nothing all day long except attend any event where there was an excuse for a drink. This ranged from following the hounds in the hunting season, attending every drinks party that anyone ever gave and, when absolutely desperate, coming to wine-tastings such as this one. He was of medium height, very upright, wearing an ancient pinstripe suit. Tufts of ginger hair stood on each side of an otherwise bald head. His face was reddened by drink and fresh air, the two main components of his existence as far as I knew, setting off very blue eyes.

'Evening, Eck,' I said.

'Wilberforce! Good God! They've let you out of your office early. Or have you been sacked?'

'Not so far. How are you?'

'Can't get near the drink, there's such a scrum around the table. I've been here twenty minutes and all I've had is one glass of very moderate claret. There's never anything decent at Francis's wine tastings. Either he keeps all the good stuff for himself, or he hasn't got any in the first place.'

'If he offered you good wine, would you buy it?'

'Never had the opportunity to form a view on that, old boy. Let's make a sortie.' He charged into the crowd and, not knowing what else to do, I followed him. He took my half-full glass, without being asked to, chucked its contents into one of the spittoons, and came back with two glasses of red wine.

'There,' he said, 'as far as I can tell that's the most expensive wine Francis has condescended to open for us tonight.' He tasted it. 'Mmm. Might do for a lunch party for not particularly close friends.'

'What are you up to, Eck?'

'In February? Not much, now the shooting season has ended. I follow the hunt when I can. Might go skiing, if anyone asks.' Eck was always asked to anything that was going.

'Eck, is Ed Simmonds here?'

'I haven't seen Ed. His bird is here, though.' Eck always used words like 'bird' that had been only just still current ten years previously, when he was a young officer going to deb dances.

'Catherine?'

'Yes, Catherine. I heard things weren't going too well there.'

'Really, Eck? You know everything.'

He looked at me consideringly and I felt uncomfortable. 'But then, if they weren't, you'd know all about that, wouldn't you?'

'I don't know what you're talking about,' I said.

'Come off it, Wilberforce. Ah, there's Teddy Shildon. He owes me money.' Eck turned away from me without much ceremony, took a sidestep and brought his arm around the Earl of Shildon's broad, tweed-clad shoulders, shouting in his ear as he did so, 'Cough up, Teddy. Twenty-five quid you owe me for that horse of yours that lost at Thirsk.'

I turned away and stood by myself, clutching my glass of

red wine. I couldn't see anyone else I particularly wanted to talk to, unless it was Catherine. She was surrounded by a circle of men, taking advantage of Ed Simmonds's absence to try to flirt with her. I did not care to join in. I considered Eck's remark for a moment. Was that what people were saying – that I was something more to Catherine than a friend, and something less to Ed than a friend should be?

Then someone else came and talked to me, breaking into that disquieting train of thought, and not much later I saw Francis start to make shooing noises with outstretched arms, like a farmer trying to manoeuvre a flock of sheep through a gate. The party started to break up. Within fifteen minutes, without much fuss, Francis had got rid of everyone, even Eck – everyone, that is, except Catherine, who now came up to greet me and kiss me on the cheek.

'Wilberforce,' she said. 'I saw you in the crowd, but you didn't bother to come and rescue me from those dull people, did you?'

'You didn't look as if you needed rescuing,' I told her.

'Ah, but I did.'

Francis came towards us. He looked exhausted, with dark circles under his eyes, but he was smiling. Campbell pattered behind him. 'Thank God that's over,' he said.

'How did it go?' I asked.

'I suppose I sold fifty or sixty cases of wine.'

'They were all terribly rude about it,' said Catherine.

'They always are, aren't they? But they know they have to keep me going, otherwise where would they get the decent wine from, when they want it? Most of them don't know the difference anyway; they just like to have the right labels on the bottles that appear on their dining tables.'

Francis turned aside, went to his desk and picked up a bottle of red Bordeaux. It had already been opened. 'Now, try a glass of proper wine,' he said.

It was a Cissac, I think. I was still learning about wine. Francis poured a glass for Catherine and me, and handed them to us, then poured one for himself. He raised his glass towards us, as if he were proposing a toast to the two of us. Perhaps he was – I don't know. We sipped the wine: it was delicious, tasting of blackberries and other notes too subtle for me to identify.

'Where's Ed tonight?' Francis asked Catherine.

'Oh, I don't know. Somewhere,' she replied, and bent her face towards her glass again. I couldn't make out her expression, or read anything into the indifference in her voice, but it was the first time I had ever seen Catherine anywhere without Ed.

Francis made no comment, his face set in its usual immobile, ironic cast. Then he said, 'Wilberforce, can you come and see me tomorrow? There's something I want to talk to you about.'

'Of course,' I said, wondering what that could be. I often came and sat and talked to Francis these days, about his wine or his misspent youth. This sounded particular.

'You can talk now, if you like,' said Catherine. 'I was just going.' She sipped again at her glass, and then put it down.

'No, Catherine, don't rush at your wine like that,' said Francis. 'Stay and enjoy it, and then you can both go, and I'm going to clear up and go to bed. I'm shattered from pouring out drinks for all these people.'

We stayed for quarter of an hour, three friends talking about not much, and enjoying the wine. Francis poured us another glass each, and then, when we had drunk that, we said goodnight to him and stepped out into the cool evening. It was quite dark now. Catherine was looking for her car keys in her handbag under the light outside Francis's shop when I said, without knowing beforehand that I was going to speak at all, 'What are you doing now?'

She looked up in surprise, and brushed her hair away from her face. 'Home to scrambled eggs, I suppose.'

'Come and have a bite to eat with me. There's quite a good little Indian restaurant down in the valley, about ten minutes from here.'

There was a pause, not longer than a heartbeat, before Catherine said, 'All right: that would be lovely. Shall I follow you down the hill?'

'That would be best.'

Twenty minutes later we were sitting opposite each other in the cramped space of Al Diwan, eating poppadums and sipping water. Neither of us felt like drinking more wine.

'I haven't had Indian food for years,' said Catherine.

I had Indian food about twice a week, because I couldn't be bothered to cook, and because Al Diwan was five minutes from the office, friendly, and cheap. I could imagine that Ed and Catherine would not often find themselves in places like this.

'This is such fun,' she said, in a more animated tone of voice than she had used so far that evening. 'What a charming little place! How on earth did you find it?'

'It's more or less the office canteen,' I told her. 'Andy and I come here sometimes.'

'Who's Andy?'

'Andy is my right-hand man at the office. He's the finance director. I'd be lost without him: as a matter of fact, it was he that brought me here first.'

'Why haven't we met him?' asked Catherine. She picked up her poppadum and bit into it, showing her relative inexperience of Indian food, as it fragmented into about a dozen pieces all over the table.

I couldn't help smiling.

'I'm not used to these things,' she explained. 'But why haven't we met Andy?' She spoke as if we were all members of a close family, and I had sinned by failing to bring him to Caerlyon to be inspected.

'Work friend, I suppose.' I felt awful as I said that: someone was either a friend, or they were not a friend – weren't they?

'So are we all just your play friends? Am I your *play* friend?'

The waiter arrived just then, so I did not have to answer this difficult question. I ordered something for both of us and then said, 'I hope you'll like it.'

'I'm bound to like it. This is such fun, Wilberforce. Wilberforce, why does no one ever call you by your first name? Or is Wilberforce your first name?'

'No, it's my family name – that is, my parents' name,' I explained.

'Are your parents not the same thing as your family, Wilberforce? You are very mysterious. I'm so glad Ed isn't here. I've always wanted to ask you about yourself, ever since I met you, but Ed doesn't approve of girls asking lots of questions.'

I couldn't decide whether she was serious or not. Catherine was one of those people for whom irony was the most habitual mode of expression, and it was often very hard to tell when she was joking, and when she was not.

'No, they are my foster-parents. I don't know who my natural parents were.'

Catherine stared, and then put her hand to her mouth, in a parody of someone being astonished. Perhaps she was. Then she clapped her hands together and said, 'I bet Francis is your natural father, Wilberforce! We all say how he has more or less adopted you. I mean, I've known Francis since I was about three. He started out in the wine trade selling wine to my father and Ed's. Eck is his godson. But you – you're his favourite now. He adores you.'

I felt uncomfortable, as if she was suggesting I had gate-crashed a party.

She must have caught something in my expression because she said quickly, 'No – you think I'm joking. I mean it. You're really like the son he never had. You care more about his wine than anyone else he knows. You're always up there. Every time I've been to Caerlyon in the last few months, you've been there. It does Francis so much good to have someone who's interested in his beloved wine, someone he can really talk to; someone who's intelligent enough for him. The rest of us are terribly thick by Francis's standards, you know.'

'Francis has been very kind to me,' I said. My voice sounded stiff even to me.

'But Wilberforce, what were your foster-parents like? Do you still see them?'

'My father – my foster-father – is dead now. He was a university lecturer. He spent most of the last years of his life writing a book about Bismarck. It was never published.'

'That's what he *did*. What was he like?'

I struggled to find an answer to this. The truth was that my foster-father had never had any time for me. As far as I could work it out, when I grew to an age where one began to look for explanations of why life was like it was, he had never really liked me. My foster-mother couldn't have children. She'd wanted to adopt a child, and given my foster-father no peace until he'd let her.

'He was a bit remote.'

'And your foster-mother?'

'She was rather quiet. She watched television a lot.'

It was true. My foster-mother had become disenchanted with the idea of babies at quite an early stage – certainly for as long as I could remember. She had always seemed to live in a world spent in front of the televison, or reading Catherine

Cookson novels. I don't know what she did before she had a television set to watch; she probably gazed at the spin-dryer.

'It sounds a terribly lonely childhood, Wilberforce. Was it?'

'I suppose it must have been,' I said. 'How was I to know any different?'

The food arrived, so I didn't have to make any further comment about my childhood, a subject that always made me uncomfortable on the very few occasions someone asked me about it. The past was walled off. My childhood had been bricked up somewhere deep inside me.

Catherine had a first forkful of chicken balti. 'Mmm,' she said. 'This is absolutely delicious. Oh God, give me some water.'

Catherine became preoccupied with her food. She ate with enthusiasm. I watched her enjoying it.

'If I lived nearer,' she said between forkfuls, 'I'd come here every night.'

'You've eaten Indian food before.'

'Not often. Ed likes Italian food. But he doesn't really like going out at all. He likes very long evenings with lots of his friends in chilly dining rooms, where the men all wear nice warm smoking jackets and the girls freeze to death in their frocks. That's the sort of evening Ed likes.' She raised her face from her plate and stared at me again, with a questioning look I had seen once before on her face, as if she was seeing me for the first time.

I began to wonder about Eck's remark earlier in the evening. Ed and Catherine were, so far as I knew, engaged. Now she spoke of him like some familiar thing, such as a black labrador, which had failed to come up to expectations.

'And what made you become a computer expert?' asked Catherine. 'Ed says you're a genius with computers.'

'I liked doing sums at school,' I said. 'Sums are like a

landscape to me. I see patterns in numbers that other people can't see, or take a long time to see. That's how I became involved in software in the end. It's a language of numbers. I happen to be good at it.' It was a landscape I had gone to live in a long time ago.

I could see Catherine did not really understand what I was trying to tell her, but the reply intrigued her. 'It must be so brilliant to be really good at something,' she said. 'No one else I know is any good at anything or, if they are, they would never admit it.'

After a while Catherine started forking in the food at a slower rate than before, and finally put her fork down on the side of the plate, and with a comical little explosion of breath said, 'I can't finish it. I've tried, and it was wonderful, but I think I might explode if I ate another thing.'

'That was the starter,' I said.

She stared at me again and then laughed out loud. 'Wilber-force! You mustn't joke! I was really alarmed, for a moment.'

'Nobody ever finishes Indian food,' I reassured her. 'That's the whole point. There's always just a bit more than you can manage.'

After a moment I asked, 'Is everything all right between you and Ed?'

'Of course it's all right. Why do you ask?'

I shook my head, regretting that I had spoken. 'I don't know. Just something to say, I suppose. It's none of my business, anyway.'

'The words "all right" define my relationship with Ed,' said Catherine with sudden seriousness. 'We've been going out for so long I can't remember when we weren't. If I've ever gone out with anyone else, it was so long ago I can't think who it was.'

'Why don't you get married?'

'I suppose we will, some day. We need to become engaged, first.'

I was surprised by this. 'I thought you were engaged. I'd always assumed you were. Everybody seems to think so.'

'Well then, we must be, mustn't we? Only it's never got as far as the columns of the *Daily Telegraph*.'

The waiter brought the bill; I paid, and we stood up to go. As I put my hand out to pick up my credit card from the plate on the table, Catherine suddenly reached down and put her hand over mine and said, 'Thank you, Wilberforce. That was a very special treat. I've had such fun. Thank you so much for asking me.' Then her hand was gone and the waiter was helping her on with her coat.

Outside, I walked her to her car. It was a clear night. I glanced up at the sky and saw that the stars were out: thousands upon thousands of points of light glittering in the dark. We reached her car and Catherine turned to face me. We stood looking at each other, without speaking. The questioning look was back on her face, as if she was searching my own expression for some clue as to what would happen next.

Then I said, 'Can we do this again some time, if you're ever at a loose end?'

'I don't think we ought. Ed might take it the wrong way.'

'I'd like to, though.'

Catherine smiled then, and said, 'If you promised to tell me your first name, I might think about it.'

'I couldn't do that. It's a trade secret.'

'Oh well, there you are then.' She leaned forward and kissed me on the cheek, and before I could return the kiss, she had slipped away and was sitting in her car. The lights came on, the engine revved briefly, and then she was gone, with a wave of her hand.

I walked down the hill to where the Range Rover was parked. What an unexpected evening: full of surprises. I wondered what Ed would think of it all, when he heard about it. Probably nothing: Ed knew he could trust me. We had been friends for over a year now. We saw a lot of each other – Ed, Catherine and me. If Ed couldn't trust me, I thought, I'd like to know who he could trust.

But could I trust myself?

Two

The next day in the office Andy said to me, as I came in, 'Good party last night?'

'Party? Oh, the wine-tasting: yes, it was fun.'

'Did you buy anything?'

'The awful thing is, I forgot to.'

It was true. I of all people ought to have bought some of Francis's wine. Never mind: I would buy a few cases from him this evening, when I went up the hill.

'Then it must have been a good party,' said Andy, smiling. He turned back to his computer and I went on to my office and switched everything on.

I looked at my watch. It was half past eight in the morning. Andy would have been here since seven, or maybe seven thirty at the latest. A minute or two later, as I was sitting at my computer checking emails, he came in with two cups of coffee and handed one to me, then sat on the corner of my desk.

'I talked to Christopher Templeton last night, after you left.'

The last three words hung in the air for a moment, like the hint of an accusation.

'And . . . ?'

'And . . . and Christopher says, that if we want to float the company next year we need to start doing something about it now. There's a queue, and we need to be in it. That means appointing advisers, making a plan, setting a budget.'

'Oh, right.'

'Yes, right. Wilberforce, we can't keep putting this off. We need to start thinking about acquisitions. Not big ones, but small ones, and lots of them. We need to raise capital to do that.'

'Our cash flow is strong enough, isn't it?'

'It's excellent, but it isn't enough to fund an acquisition programme.'

We had had these conversations many times in the last few months. I sipped my coffee and wondered why we needed to have another.

'We need to keep talking about this, Wilberforce. I know you hate it. Your body language isn't hard to read. But we can't stay where we are. A business of our size either gets bigger slowly, or smaller quickly.'

'I don't hate talking about it,' I lied; 'it's just I have a lot to do this morning.'

'Give more work to Steve,' said Andy. Steve was head of programming, but he wasn't as good as I was. 'Talk to me for a while. This is real life, not a program. Wilberforce, we've built a great business here, but we're still only a ten-million-a-year company. To survive in our market we need to be three or four times as big. Now, we've got the track record to float the business. If we float we can raise new capital and start buying some of our smaller competitors. You know, we've both done quite well so far, and you've never had bad advice from me yet. Trust me. If we float, I know who we could buy and how much it might cost. We could be seriously rich in a year or two.'

I swivelled my chair to face Andy.

'There,' he said. 'Now I've got your attention.' He smiled again, his eyes crinkling at the corners. But it was a hard smile.

'Andy, I don't know that I want to go on working twelve hours a day for the next ten years. I wouldn't mind taking life a little easier.'

'Then step up to become chairman. Let me do the work. Make me managing director. It's virtually what my job is nowadays. I know ten customers for every one you ever meet. I'm not getting at you, but it's true. Step up to chairman, go part-time, collect the dividends, and spend more time with your smart friends at the top of the hill.' Andy laughed as he said this, to take the sting out of his words.

'What's wrong with my friends? You haven't met them.'

'I'm sure they're absolute sweethearts. I'm sorry I mentioned them. I don't know why I did, except that you seem to spend as much time up there as you used to down here. Let's not get off the point. I would like you to agree that I should start laying down a proper plan for floating this business on the stock market.'

For a moment I said nothing. The truth was, Andy was right in one thing: we had to do something – either put the business up for sale or float it. It was exactly the wrong size: too big to be a niche business, too small to compete with the big players.

'Well, I'll think about it,' I said.

Andy shook his head. 'Do,' he said, and left my office. We barely spoke again for the rest of the day. I hadn't yet told Andy about the letter I had in my desk at home from an investment bank based in the City, asking me if I'd consider selling the business to an unnamed trade buyer.

That evening I drove up the hill again to Caerlyon. The lane was quiet and empty; no lights were on in the big house; the Gateshead Community Outreach Centre showed no more signs of activity than it ever did. The light was on in the yard above the entrance to Francis's shop, and I parked my car in the yard and went inside. The lights were on in the shop, but Francis was not in sight.

'Anybody at home?' I called.

From some distance, I heard Francis's reply: 'Wilberforce, if that's you, come on downstairs to the undercroft. If it isn't you, bugger off.'

I went downstairs. Francis had a clipboard with a sheaf of dog-eared bits of paper attached to it. His spectacles were on the end of his nose and he was checking the contents of a rack of wine and marking it off from a list on the clipboard. Campbell was sitting near him on top of a case of wine, licking a paw.

'What on earth are you doing?' I asked. I had never known Francis do anything like a stock-take before. He relied on his extraordinary memory, which could lead him unerringly to a far corner of the undercroft, where a case of Château Pessac-Léognan would be buried under half a dozen cases of other wines. He looked up, his face lighting with a smile as he saw me. As I looked at his thin figure standing beneath the vaulted arches of the undercroft, the recesses of the stone ceiling hidden in darkness, the whole vast, gloomy, mysterious space illuminated only by weak yellow bulbs of light in metal sconces at intervals along the walls, I thought there was something spectral about him. It was as if he were condemned for ever to wander between the pillars of wooden cases, along the racks, into the strange side chapels protected by locked grilles, where the rarest wines were.

'I'm doing a valuation,' he said. 'I've been at it for days, on and off. But I'm getting there.'

'Why are you doing a valuation?' I asked. A cold sense of dread filled me as I spoke. Surely Francis was not going to sell his wine. Yet such a thing was very likely: Francis was hard up, he had no other visible means of support except for his wine merchant's business, and I could not imagine he made much money from that. Almost no one ever visited the shop. Very few people even knew it existed. He never advertised; he never sent around catalogues or even lists of the wines he had for sale. A few loyal friends of means, such as Ed Simmonds or Teddy Shildon, would buy a couple of dozen cases of good wine from him a year. Lately I had begun to do the same. But I knew from personal experience that Francis hated selling the wine. He liked to drink it in moderation, he enjoyed talking about it if he could find anyone to listen to him, but above all he liked to look at it. He liked to walk among the columns of wine cases, recalling past vintages, forgotten fragrances of some noble claret whose name and year he saw stencilled on the side of a case, or picking up a bottle from one of the racks, reading from the label a story few other men would have read, for Francis had told me that in his time he had visited most of the vineyards from which he bought wine: he might recall the firm handshake of this grower, the cellars of another.

All this brought in Francis less money than I imagined even he spent. He lived frugally in a two-bedroom flat at the back of his former family home, Caerlyon House. He never entertained except with a bottle or two of wine in his shop, or the occasional kitchen supper in the flat for a handful of friends; he never appeared to buy new clothes, although he was always well turned out in his dress. I think he received a peppercorn rent for the rest of Caerlyon House, but he once told me he had virtually given it away to the Council on a ninety-nine-year lease, in return for them taking on its upkeep. If he had any other income, I did not know where it came from.

'Come upstairs. I want to talk to you.' We left the undercroft and went upstairs to the shop. Francis went to the door and flipped over the 'Open' sign, to read 'Closed', then locked the door. 'There,' he said, as if he had just prevented, in the nick of time, a stream of customers from entering the shop. 'That should give us peace and quiet.'

On his old wooden desk was a decanter of claret and glasses. He filled two and handed me one. I sipped the wine.

'Well?' asked Francis.

'Is it a Margaux?'

'Very good, Wilberforce. Very good indeed. Right first time. You wouldn't care to say which one, would you?'

I shook my head. 'I'm not ready yet,' I told him.

'You're not far off. It's a Château Lascombes. Not everyone would have guessed that. You don't give yourself enough credit. You really are showing signs of knowing about wine. Now, tell me what the year is.'

That was easier. I knew Francis would have opened a classic vintage, and would not have tested me on some obscure year when the wine was thin and uninteresting. I sipped the wine again. Its taste was smoky and flowery at the same time.

'Nineteen eighty-two?' I asked.

'In the bull again, Wilberforce. Well done. It is a 1982, one of the last really great wines they ever made at Lascombes in the 1980s.' Then he sipped his glass at last, and motioned to me to sit down in one of the chairs next to his desk. He pulled up another for himself and sat down opposite me.

'Why were you doing a valuation?' I asked again.

Francis put his glass down on the desk and steepled his fingers together and looked at me. 'Because I want to know how much it's worth.'

'You're not thinking of selling up, are you?'

'That's exactly what I'm thinking of doing,' said Francis. His gaze was steady on me, watching my reaction.

It couldn't have been hard to read. I was horrified. 'But . . . Francis . . . you can't . . . you mustn't. What would you do? Where would you live?'

Francis shook his head, as if these questions were un-important. Then he asked, 'How's your business going, Wilberforce?'

'Very well,' I said. Francis had asked me a few times in the past months about my business. I don't know that he understood what it was I did for a living. He was fascinated by the idea that wealth could be created from the abstractions of software programs.

'You know, the last member of my family to make any real money was my great-grandfather,' said Francis. 'He did it by employing a lot of imported Welshmen to dig coal out of the ground. We had a colliery a few miles to the south of here – a deep seam. The only people who were prepared to go that deep were from the Welsh valleys. My great-grandfather had the energy and the imagination to make it all happen, and he made a good deal of money. When he had made his pile, in his later years, he bought his own steam yacht and spent a considerable amount of time chugging around the Isle of Wight and sitting on deck smoking cigars.'

I smiled. Francis was a fund of stories of the glories of a bygone age. I could tell that the image of his grandfather, sitting on the deck of his yacht with a rug over his knees and smoking a Hoyo, was more real to him than the idea of me making money from software. I don't think Francis ever quite grasped what 'software' was.

'You're a clever man, Wilberforce,' said Francis. 'You create wealth too, but as far as I can tell, it all comes out of your own head, like a musician or a playwright.'

'It isn't just me,' I said. 'We have a lot of very talented people working for us, these days.'

'I dare say. I suppose they are there because of you. You make money, Wilberforce, and I have always spent money. That's the difference between us.'

'You've built up all this collection of wine,' I said. 'That counts for a lot.'

Francis stood up, so I stood up too, and followed him as he went down the steps again into the undercroft. He switched on the lights and walked down an avenue of wooden cases into a space in the centre, a point from which, like Oxford Circus, other avenues of cases radiated away into the darkness. He stood in the centre and said, 'Yes, I have my wine, but what will I do with it? I have no children.' He spread his arms wide to show the extent of his collection, standing tall and thin at the centre of his kingdom. The gloom of the cellar was hardly dispelled by the weak light bulbs, and in the uncertain light the number of cases looked vast. One could never tell how far they really extended.

'But you must feel pleased with what you have achieved,' I said. I thought Francis's collection might be the greatest in Europe – or in the world. At least, that is what I felt whenever I went down there.

Francis dropped his arms to his sides and reminded me, 'I inherited quite a lot of it, you know.' He had told me this before. 'I'm afraid I have not been very good at hanging on to the things that were left me. But I've managed to hang on to this.'

'Well, it's more interesting to look at, and a lot more fun, than a load of computer programs,' I said.

Francis laughed briefly, and then we went back up the stairs again to the shop. He sat down in his chair again and looked at me. He said, 'You ought to work less hard, settle down and marry someone, and start to lead a proper life.'

'Francis! Who on earth would marry me?'

He ignored my question and said, 'I should have married. I almost did, at one point, but . . . it didn't work out.'

'I'm sorry,' I said. 'I haven't even got that far.'

Francis looked at me. The strong arch of his eyebrows gave

his face a quizzical look at times, and now I thought he was quizzing me. 'I think you'll be married before the year is out.'

'I'd like to know who to, if that's the case.'

There was a silence and then Francis said, 'You do know. Of course you know. But you asked me about my selling up the wine a moment ago, if you remember. I am selling it.'

I couldn't help myself. I put my head in my hands and said, 'Oh God.'

'I'm selling it to you.'

I looked up. He was smiling, but not as if he was teasing me.

'You're what?'

'Wilberforce, I've got cancer. If I live for six months it will be longer than the doctors expect at the moment.'

I stared at him, appalled. I had noticed that Francis wasn't well, for the last few weeks, but I'd never dreamed for a moment that it was something serious. I think I said something, about how sorry I was – was there anything I could do? but he brushed aside my words with a wave of the hand.

'Let's concentrate on the matter in hand. As you know, I've no living relations that I know of. That has never troubled me much, but lately I have been giving it some thought. I find, after all, that it is a trouble to me that, when I die, my life's work, my life's passion, will be sold at auction by ignorant men to other ignorant men, that this collection of wine which my grandfather started and which my father built upon and which I inherited and added to, should be dispersed on my death. This collection of wine has become my life. I can't bear the thought it should go under the hammer. I've been to auctions like that myself, as a buyer – dealers looking to make a quick turn, or rich businessmen wanting trophy wines.'

I shuddered at the thought. I supposed Francis thought of me as a rich businessman. At least I had begun to appreciate what he gave me to drink. 'I couldn't bear that, Francis,' I said. 'I'd sooner buy it all myself. But I haven't got that kind of money.'

'Haven't you? You don't know what the price is yet, do you?'

Francis poured us both another glass of wine, then sat back in his chair again. 'There's another thing: Blacks have lived in this house for over four hundred years. That's quite a long time, even in this part of the world. I used to tell myself all that meant nothing to me. But when I inherited the house, it was in bad shape and needed a lot of money spending on it. Half the estate had been sold. I think we were down to two thousand acres when I inherited, and ten or a dozen farmhouses. We used to own all of that valley where you work, you know. We managed to sell most of it to the Church Commissioners in the 1930s. They took it off my father's hands as a favour.'

I looked at him in astonishment. The building in which I worked on its own had a freehold value of several million pounds. Unfortunately I was only a tenant. Francis's family had given away land that had a present value of tens of millions.

'The Black family has not managed its affairs well. We became rather too keen on collecting wine and, in my father's case, drinking it. My father and my grandfather were both very fond of drinking wine. They spent a fortune on building up this cellar; and drinking the stuff. When I inherited Caerlyon it already had an enormous mortgage, which I haven't exactly been able to reduce. I've never drunk that much. Unfortunately I had what they call a misspent youth. I used to gamble quite heavily when I lived in London.' Francis sighed. 'When they hand out sainthoods, I won't be anywhere near the front of the queue. It's a little late to put things right.' He rubbed his forehead with his hand. His voice sounded flat.

'There has been a Black living in this house, or in the houses that were here before, since 1540. In a few months' time, that will all come to an end.'

He looked up at me again, and I saw now the infinite sadness that had always lived behind his eyes, but which I had never recognised before. I had taken Francis at face value: I had read the urbane, reserved, ironic expression and never looked behind it. Now, his face thinner than before and with dark circles under his eyes, there was no mistaking how he really felt.

'I think I would die easier if I had done something to preserve what's left to me. That's what I want to talk to you about.'

I said nothing. I couldn't think of anything to say. This was strange territory he was taking me into.

He went on, 'Wilberforce, I'll sell you my wine for one pound.'

'A pound! You mean a million of them, don't you?' For a moment I wondered whether Francis's illness was affecting his reason. Or perhaps he was on some very strong medication – that might be it.

'There is a catch. Two of them, in fact,' Francis said. 'They depend on your being as well off as I think you are. The first catch is that to get the wine you have to buy Caerlyon itself. That means paying off a mortgage of nearly one million pounds. At the moment the rent from the Council doesn't even cover the interest. The second is, I want you to open negotiations with the Council after my death, and buy them out of their lease. I know they'd take your hand off if you made them an offer. This place is a white elephant as far as they are concerned. There was a fashion amongst local authorities for taking on buildings like this a few years ago, but now they want to get free of them whenever they can. They hardly ever use it nowadays. Anyway, I want you to find a

182

way to get them out and then live in the house when I am gone.'

I decided Francis wasn't speaking under the influence of drugs. His voice was as clear, as sharp as ever. It was only that nothing he said made any sense. 'Me? Live here?' I asked.

'You were adopted, weren't you?'

'I was brought up by foster-parents. I never knew my real mother or father.'

'Then it's not as if you are going to inherit a family home, is it?'

I shook my head.

'Make this your home, then. Live here as if you had been my heir. Except that all you are inheriting is debt. But if you can pay off the debt, and prevent the house and its contents being sold, then this can become your home. Everyone needs to belong to somewhere, Wilberforce.'

I couldn't think what to say to this proposition.

'Then, even if no Blacks will ever live here again, I can die knowing that someone's family will live here. Future generations of Wilberforces,' said Francis, with his dry laugh, 'might live and prosper here. I'd rather it was you than anyone else.'

I shook my head. This was too much to take in. I wondered how to let Francis know that all of this was impossible. I was well off, I suppose, with a good income, but there was no way in which I could raise more than a million pounds in the next six months. Even if I could, what would I do, rattling around in an enormous house like Caerlyon? My two-bedroom flat in Newcastle was too big for me. I'd never been inside the Council-occupied parts of Caerlyon, but Francis had told me it had twenty bedrooms, a drawing room, two dining rooms, a smoking room, and numerous other domestic rooms, offices and studies. The thought of living there on my own was preposterous. I would go mad.

What was I to say? How could I let Francis down without hastening his death? I had no doubt that my refusal would bring the end nearer. I had no doubt that I represented the last throw of the dice for Francis, a man confronted with the prospect of his own untimely death and forced to reckon up the wasted years of his life. I chose my words as carefully, with as much kindness as I could.

'Francis, I'm afraid that's just . . .'

He held up his hand. 'Don't say any more, Wilberforce. It was unreasonable of me to suggest it. I know it was the most presumptuous suggestion. I know I should never have made it, except that I also know how much you have come to care about my wine collection. I hope you will not think the worse of me for speaking as I have done.'

'I'll do it,' I said, 'I'll sell my company, raise the money, buy the house and keep the wine.'

Francis did not speak for a few moments. Then he said, his head bowed, 'You don't mean it.'

'I've never been more certain of anything in my life. It has just occurred to me that it is, after all, the best possible thing I could do. I can't explain it all now, but I have never meant anything more certainly in my whole life. Of course I'll do it.'

As I spoke, a huge weight was lifted from me that I had not realised I had been carrying. My business, which had once been my whole life, now stood in the way of my life. I didn't enjoy it any more. It had become too big, too grown-up, too much about money, too demanding of every part of my life. I couldn't even drive up the hill to see Francis without Andy making me feel guilty, as if I was spending time that belonged to him. And then there was the wine. As soon as Francis had talked about selling it, I knew I could never let that happen. It had taken a few minutes for the consequence of that truth to work its way into my conscious mind, but now I knew: I needed that wine; I couldn't bear the idea that it would be dispersed, disappearing into other men's collections, other men's cellars, being sold in hotels and restaurants. I needed it, and I had to have it.

Then Francis poured us both the last of the wine from the decanter and raised his glass to me in a toast. He said, 'Drink this, in remembrance of me.'

A few days later I met Ed and Catherine at another of the many supper or dinner parties that I went to that year. There were the usual people there, including Eck. We were having dinner with someone called Bilbo Mountwilliam, who lived in London but had a house in the county. Before we went into dinner, when she didn't think anyone was watching her, Catherine turned to me and made a ridiculous little mime of someone eating a poppadum, and then put her finger to her lips. I almost burst out laughing. I knew that she meant I wasn't to say anything about the two of us having had supper together in Al Diwan. That meant she had not told Ed about it. I smiled and nodded and then we were going through to the dining room and I found myself sitting next to Annabel Gazebee, who immediately engaged me in conversation. No one around the table seemed to have heard of Francis's illness, so I said nothing about that either.

But while Annabel was talking to me, I wasn't really thinking about what she was saying; I was thinking about the feeling that had been almost like an electric shock, when Catherine had turned to me and put her finger to her lips. It was the sense of a conspiracy: it was the sense of a connection. I shook my head to clear it of its treacherous thoughts and tried to concentrate on Annabel's very long description of an opera she was organising for a Red Cross fund-raising event.

Later in the evening I saw Ed casually drape one arm over Catherine's bare shoulder, without turning his head to look at her. The act of possession made me flinch. Then my neighbour on the other side asked me a question, and I realised she had spoken for a second time. I made an effort and turned to talk to her.

The following morning Catherine rang me in the office. I hadn't even known she had the number. 'We need to talk,' she said, without any preamble.

'Oh. Well, yes, of course. When?'

'Are you free now?'

I smiled to myself at Catherine's assumption that, like her other friends, I couldn't possibly have anything more important to do than go and talk to her. Then it occurred to me that it would be very nice to leave the office for a couple of hours and spend them with Catherine, if that is what she wanted. I clicked open the diary in my computer and looked at what was in it for the afternoon.

'Hold the line,' I said to Catherine, 'I'll see what I can sort out.' Then I buzzed Andy on an internal line.

'What's up, doc?' he asked, as he picked up.

'I need to free myself up this afternoon. Something's come up. I've got a presentation to the people from Miller Ltd, who are coming in about three p.m. to look at the new project-management software package. Can you do that for me?'

'Sure thing. Are you back in later? I want some time with you.'

I knew what that would be about. 'Thanks. I'll let you know if I'm not going to make it.'

I picked up the parked call again and said, 'That's fine, Catherine. Where do you want to meet?'

'Come here, if you don't mind.'

'Here' was Coalheugh, Catherine's family home, about fifteen miles south-west of Caerlyon, deep in the Pennine dales. Her parents were not often there at this time of the year, spending most of the winter in Bermuda and the spring in their house in Antibes.

'I'll be with you in half an hour or so.'

I drove south, into the bleached winter landscape. A low sun shone on quiet fields mostly bare of stock, the cattle in their sheds for the winter, most of the sheep penned up for the start of lambing. All the colours were pale: the fields almost yellow, the woods on the sides of the valley brown except for the dark green of spruce here and there. A few patches of snow could be seen higher up on the hills. As I drove, I wondered what Catherine could possibly want to talk to me about. Then I wondered if Ed would be there. I turned off the road between the drive gates, along a drive that turned this way and that through parkland planted with great oaks and ash, with patches of snowdrops here and there, nodding in the breeze. After a while Catherine's house came into a view: not as large as Caerlyon, but big enough – a large Victorian house built from dark-grey stone, of no great beauty, ornamented only by a crenellation that ran along its front.

Catherine must have been watching for my arrival because as I parked the car at the front of the house she came down the steps to greet me.

'Thank you for coming, Wilberforce,' she said, kissing me on the cheek. 'There's no one at home so I thought I'd better come and let you in myself. It's the housekeeper's day off.'

Ed Simmonds evidently was not there; otherwise he would have come out to meet me too.

'I'm sorry you've been put to the trouble of opening your own front door.'

We went inside, into a large hall, and then into a drawing room. There was a fire burning in the hearth, but the room was very cold.

'Come and stand by the fire,' said Catherine. 'Not many

people can cope with the temperature in this house. My father has all the bills sent to him, and he checks the central-heating bills to the last penny. If he thinks I've had the heating on in the daytime, he gives me absolute hell. Of course if he and my mother were ever here at this time of the year, it would be on all the time.'

She went to a table where a bottle of wine and two glasses stood on a tray. 'It's too late for coffee, and too early for tea, so would you like a glass of wine?'

'If that's what you're having.'

'I think so. Oh, perhaps you'd like something to eat? Have you had any lunch?'

'I don't want anything, thank you.'

Catherine poured the two glasses of white wine and brought them across. 'Not up to the standards you are used to at Caerlyon,' she said.

'Delicious,' I said politely. It was not delicious, but it was icy cold, the same temperature as most of the room, and drinkable. A year ago I wouldn't have known the difference. Now, thanks to Francis, I knew it very well.

As if reading my mind she said, 'It's Francis I wanted to speak to you about.'

I waited.

'Did you know how ill he was? Did you know that he was dying?'

'Yes. He told me a week ago.'

'And you didn't let me know? Or Ed?' Catherine looked hurt as she said this.

'I didn't think it was my business to tell anyone. I thought it was up to Francis to decide who he was going to tell, and when he was going to tell them.'

Catherine considered this and then said, 'You know, you're right. I shouldn't have expected you to call. Anyway, he told Ed about it the other night and Ed rang and told me this morning. I've been thinking about it ever since. That's why I had to speak to you.'

I waited.

'We must do something, Wilberforce,' she said. She walked across to the window, and I followed her and we looked out across the park. Great banks of cloud were blowing across the sky, and the light was darkening. I wondered if it might snow.

I said, 'I don't think there's anything we can do. Francis is seeing one of the top oncologists in the North-East. He's being looked after as well as he could be, but he's been told there's no chance of any remission. He didn't go to the doctor until it was far too late.'

'That is so typical of Francis. But I didn't mean about that. He told Ed that he wasn't expecting to live six months.'

'He told me that, too.'

She said, still staring out of the window, 'No, I meant about his wine. It will kill Francis before his due time, soon as that is, if he thinks everything will be sold up after he dies. It would be an absolute tragedy. We must do something about it.'

'Like what?' I asked. I felt uncomfortable at the direction the conversation was going in.

'Well, I haven't talked to anyone about it – not even Ed, although it was something he said that gave me the idea. He said: Somebody Francis likes should buy his wine. Ed says some of it is absolute rubbish, but the older wine he thinks is well worth having. But whether it's rubbish or not, it's a lot of wine.'

'I don't think I would call any of it rubbish,' I said. 'Francis is a very great collector. But Ed is right about there being a lot of wine.'

'So then I thought: Why don't a few of Francis's friends form a syndicate to buy the wine? It's too much for any one person anyway. And you're a businessman. I thought you would be the best person to organise it and make something happen. If Ed organised it, we'd still be messing around trying to decide how to do it a year from now, and it would be far too late. If you got involved, I'm sure Ed would join in, and Eck, and Teddy, and half a dozen others. Then it wouldn't be too much each, and Francis would know it would all go to good homes. I'm sure he'd die so much happier, if only we could do that for him.'

'I'm sure he would,' I said. 'Look, it's starting to snow.' A few flakes were hurrying slantwise across the park. As we watched, snow started to fall in flurries.

'Yes, it is. I hope you can get back all right. But what do you think of my idea?'

'I think it's a brilliant idea,' I told her. I turned to face her and said, 'Catherine, it's too late.'

She stared at me in surprise and then asked, 'What do you mean, it's too late?'

'I mean that I'm going to buy all the wine.'

Now Catherine was looking at me in absolute astonishment. I told her about the compact I had formed with Francis, in as few words as possible. It still took quite a while.

'You can't really mean it,' she said at last. 'You're going to sell your company and give up your career, just in order to save Francis from dying a wretched man?'

'That's what I've said I'll do. You think I'm mad, don't you?'

'I think that would be about the best thing I ever heard anyone ever do. Are you actually going to go through with it?'

'Francis is having a new will drawn up, to leave everything to me on various conditions which I have agreed with him. One of them is paying off the mortgage. He's probably changed the will by now. And I'm going to have to get my skates on and sell my company, otherwise I won't have the money to do it all.'

'But what will you live on?'

'Oh, I'll probably have to go on working for whoever buys my company, at least for a while. Anyway, I'm hoping that my share of the proceeds will be worth quite a lot more than even Caerlyon will cost me.'

Catherine went and sat down on a sofa, and cupped her wine glass between her hands. She stared into the fire for a moment, thinking.

'You're going to live in Caerlyon and look after Francis's wine: it's better than a fairy story.'

I said nothing. Sometimes, when I thought about what I had committed myself to doing, I broke into a cold sweat. This was one of those moments. What on earth was I doing? Then something happened to change that. Catherine put her glass down, stood up, and walked across to where I stood beside the window, looking at the snow.

'Wilberforce, I think that is the most wonderful story I have ever heard,' and she put her arms around me and kissed me. The odd thing was, I don't think either of us expected what happened next. I don't think she intended anything more than a sign of affection, a sign of gratitude for what I was proposing to do for someone she had known and loved since childhood. But then we were in a tight embrace, and I was returning her kiss, before either of us had any idea of what was happening.

If we had not both heard the noise of a car coming along the drive, I don't know that we could have stopped. We broke apart and Catherine looked out of the window. She was trembling, holding her arms and hugging herself, as if to wake herself up.

'Oh God, Wilberforce, I didn't mean to do that,' she said; 'I don't know what happened.'

'Catherine . . .' I began. I'm not sure what I would have said, but she interrupted me anyway.

'It's Ed,' she said, in a different tone of voice.

We went into the hall to meet Ed, who parked his car, bounded up the steps and let himself in.

'Hello, darling,' he said. 'I thought I'd come over and make sure you were all right, in all this dreadful weather. It's really beginning to snow hard.' Then he saw me standing just outside the drawing-room door and said in a surprised voice, 'Wilberforce! I thought you were a working man. What on earth are you doing here?' He did not sound particularly pleased to see me.

'We've been talking about Francis,' Catherine told him. 'I had an idea and I wanted Wilberforce to come out and listen to it. But he's had a much, much better idea.' She turned to me and said, 'I know you probably don't want to talk about it, but you have to tell Ed.'

So then I had to tell Ed the whole story all over again. Ed listened intently, once exclaiming in surprise when I told him my decision. He wasn't just intent on me. Once I saw him look at Catherine, as she sat there, rapt, watching me tell the tale of my folly over again. Then he looked back to me.

When I had finished he said, 'You must be completely mad, Wilberforce. Certifiable.'

'Oh, don't say that,' said Catherine. 'I think Wilberforce is being absolutely wonderful.'

'I rather agree with you, Ed,' I said.

'But it is an amazing thing to do. You're a dark horse, Wilberforce,' said Ed. We talked about it all for a few minutes longer and then, looking at my watch, I said, 'I need to get back. We'll see each other soon.' I didn't know whether I was speaking to both of them, or just Catherine, as I said this.

'The roads aren't too bad,' said Ed, 'but take it easy.'

As I drove away, the tyres crunching on the newly fallen snow, I saw a daffodil had come out beside the drive and was poking through the snow. It was winter now, but spring could not be far away after all. I wondered what the year would bring, whether it would all really happen or whether I would come to my senses and tell Francis I had to forget the whole absurd idea.

I wondered what had just happened between Catherine and me. Then I wondered what would happen next.

Three

I did not see Andy the afternoon I returned from Catherine's house. Instead, I drove straight home. It took me a long time to drive back through the snow, but by the time I got back to the city what little had fallen there had turned to slush. When I arrived back in my flat, I made myself a mug of tea, sat on the sofa in the living room and replayed the scene that had just taken place between Catherine and me, about twenty times. I still did not understand what had happened. Of course, Catherine was Ed's girlfriend, she had always been Ed's girlfriend, and soon they would be married. What had happened had been one of those odd, embarrassing accidents: you set out to plant a kiss on a girl's cheek, she moves her head and by chance you have touched her lips.

Then I imagined how I would feel if I heard they were going to be married. It was not a good feeling.

After an hour of this I thought I might go mad if I didn't do something. I had a computer at home from which I could access the server at the office. I thought I might log on, check my emails and do some work. On the way to my computer I opened the drawer of my desk and decided to pull out the letter from the investment bank in London who had written asking whether I would be prepared to discuss selling the business. I had often received letters of this sort, but something about this one made me feel it was quite serious, not just a fishing expedition. I found it, and read it again. The writer was someone called Bob Fulford. Then I sat down at my desk, picked up the phone and dialled the number.

'Andromeda Investments,' said a girl's voice.

'Bob Fulford, please,' I said.

'Who's calling, please?'

'My name's Wilberforce – from Wilberforce Software.'

After a pause, I was put through.

'Mr Wilberforce?' said a pleasant voice.

'You wrote to me that you knew someone who might be interested in buying my company?' I asked him.

'Yes. I remember. I was going to give you a call to follow that up, if you hadn't got in touch. I have a client who is a great admirer of what you've done with your business.'

'I'd be willing to meet him, but not up here.'

'I'm delighted to hear it. There's nothing lost by having a conversation, is there? You just tell us what suits you, and we'll make an arrangement.'

A few minutes later, when I put the phone down, I had agreed to go to London to meet the representatives of Bayleaf Corp, a huge US company based in Houston. As soon as Bob Fulford told me the name, I recognised it, and I knew why they would be keen to buy us. We would be more of a snack than a main course for them, but still, I could understand why they might have an appetite.

The next morning, as soon as I arrived at the office, Andy came in. He looked ill at ease. He handed me a mug of coffee and sat on the corner of my desk. He made as if to pat me on the head. 'There's a good boy, now,' he said. 'Go and sit in your basket.'

'What is it, Andy?'

'While you were out yesterday – oh, by the way, I made a sale to the Miller people – I decided to take some action.'

'Well done, Andy. What action?'

He wasn't looking me in the face for once. He stared at the picture of Bill Gates that I kept on the wall, and then said, 'I called Christopher Templeton last night. I've arranged a meeting in London tomorrow to discuss floating the business on the stock market. Will you come?'

'No, I won't come,' I said. 'It's your project. You do it.'

'But you've no objection to me going, and spending a few thousand pounds on fees if we need to, just to map out a plan?'

'None at all. Only don't expect me to be wild with enthusiasm about it. Go and see Christopher, and then come and tell me what it will all cost and what we get for our money, and I promise I'll think about it.'

'Wilberforce,' said Andy, standing up, 'I don't think your heart's in this business any more – not the way it used to be. That worries me. I get a good salary here, but that's all.'

'You have twenty per cent of the equity,' I reminded him.

'No I haven't. Not right now. The way it's set up, I have options over twenty per cent of the equity if you decide to sell the business, or we decide to float it. Then I can cash in, not before. And I've got to a stage in my life, and you and I have got to a point with this business, where I know it's now or never. I'm prepared to put in another ten years of hard graft to build this business up into a really big company. But the way forward is acquisitions, using our shares to buy businesses. That's what I want your agreement for.'

I thought about my own telephone call, and my own planned meeting with the London investment bank and its American client. I wondered whether I shouldn't tell Andy about it. I decided I would not, until I was certain there was something in it. Even as I made that decision, I thought: That's the first time I've kept something back from Andy.

Andy looked at me sharply. 'Is there something on your mind?'

'Nothing special,' I told him.

'And you're not pissed off with me for taking unilateral action?'

'I've said I've no objection. If you think it's the right thing to do, go and do it. You're the finance man. Just don't sign on the dotted line without talking to me again.'

Andy shook his head. 'I'd never do that,' he said. 'I know I have my faults, but stitching up one of my friends isn't one of them.'

The next day Andy went down to London. I went to the office, and sat at my computer all morning, but I didn't get much done. I spent the whole time thinking about the promise I had made to Francis. Had I gone mad? Had he hypnotised me? I couldn't believe what I'd done. How on earth was I going to get out of it? And if I did manage to get out of my promise – and, of course, I had to get out of it – what would Ed and Catherine think of me? What, in particular, would Catherine think of me?

I decided I would go up to Caerlyon early that evening and see Francis. With luck, he would be on his own. I would just have to look him in the eye and lie to him. I would make up some story about why the company couldn't be sold – something about bankers, or contracts. He would never know any different. Francis's knowledge of business was slender. He would listen, he would try not to show his dejection, but I felt sure he would acknowledge to himself that there never really had been any chance that I would be able to fall in with his ideas.

As I sat at my desk, my phone rang. I picked up, knowing who it would be even before I answered it.

'Are you busy?' asked Catherine.

'I'm never busy,' I told her.

'I must see you. We need to talk.'

'Fine. When did you have in mind?'

There was a pause and then she said, with a sheepish note in her voice, 'I'm downstairs, parked outside your office.'

I told her to wait, pulled on my jacket, called across the office to my secretary Mary that I had to go out for a couple of hours, and ran down the stairs.

As soon as I came out of the entrance to the office, Catherine gestured to me to climb into her car. The moment I was inside we shot away from the kerb and swerved into the traffic. Catherine drove fast, but well.

I asked, 'Where are we going?'

'There's a place I go sometimes. It's by the seaside, at the mouth of the Tyne. My parents used to take me to lunch near there when I was little, and then make me walk on the beach with my nanny for half an hour. They thought the sea air might do me good.'

'I'm sure they were right.'

Little more was said while we were in the car. It was not until we had parked and walked down the front street of Tynemouth, and on to the grassy bank that looks down over the ruined priory and the giant breakwaters that protect the estuary from the bitter surf of the North Sea, that Catherine finally spoke.

'I'm sorry about what happened the other day.' She had stopped, and had turned about to face me. Behind her the river was like a sheet of glass. There was not a breath of wind. A thin mist was rising from the water, shrouding the wharves and the cranes upriver, turning them into vague shapes of uncertain meaning.

'What did happen?'

'We – don't embarrass me. You know what happened. I didn't mean anything by it. It was just a moment when I forgot myself. You were being so kind and good about Francis. I couldn't help it.'

I thought about my own resolve to tell Francis that very

evening that I would have to go back on my promise, and said nothing for a moment.

Catherine started to speak again. For some reason she appeared to be on the verge of tears. Her face looked white and strained. The confident, amusing person I thought I knew she was had disappeared for the time being. 'The thing is, Wilberforce . . . The thing is, I'm going to marry Ed. I've always known that. He's always known that. My parents dote on Ed. All my friends think I should marry Ed. My mother longs for the day when her daughter will be Ed's wife, with a title and an estate.'

'And what do you want, Catherine? Do you want a title and an estate?' I asked her.

'I think all that is a distant second to the question of whether one loves the person one is meant to marry. Don't ask me any more questions, please, Wilberforce. Just listen for a moment.'

But she did not speak for a while. She was trying to tell me something, but I could see the words would not come. Then at last she did speak again.

'Ed asked me to marry him after you left me the other day. That was why he had come round. It was nothing to do with worrying about me being snowbound. Almost as soon as you left he told me that his father is dying. Poor Simon Hartlepool. He's got the most awful cocktail of illnesses. It's the result of burning the candle at both ends for a lot of years. Ed didn't exactly get down on his knees. He just stood there and said, "My pa is dying. I want us to get married before he goes. It would mean so much to him." '

'And what about you?' I repeated. 'Do you want to get married to Ed?'

Although I said these words very calmly, inside I was terrified of what she would say next. If she told me that to marry Ed was her dearest wish, of course that would be the end of it. The end of it? There hadn't really been a beginning. All the same, my heart started to pound, as if a ghost stood in front of me. Catherine might have been a ghost, for that matter. She was so pale I wondered if she was about to faint. I took her arm and steered her to a nearby bench. We both sat down, and stared at the glassy river.

'Thank you,' she said. 'I thought my knees were going to give way.'

'What did you tell Ed?' I asked. I didn't apologise for not minding my own business. I think she could hear the desperation in my voice.

'I told him I would have to think about it for a little while. He got quite stroppy. Ed doesn't like the thought that anyone – even me; especially me – could think twice about falling into his arms. And why should he? He's got all the things a girl ought to want. Ed is very sweet, even if he can be a little self-centred at times. You like him, don't you?'

When was Catherine ever going to answer my question? I muttered something between my teeth about how nice Ed was, and then she said, again, 'The thing is, Wilberforce, I know there could have been something between you and me. But it's impossible. My life has been mapped out for me. I would break the hearts of my parents, of old Simon Hartlepool, and especially I would hurt Ed, if I suddenly changed my mind. That's not how one behaves. One's not allowed to do the unexpected. Life isn't allowed to be unexpected.'

I stared rigidly in front of me. I couldn't speak.

'Next time Ed asks me,' she told me, 'I'll say yes. I would have said yes the first time, only . . . I had to speak to you first.'

She had finished telling me what she had needed to say, and we both sat together on the bench. A chill rose from the river and numbed me. Then, in the mist, I glimpsed something coming downriver, and at the same time heard the blast of a ship's siren. We both rose to our feet. Slowly, like some great Jurassic beast, an enormous shape was coming towards us, through the wreaths and tatters of fog. Four tugs, two aft and two astern, towed the structure. The constant blasts from the foghorns suggested the mournful hooting of some vast predator, stalking through a primeval forest of cranes, dimly outlined against a pearly sky for one second and then again obscured as the mist rolled back in. As it approached, Catherine gripped my right arm as if the beast might attack us, but it was only an oil-production platform – a giant structure of decks, and helicopter pads, taller than ten houses, larger than any building, on four enormous columns, with drilling rigs reaching up through the decks and into the mist, moving slowly towards the mouth of the river.

'My God,' said Catherine.

I put my arm around her shoulders and she relaxed into me. We stood like that for a long time, watching the giant steel skeleton pass through the piers and out to sea, and the strangeness of the moment made us forget, for a time, all that had just been said.

That night I went up the hill to Caerlyon, to break the news to Francis. The light in his shop was not on and the door, when I tried the handle, was locked. I walked across the cobbled courtyard to the entrance to Francis's flat. The door was unlocked, so I opened it. Inside, everything was neat, tidy and austere. There were few ornaments or pictures. On one table I saw one of the few pictures Francis did possess. It was a photograph of him standing with his arms around Ed and Catherine. I had taken that photograph, one day when we went grouse-shooting on Ed's moor at Blubberwick.

I called out, 'Francis?'

There was no reply. I went to the foot of the stairs and called again, and thought I heard a faint reply. I hurried up the stairs and knocked on a closed door that I supposed was Francis's bedroom. I had never been upstairs in his flat before.

'Come in, dear boy,' said Francis's voice. He sounded hoarse, and faint.

I opened the door and put my head around it. Francis was lying, fully clothed, on his bed. The spaniel Campbell was curled up beside him on the bedspread. His bedroom was as neat and impersonal as the rooms downstairs. All of Francis's life was next door, in the undercroft.

'Are you all right?' I asked. 'Can I get you anything?'

'I'm just having a rest,' said Francis. His skin looked yellow, his face tired to death. 'I'll be down in twenty minutes. Go and select a bottle of wine from the cellar. It's the only food I want nowadays, so find something that won't disappoint me, and bring it up to the shop and open it. I'll join you there.'

'The keys?'

'On the kitchen table, as far as I remember.'

I went downstairs, found the keys and opened up the shop. There was no burglar alarm, and once you were in the shop, the door at the bottom of the stairs that went down to the undercroft was never locked. An enormous iron key stood in the lock of the undercroft door; it had rusted itself solid and was impossible to remove or turn. I thought to myself that the first thing I would do when all the wine became mine would be to put in a really first-class alarm system, CCTV, direct phone links to the police station and all the rest of it. A steel door and Chubb locks at the foot of the stairs wouldn't be a bad idea either. What about the risk of fire? There would need to be a sprinkler system installed, and proper climate-control too.

Then I remembered I had come to tell Francis that I couldn't, after all, take on Caerlyon and buy his wine. I did not quite know how best to tell him. There probably was no good way to do it. Poor Francis: he looked frailer this afternoon than I had ever seen him. I went down the stairs into the undercroft and flicked on the lights. There, in the half-gloom, was one of the great collections of wine, perhaps one of the greatest that had ever been assembled. I remember Eck telling me, not long after I had first met Francis, that over the last thirty years Francis had sold off the last of the Black patrimony: two thousand acres of farmland, and ten farmhouses. Eck supposed most of the proceeds had either gone to pay gambling debts, or else had been spent on acquiring more wine. Eck said that Francis used to be part of a very fast set that played cards at Aspinalls or the Clermont. Most of them were a good deal richer than he was, and he had got seriously out of his depth. Then his parents had sent him away to Austria to live with Heini Carinthia, in order to get him away from London. It was Heini who had got Francis interested in wine.

Now I, too, stood in the half-light, looking at the thousands of bottles, gleaming jewel-like from the racks, for Francis dusted his bottles all the time. The aisles of cases with their magic names spoke of warm hillsides in a far country: Latour-Martillac, Rauzan-Ségla, Léoville Las Cases, L'Eglise-Clinet. The enchantment was all around me. I heard, in my mind, Francis whispering the names and vintages of this fabulous treasure, in which the sunlight of fifty years was captured in the grapes from a thousand vineyards: a secret world of experience few could understand and fewer would ever enjoy, and which could only ever be possessed by one person: me.

I found a bottle I thought Francis might like and took it upstairs to open it. Francis was already in the shop, sitting in a chair.

'You were quick,' I said.

'You were slow,' he replied. 'You've been down there at least half an hour, by my watch.'

'Was I really?' I said, in surprise.

'Yes. The undercroft can steal your time in that way. What have you brought up?' He took the bottle and looked at it and said, 'Yes, I think I might have chosen that myself if I'd seen it. Decant it first, please.'

I decanted the wine and poured two glasses out.

'No second thoughts?' asked Francis. 'Every day I expect to hear from you that you've changed your mind about Caerlyon. You know, I would forgive you in an instant if you did. I only hope you will forgive me for putting you in such an impossible position.'

I was silent. I had finally come to the banks of the Rubicon. I had to cross it now, or turn aside for ever. I had come here to tell Francis I couldn't help him; I couldn't make the commitment he was asking from me. And now he himself had offered me, in the kindest and most tactful way possible, the way out that I needed. Francis said nothing, but sipped his wine while I sat and thought about it all over again.

I thought about the store of wine below. How would I feel the day the sale was announced? I would creep to the back of the room and be the underbidder on one or two small parcels of wine, while the dealers and the collectors bid it all out of sight. For what: to repay a bank loan on a house nobody wanted?

'Francis,' I said at last, 'I will admit I've been having second thoughts. It's a big change to my life, and a huge responsibility. But I'm going to go through with it. Don't ask me about it again. There's no need. I've tried to walk away from what you have offered me. I can't.'

Francis smiled, with a touch of sadness. 'Wilberforce, I'd no right to ask you to do any of this, not even if you had been a member of my own family. But I'm so relieved to hear you say you will do it. It is such a responsibility to ask you to accept. Once it is all yours, you will find that it is a question of whether you own the wine, or the wine owns you. Now we shall open a second bottle, to celebrate. What were we drinking just now? A Pomerol? Go and bring up a bottle of Château La Fleur de Gay. There are some 1980s in the rack on the left-hand side, about halfway down, top row.'

This was the first time I had seen Francis drink more than a glass or two. We drank the Pomerol and, later, half a bottle of Château Gazin. I drove home very late, and very slowly.

A day or two later I received a postcard from Ed Simmonds. It said, 'I'm having one or two people in for drinks at seven p.m. this Thursday night. I'd be very disappointed if you did not come.' Of course I rang up and left a message saying that I would be there.

On Thursday evening after work I drove across country to Hartlepool Hall. It was about five miles from where Catherine lived, but altogether grander and larger, with an ornate lodge at the drive entrance and stone griffins holding emblazoned shields up on the top of each gate pillar. I had been there often before, but now I realised it was several weeks since Ed had invited me there, when once I used to be in and out of the place. The bulk of the hall was picked out against the night sky by a few lights here and there. I wondered which of them the old marquess's bedroom was, and whether he still clung to a thread of life. I hadn't heard to the contrary.

Although it was after seven, I saw to my surprise that, apart from Ed's Land Cruiser, there were no other cars there yet. I parked and went up the steps. Horace, the butler, opened the hall door for me and showed me into the library where a tray with a couple of bottles and a few glasses showed it was going to be a very small party indeed. Ed was sitting on a fender beside the fire, reading the papers. The library was an enormous, gloomy room full of leather-bound volumes. Some of the shelves housed glass cages with stuffed owls and other creatures in them, to break up the monotony of the rows of books.

'Oh, good evening, Wilberforce,' said Ed. 'So glad you could make it.' He was wearing jeans and rather an old jumper with its elbows out: even for Ed, he was dressed somewhat informally for a drinks party.

'Am I the first?' I asked, as Ed poured me a glass of white wine.

'Well, Eck and Annabel are looking in a bit later, so it's just me for the moment, I'm afraid.' Ed looked a bit awkward as he said this.

I wondered if he had asked them for supper, and was finding it hard to explain why I hadn't been included. I lifted my glass and sipped it, and, not quite looking at Ed, I said, 'Is Catherine coming?'

'Well, no, she's not, just yet. To tell the truth, Wilberforce, I've got you here under false pretences; not that it isn't always a joy to see your cheerful face. I wanted a word with you.' Ed stood up as he said this and looked me in the eye, and now there was no longer anything diffident about his manner.

'Oh, really?'

'Really,' said Ed. He put his glass carefully down on a table. 'In point of fact, it's about Catherine I wanted to have that word.'

'What about Catherine?' I asked.

'You know the two of us have been going out together for a very long time.'

'Of course I do,' I replied.

Ed's voice became sharper, and a little louder: 'You know we're going to get married, I suppose.'

'I didn't. Congratulations. When's the happy day?'

Ed shook his head in irritation. 'No date has been fixed.

But the general idea is, that Catherine and I are going to marry and I should think it will be sooner rather than later.'

I wondered if Ed had proposed to Catherine again since I had last seen her a day or two ago.

Then he said, 'However, there's a snag.'

'A snag?'

'Don't pretend not to understand me, Wilberforce. You've been seeing Catherine behind my back and you've muddled her up. She's still very young, and she hasn't known many men apart from me, and she thinks she likes you just because you're someone new.'

'I'm not exactly new, Ed,' I objected; 'it's been well over a year since we all first met.'

Ed gave me a hard smile that was almost contemptuous. I had seen it before once or twice, when someone or something made him forget to be the engaging, unselfconscious young man he normally appeared to be. 'Believe me, Wilberforce, a year or two *is* new – very new. You've wandered into our lives, and we've befriended you. Now I find Francis is leaving you all his wine, and you want to take Catherine away from me, and presumably set up house with her at Caerlyon. It's a joke.'

I felt myself going red. This sneer, this implication I had insinuated myself into their lives, was very distasteful to me. Ed could scarcely have found a more hurtful thing to say to me.

'I'm sorry if Catherine thinks she likes me more than you think she ought to. I don't know what else to say about it. If that's true, all I can say is that these things happen.'

'I want,' said Ed, almost grinding the words out between his teeth, 'I want you to stop seeing her.'

'I'm not seeing her – not in any regular way.'

'She says you've been with her three times in the last fortnight. What do you call that?'

'I don't call it anything. I go about my life, and Catherine goes about hers. If we meet, it's rather up to her, wouldn't you say?'

I don't know if Ed was contemplating physical violence. There certainly was a look in his eye, and I might have stepped back, only there was a sofa behind me and I would have ended up sitting down rather abruptly. Just then, Horace came in and announced the arrival of Mr Chetwode-Talbot and Miss Gazebee, and then withdrew again.

Eck came in to the room, beaming all over his red face. 'Ed!' he said. 'Wilberforce! The delightful Annabel will be here in a moment, only she's wandered off somewhere with Horace.'

'Eck,' said Ed. 'There's wine, or there's anything else.'

'Whisky and soda, please, Ed.'

Ed went to another table where a decanter of whisky and a siphon stood, and poured a whisky and splashed some soda into it. While he was doing this Eck looked at me and raised an eyebrow. I shrugged. The tension in the room had diminished as soon as Eck had come in, but it didn't take a psychic to know that something was wrong.

Ed came back with a large tumbler and handed it to Eck. Just then Annabel came in. She saw me, and came and kissed me briefly on the cheek, then went and embraced Ed with rather more enthusiasm.

More drink was supplied. I wondered how soon I could leave without causing comment.

'How's your pa?' Eck asked Ed.

'Not making much sense.'

'Poor old boy,' said Annabel. 'It must be ghastly for him. He was always such an active man.'

'That's what all the girls used to say,' said Eck; 'not such a bad epitaph, really.'

Ed looked amused. 'You wouldn't say that, Eck, if my mother had still been around.'

208

'I wouldn't have said anything at all,' replied Eck. 'She used to terrify me. Remember that party you had when you were eighteen, when she caught me passage-creeping?'

There was laughter. I felt excluded. They were sharing jokes that I could not understand, remembering days when I had been sitting at home alone and trying to teach myself how to write computer programs, trying to find a future for myself.

I put down my glass. 'Ed, if you'll forgive me, I'm going to push along.'

'But we've only just come,' said Annabel. 'That's terribly rude.'

'Aren't you staying for supper?' asked Eck. 'And where's Catherine?' I think Eck was being mischievous. He enjoyed stirring the pot.

'Catherine will be along a little later,' said Ed. 'Wilberforce has already turned down my supper invitation, haven't you, Wilberforce?'

'Ed, you're always more than kind, but I really have to go.'

Eck smiled at me and raised his glass in my direction: 'Wilberforce, you work too hard. Money, money, money.'

I said nothing. I smiled and said, 'Ed, thank you for the drink. Good to catch up. I'll see you soon, I expect.'

'You'll see yourself out,' said Ed. 'I've no idea where Horace is. He's probably heating up supper – its cook's night off.'

He turned and said something to Eck and Annabel as I left, and there was an explosion of laughter as I went out of the library. Horace was in the hall, after all. He opened the door for me and said, 'Good night, Mr Wilberforce. We will see you again here soon, I expect.'

I was always a favourite with Horace, for some reason.

Four

I opened a second bottle, this time of Château Smith-Lafite. We were both sitting on top of boxes of wine in the under-croft. Francis was not drinking much wine. Since the evening when we had celebrated my affirmation that I would look after Caerlyon and its contents after his death, he had become even more frugal than ever. He sipped half a glass of this, half a glass of that. But he encouraged me to sample as many different wines as I could manage, and as I drank them he told me what he knew about them: which wine critic had said what, what score the wines had been given, how the wines were made, which years were good and which less good; sometimes he would describe the grower's own knowledge of wine, his house and his family, the colour of the earth in the vineyard, the way it looked on a sunny day.

If I ever showed signs of not wanting to finish a bottle I had started to drink – and at first I very often felt that two-thirds of a bottle was far more than I could manage – Francis would simply say, 'Don't waste it. Think of the love that went into making it.'

After a while it was less of a problem for me; I developed a tolerance for drinking the wine, even a certain fondness.

'You know,' said Francis, 'I don't know how much time I've got left now. Perhaps I have another month or two. I fear that this will be one of the last times we come down to the undercroft together. The stairs are becoming too much for me.'

I poured us both a glass of wine. Francis now walked everywhere with a stick, and he had persuaded someone to carry his bed down from the upstairs level of the flat to the dining room, where a makeshift bedroom had been made up. Fortunately there was a small bathroom on the ground floor.

'Don't say that,' I told him.

'My dear boy, one has to face facts. The comfort is, that you are learning so much about wine in these hours you very kindly give up to me that we are coming to a point where there is not much more that I can tell you.'

'I am sure I will never know half of what you know,' I said.

Francis did not reply. He looked around the great vaulted space, with its rows and columns of bottled treasure, and said, 'You will find that, no matter how much wine you take from here, it never seems to make any difference. I have collected so much, and sold so little.'

'It sounds the ideal cellar,' I said.

'Sometimes I wonder whether it hasn't been a waste of my life, collecting wine. After all, it is only fermented grape juice.' Francis shook his head and smiled at his own absurdity. 'I think there came a point, about fifteen years ago, when I had to choose between selling a farm or selling the wine, in order to make ends meet. I simply couldn't think of any other choice available to me. I was never brought up to any trade. No one ever told me I might have to learn a living. My father and my grandfather certainly never had to. I hadn't the least idea about money when I inherited. It never occurred to me to think about the stuff. My accountant came to see me twice a year, and we drank a bottle of sherry between us. Afterwards I never could remember a single word he had said to me. Then, one day, the bank wouldn't let me have any more money.' He raised his glass of wine and drank a little from it.

'A little young, still, wouldn't you say?'

I nodded, and asked, 'So what did you do?'

'Well, I knew I had to do something. Before I came back to live here, I lived in London for a few years. I got in with what my mother called "the wrong crowd". It seemed like fun at the time, but I was in over my head and ran up some pretty serious gambling debts. My parents had to sell a couple of farmhouses. My mother had to sell some family paintings. It was hard luck on her, but then she had been very unkind to me, so perhaps justice was done, after all.' Francis stopped speaking for a moment, thinking of some memory at an infinite distance. He shook his head as if to clear it and said, 'Anyway, that gave me the idea. I sold another one of our farms, cleared my overdraft with room to spare, and started collecting more wine. After that, it was obvious: whenever my cash at the bank ran down, which it did surprisingly often, I sold another farm.'

I enjoyed these conversations with Francis. They were unlike any conversations I had ever had with anyone else. Now I was spending as much time with him as I could manage. He would die soon; I wanted to know what he knew. It was more than that: Francis was not talking to Eck, or Ed, or even Catherine, whom I knew he adored. He was talking to me.

Francis was emptying the vessel of his mind into mine, day by day. 'I learned an important lesson from that,' continued Francis.

'Which was . . . ?'

'Never run out of farms. Unfortunately, I did. Then one spring night, as I remember, you walked through the door and asked me whether I sold red wine.' Francis laughed at the recollection and I felt myself blushing. I heard a scratching noise somewhere not far away and said, 'I think we've locked Campbell out. I'll go and let him in.'

'Do,' said Francis. 'Poor little dog.'

I went upstairs and opened the shop door; Campbell

insinuated himself inside and then pattered down the stairs behind me, to go and sit at his master's feet.

'I didn't realise it straight away,' said Francis, 'but chance brought me the one person I have ever met who feels about this place, and what is in it, the way I do.'

I felt the undercroft humming with power as he spoke, as if unknown frequencies of radio waves were emanating from its tens of thousands of bottles. But it was only the wine singing in my veins.

'What will you do,' asked Francis, 'when you sell the business?'

I had shared with Francis all my plans. I had yet to tell Andy, but I could not put off doing that any later than the next morning. The American buyers wanted to see numbers; they wanted information. The person who was going to have to give it to them was Andy. I was not looking forward to the conversation. I sighed.

'Having second thoughts?' asked Francis. He reached out and briefly put his hand on my arm. It was the first tender gesture I had ever seen him make. His hand looked very thin.

'No, just thinking about all the things I have to get done before I actually do manage to sell the company.'

'I'm sure you'll deal with it all,' said Francis. 'After all, how much more difficult could it be than selling a farm? But you haven't answered my question.'

'I don't know,' I said. 'I can't see that far ahead.'

'You should settle down and get married,' said Francis. 'Don't make the mistake I made. I once thought I had found the girl I loved. Unfortunately my mother did not approve. That might sound ridiculous in these days, but it wasn't so odd thirty or so years ago. My mother was a very strong character. Formidable was the word most people used to describe her.'

I tried to imagine. Eck had once told me something about

Francis's mother. He had made her sound cruel, almost monstrous.

'I've never stopped regretting the fact that I was so weak I allowed her to take away the one thing in my life that might have been really good,' Francis went on. 'Don't you let any of your chances slip through your fingers the way I did.' His voice was very sad.

'There's no one I know who would marry me,' I said.

'You are a clever man, Wilberforce,' said Francis, with more energy, 'and you have become, as I told you, very knowledgeable about wine. But in other ways you are remarkably slow on the uptake.'

I looked at him but did not say anything.

'I told you before you would be married before the end of this year, and I said that you already knew whom you would marry.'

'I didn't understand you then, and I don't really understand now.'

Francis put down his wine glass so firmly on the box beside him that the wine splashed out of the glass. Campbell raised a paw and looked up, in case action was required from him.

'Don't be so obtuse! Look what you've made me do! Catherine, of course. Who else could I possibly have meant?'

'Catherine's going to marry Ed Simmonds.'

'She will, of course, if you sit there like a lemon and let it happen. I must say I thought that if I dropped enough hints you might get up off your arse and do something about it.' Francis was now quite animated, even angry.

'But . . .'

'But nothing. Pour me some more wine.'

I poured him another glass to replace what he had spilled, and he said, 'Catherine and Ed is an arranged marriage. Robin Plender and old Simon Hartlepool fixed it up years ago between them, over a glass of port, and Helen Plender supported it. Ed always does what he's told, and for Ed, one girl is very much as good as another provided she is pretty, which Catherine is, and amusing, which Catherine is. Ed will marry anyone who fits that bill, and who will more or less do as she's told.'

'And why should Catherine not fall in with all of this?'

'Because being married to Ed Simmonds is not what she wants to do. Ed will treat her just as his father treated his mother: he kept her tied to Hartlepool Hall to bring up children, whilst he had one mistress in London and another in Paris, and divided the rest of his time between going racing and shooting grouse. That's the way that family has always conducted itself, and Catherine knows that as well as I do. It will be all sweetness and light for six months, and then Ed will say, "I've just got to run up to London to see the Trustees," or some such nonsense, and that will be the beginning of the end. Except, Catherine being Catherine, she would never seek a divorce.'

We sat in silence for a while. I poured myself some more wine.

'Why do you care what Catherine does?' I asked him.

'Because I have known her since she was a small child. I am very fond of her.'

'Why should you ever think she would want to marry me?'

Francis said, 'I'm becoming chilled down here. Take my arm, and let's see if I can manage to get up the stairs.'

We did manage to climb the stairs, and then lock up the shop. Francis, with some effort, and holding on to my arm, negotiated the cobbles in the courtyard, and at last got himself inside his flat, where he sank with a sigh of relief into an armchair. When I thought he was comfortable, I sat down opposite him. Campbell jumped up into his lap.

Then I repeated my question to Francis: 'Why should Catherine want to marry me?'

'For one thing, she's curious about you. You're so different from the other people she knows. I think she's attracted to you.'

'That's a reason for someone to get married?'

'It's a reason. But you asked the wrong question.'

'Oh. Sorry. What is the right question?'

Francis didn't say anything for a moment. Then he said, 'Wilberforce, there's a copy of today's *Daily Telegraph* on the kitchen table. Do bring it to me.'

I went and fetched the newspaper and handed it to Francis without looking at it. He took it and opened it up, then folded it at the page he had found.

'The right question is: Why ever should you want to marry her?' he told me. 'There's something in the paper you should see.' He passed me the folded newspaper and I read it.

Forthcoming Marriages

Lord Edward Simmonds and Miss C. Plender

The engagement is announced between Lord Edward Simmonds, son of the Marquess of Hartlepool, Hartlepool Hall, Co. Durham, and Catherine, daughter of the Hon. Mr and Mrs Plender, of Coalheugh, Co. Durham.

As I read this, I felt a sensation I had previously only seen described in books: I felt as if my body had turned to ice.

'Now do you know why you want to marry her?' asked Francis.

I could not speak. I hated him at that moment.

'Because', Francis explained, 'if you don't marry her, someone else will.'

When I arrived at the office the next morning, Andy was waiting for me with two mugs of coffee. He must have poured them out as soon as he saw me parking my car. I was not in the mood for Andy. I wanted to sit at my desk, put my head in my hands, and feel sorry for myself.

He said, 'Morning, Wilberforce.' He wasn't smiling.

'Andy.'

I took the coffee and sipped it. He stood in front of me, not speaking, not smiling. I looked up at him after a few moments and said, 'OK, what is it this morning?'

He put his coffee down. 'Oh, nothing much, Wilberforce, except that I gather you're busy selling the company behind my back.'

Oh dear: largish cat out of bag.

'I'm not doing anything behind your back.'

'I rather got the impression from the man from Bayleaf Corporation that you'd already agreed a price.'

I stood up. 'Don't get at me, Andy,' I told him. 'Yes, I've had talks with Bayleaf. I didn't approach them. They approached me through a bank. You know I'm not crazy about the idea of taking the company public. I wanted to see what our other options were. I'll tell you something else: the reason the bank approached me was that they'd heard on the grapevine we were thinking of coming to market; so much for Christopher Templeton's professional discretion. He must have gossiped. So I went to see them, and, yes, we discussed possible terms. I mean, they asked me how much money I wanted, and I told them.'

'You did what? Without talking to me first? What did you tell them?'

I told him.

'Jesus Christ, Wilberforce – that's about half what it's worth!' shouted Andy. He clapped his hands to his head. It was not a melodramatic gesture: he looked as if he really thought his head might explode.

'Oh well, that's what I've told them anyway,' I said. My

head was beginning to ache as much as it looked as if Andy's might be aching. I really wasn't in the mood for this.

'I can't believe you,' said Andy: 'I've given ten of the best years of my life to help you build the business up. Then you stitch me up like this. You don't even bother to tell me about it – me, your finance director. I even thought we were friends – good friends. What a mistake.' He turned and started to leave the office, his mug of coffee forgotten.

'Don't forget your coffee,' I told him.

He turned back, looked at the mug and then at me in disgust, and then said suddenly, 'Have you signed anything?'

'Only Heads of Terms – nothing legally binding.'

'Only Heads – did you get any legal advice?'

'I didn't need it; I could understand it all perfectly well without some lawyer explaining it all to me. And it says it's not legally binding.'

'Believe me,' said Andy, putting his mug down, 'anything you sign where the other party is a US corporation is legally binding. They will sue the arse off you, if you don't go through with it – sue us, the company, as well. You're a clever man in some ways, Wilberforce, but what you have just done is the most imprudent thing that I have ever heard of in my entire business life.'

That was twice in two days someone had called me clever, when they really meant that I was stupid. I didn't enjoy it any more the second time. Andy walked out again, slamming the door, causing heads to be raised from desks in the office outside. I noticed he had forgotten his mug of coffee again.

That was the difficult beginning to a difficult few weeks. In the end, Andy and I reached an accommodation of sorts: I had to pay him an enormous bonus to get him to agree to the deal with the Americans and to help make it happen. I couldn't have sold the company without him, and Andy made sure that, if the company was going to be sold 'from under his

218

feet', as he kept saying, then he would be richly rewarded for helping me, not to mention his proceeds from his share options when the business was finally sold. What had once been a light-hearted friendship became a very sour relationship indeed. I took Andy out to dinner at Al Diwan one night in order to try to patch things up between us. We had been working very late, putting together the disclosure bundle, part of the pre-contract documentation. Asking him out was a mistake, for two reasons. The first reason was, I should never have allowed myself to hope that he would ever see my point of view. As far as Andy was concerned, I had broken his code of behaviour between two friends. I had gone behind his back.

Over a pint of Cobra and a plate of poppadums, he said, 'You know, I don't understand why you didn't talk to me before going to the Americans. At least we could have got a better price from them. We're more or less giving the company away. I promise you, in a year to eighteen months, we could have floated the company for twice what they are buying it for.'

'Yes, and then I wouldn't have been able to sell any shares anyway.'

Andy looked at me. 'Do you need cash, Wilberforce? What's going on? You earn a huge salary, you live in your flat, you don't have a mortgage, and you don't even pay for a season ticket at Newcastle United. You've got a nice car; you don't go on holiday; as far as I know you haven't got a girlfriend, and you don't do drugs. What on earth do you need cash for?'

'You wouldn't understand. That's why I didn't tell you in the first place.'

The chicken balti arrived. Andy leaned back in his chair, caught the waiter by the arm, ordered another pint of Cobra for himself, and said, 'Well, try me.'

I said, 'I need to buy some wine.'

He began to laugh, and a few grains of pilau rice shot across the table on to my tie, as he spluttered for a moment. 'Sorry,' he said, 'I'll brush those off. How much wine?'

'A lot of wine, actually.'

Andy stopped laughing. He was really puzzled now. 'But, Wilberforce, I didn't know you drank wine. I've never seen you drink very much of anything. You can't even get through a pint of lager. It must be – it must be – let me see: say you can buy good drinking wine at Morrison's for four pounds a bottle and your end of this deal is say three million after tax and fees, then you should be able to buy three-quarters of a million bottles of wine, give or take.' He started laughing again, no doubt at the idea of my wheeling trolley loads of wine out from a Morrison's store. Some of the lager went up his nose. He shook his head. I could see he was amused, and very angry at the same time.

'Much less than that: about one hundred thousand bottles, altogether. But you need to take into account that there are individual bottles which might be worth a thousand or two in the collection.'

Andy stopped laughing. He looked at me curiously, as if I had just crawled from behind a stone. 'You're serious, aren't you?'

'I've become interested in wine. I've always wanted to have a hobby, but I've been too busy up until now.'

'A hundred thousand bottles?'

'I think so.'

Andy said, 'Let me be clear about this. You've thrown away a great company, which I personally have sweated blood and tears to build up, you've trashed a good friendship, or a friendship I thought was good, and you're doing all that so you can buy some wine?'

'That's about it.'

'Where are you going to keep it?'

'I'm going to keep it where it is now: in a cellar. I get the cellar as part of the deal.'

'And where's that?'

I hesitated. I had a vision of him jumping into his car, driving to Caerlyon, going down to the undercroft and laying about it with a hammer, just to teach me a lesson. I shuddered.

Andy saw the hesitation, and saw the shudder. He said, 'You don't understand about friendship, do you, Wilberforce? I trust you, but you don't have to trust me. Is that it? Is that how your mind works? I work twelve hours a day for you, I have practically no social life, whilst you wander off every night at six o'clock to go drinking with some wine merchant friend of yours. Great. You know, when they put you together, Wilberforce, they left something out. I don't know what it is, but something's missing in you. You're not normal. I should have seen it before.'

I said nothing. It was best to let him have his say.

'You won't even tell me whose wine you are buying, or where you are going to keep it. Are you frightened I'll go and steal some?' He stood up and dropped his napkin on the floor. 'I've lost my appetite. I'm not going to waste my time sitting here with you. You pick up the bill. You can afford it.'

'But you haven't even started your chicken balti,' I said.

Andy didn't even look at me, and walked out.

I sat for a while pushing the food around on my plate, but there no longer seemed much point in eating any.

He and I never really spoke again, after that evening.

The second mistake I made in going to the Al Diwan was: it reminded me of Catherine. The last time I had been there was with her. That had been several weeks ago. Time, the great healer, was not doing much healing as far as I was concerned. I used to wake up in the night, burning with the thought that Catherine was going to be someone else's. The idea overwhelmed me. I could not stand it. I knew I ought to call her, or write to her, or do something that would let her know how I felt, that might somehow induce her to change her mind.

I did nothing. Every night, I awoke thinking about her. I sat in the dark on my bed, full of neediness, and I did nothing.

A day or two later I went to see Francis again. I had been less diligent in going to see him lately, partly because of the pressure of work and partly because we could no longer go down to the undercroft together. Now Francis spent most of the time in bed, and he was taking a lot of morphine under the watchful eye of a nurse from the hospice. Francis was not often lucid these days. He made simple mistakes when talking about wine, confusing châteaux and years in a way I found unsatisfactory, when I remembered how diamond-hard his memory had once been.

Perhaps there was not much more he had to tell me anyway. He was beginning to repeat the same stories for the second or third time. He talked about his grandfather. He talked about his mother. He told stories about them with a mixture of unhappiness and pride. They weren't as interesting the second time, and became tedious on the next repetition. There wasn't a lot left for him to say. Like some of his older wine, he was going over. Soon he would be undrinkable.

There wasn't a lot left for me to say either. What can you say anyway, to someone who is dying and who, at the end of the day, you don't really know that well?

From time to time I still made the effort to go and see him. I didn't want Francis to think I had tired of him. I didn't want to take the risk that he might suddenly revise the terms of his will and somehow leave the wine away from me. I don't think he would have done that, but you can never be sure.

When I arrived, the first thing I noticed, or rather didn't notice, was Campbell. 'Where's Campbell?' I asked Francis. He was lying in bed, very pale, very gaunt. Under the sheets he seemed as thin as a wafer of chewing gum, as if everything below the neck had wasted away. Perhaps it had.

'Had to give him away, dear boy. I can't look after him, and the nurse won't. Teddy Shildon has taken him in, thank God.'

'That's sad,' I said. 'I liked Campbell. I would have taken him if you'd asked.'

'Wilberforce,' said Francis, 'you don't know the first thing about dogs.'

I said nothing, then, 'I'm sorry I haven't called for a bit. I've been very busy. But all in a good cause.'

'All in a good cause,' echoed Francis, faintly. He hadn't any idea what I was talking about. 'And how is the sale of your company going?' he asked.

'That's what I meant. That's what is keeping me so busy. It's going very well.'

Francis half-sat up in bed and gripped my arm. His grip was weak, but his hand felt hot through my shirt sleeve. 'You must do it soon. If the money isn't there, the executors will have to sell the wine to pay off the Caerlyon mortgage. I won't last much longer, Wilberforce.' He had raised his voice. He sounded desperate, quite unlike the old, languid Francis I remembered. I didn't like this new version of him: corpse-like, feverish, waiting for a transfusion of my money.

The nurse put her head around the door. 'Now, we're not getting all excited, are we, Mr Black?' she said.

Francis gave her a ghastly smile and sank back on the pillow.

The nurse looked at me, and said, 'Two more minutes. You mustn't tire him out.'

When she had gone down the stairs, Francis asked, 'Have you seen Catherine?'

'No.'

'It won't be long now. Simon Hartlepool is in the same condition as me. I don't believe he'll live much longer, and Ed wanted to get married while his father was still alive. I don't think he can now. I think he will have to wait until it's all over, after all.'

There was a silence, and Francis's gaze wandered away from me. I thought he had forgotten I was there, or was slipping back into a morphine dream.

Then he turned to look at me again, and said, 'We won't speak many more times, Wilberforce. I am losing the battle. I can't manage without the morphine and it's making me very confused. But there's one thing I've always wanted to know about you.'

I said, 'You can ask anything you want, Francis. There's nothing much to know.'

'What's your first name?'

I hesitated. He had asked me the one thing I really did not want to answer.

'I can't die not knowing your given name, Wilberforce,' Francis told me.

'It's Frankie,' I told him.

Francis's face slowly spread into a rictus, the lips drawn back from his teeth in a death's-head smile. 'But what were you christened?' he asked.

'Francis,' I said. Then the corpse on the bed began to shake with laughter, until tears ran down its cheeks. I couldn't bear to watch. I heard him heaving with laughter and between gasps saying, 'Frankie – Francis – Francis Wilberforce. Oh God, that's priceless.'

I gave a surreptitious glance at my watch. I wanted to be out of here. I hadn't wanted to tell Francis that we shared the same name. It was another invisible bond between us, and maybe one too many. I had a meeting at the solicitor's in half an hour to discuss the sale and purchase agreement. It was an excuse to get going. I stood up.

Francis stopped laughing, and put his hand on my arm for the second and last time. 'Don't go,' he said. 'Stay with me a while longer.'

I muttered something about having to go to a meeting and said I'd look in again very soon. I went next door into the kitchen. The nurse was reading the *Daily Mail*. She looked up as I came in. From the dining room where Francis lay on his bed I could hear that he had started laughing again. I could catch the words between the whoops: 'Frankie! Francis! Oh, my God.'

'You seem to have cheered him up, anyway, dear,' said the nurse. I nodded and made for the door but she called me back. 'Have you a mobile phone?'

'Yes.'

'Give me the number, and keep it on. It won't be long now.'

I nodded and went out to my car. How thoughtless of Francis to want to detain me. He should have known that nothing now was more important than concluding the sale of my company.

Five

When you're in trouble, go and see your mother.

I was too busy for the next few weeks to go and see Francis. I suppose that's a lie: there must have been half an hour here or there. Somehow I never got round to it. I was too absorbed in the sale of the company. There were meetings, and then more meetings. There were histrionics from the solicitors on both sides. The purchaser walked out of the room once and said he would be on the next plane back to Houston, and half an hour later was back in the room joking and laughing as if nothing had happened. Nothing *had* happened: someone changed some words in a clause, and the party moved on. When I did surface for a few hours, it was to feel utterly wretched. If this deal fell through, I wouldn't get the wine; worse than that, if anything could be worse, I thought about Catherine marrying Ed. I started taking *The Times* and the *Daily Telegraph* in case the wedding was announced in either newspaper. I saw nothing about it. I didn't talk to any of my Caerlyon friends. I rang none of them; none of them rang me.

Except that one day, Teddy Shildon did ring, as I was leaving the flat to go to the office. 'Wilberforce,' he said. 'Sorry to call you so early.'

'Not at all, Teddy,' I said. 'How's Francis? I haven't seen him for a couple of weeks.' It was more like six.

'He's sinking fast, poor old boy. That's what I was ringing about.'

I waited for an explanation.

'You know, of course, that I'm one of Francis's executors?'

'Yes, he told me.'

'And of course I know about your amazingly generous offer to pay off the mortgage at Caerlyon, and take over Francis's wine. I suppose I've got that right, haven't I? It's not something Francis has dreamed up on his own?'

'No, that's exactly right.'

There was a pause, and then Teddy Shildon said, 'Slightly indelicate question, this, but I have to ask it. As soon as Francis dies – and it won't be long – the bank will want to call in their mortgage. That will mean the house and its contents will have to be sold at auction. So you see, it's really rather important . . .' He did not finish the sentence, but allowed me to complete it by saying. '. . . that the money's there.'

'That's about it.'

I said, 'Teddy, one can never be sure about these things, but as far as I can tell at the moment, the money will be there. We're expecting to complete the sale this week.'

'Jolly good. That's what I was hoping to hear. Well done. Keep me posted.'

'I will.'

I was about to hang up when Teddy added, 'Poor old Simon Hartlepool is in a bad way too. I think there will be two big funerals in the same week. One last thing I wanted to mention to you, Wilberforce: as I'm an executor of Francis's estate, I'm responsible for organising some sort of knees-up after the funeral. I thought I would open a few bottles of wine in the undercroft, clear a space and have drinks down there. The sort of send-off Francis would have appreciated, don't you think?'

I did not think that Francis would have liked people poking around in his wine cellar and drinking his wine indiscriminately. Unfortunately, it was not yet mine, so there was nothing I could do except agree with the suggestion. I said I thought that would be fine, and hung up, angry with myself for not having the courage to tell him it would be a waste of Francis's wine.

We did complete the sale of Wilberforce Software Solutions that week. After all the tedium and tension of the preceding weeks and months, it was a remarkable anticlimax. We all sat in a huge boardroom at the solicitor's offices, while piles of documents were moved from one place to another, as if in an enormous game of patience. Occasionally Andy and I were asked to sign some of them. We sat in silence, sipping cups of coffee and then glasses of water, as the day moved on. Now and again he would cross the room and join the Americans in confidential conversation. They had asked him to stay on after the sale, but as managing director. I was to be a 'consultant' for a year, but I had a feeling Andy would not be able to find any office space for me. People spoke in hushed tones, occasionally making phone calls to banks to check on the departure of large sums of money from one account, and on their arrival in others. At four o'clock it was done. There was brief applause from the lawyers and the man from Bayleaf came and shook my hand and said how pleased he was. Someone else took a photograph while he did so.

Then Andy came across and said briefly, 'Well, Wilberforce, you can go and buy your wine now. I'm taking Chuck to the airport. I'll see you in the morning for a handover session. Be in my office at nine o'clock, please.'

Then they left and, after a few valedictory words with my solicitor, I wandered out into the street.

For the first time in fifteen years I had nothing to do. At last I was free to do whatever I wanted. I felt as if I stood on the edge of a giant void. I was suddenly terrified by the emptiness in front of me. I might live another fifty years, and I had nothing whatsoever to do in all of them. I had no other life, apart from what might await me at Caerlyon. I did not like football or cricket; I did not make model airplanes or collect stamps. I had no friends outside work apart from my Caerlyon friends. Since I had quarrelled with Andy, I thought I might have no friends inside work either. In any case, I felt sure I would not spend many more days at the office. What on earth was I going to do with myself?

I went to see my foster-mother.

She still lived in the house I had given her and my foster-father five years ago. It was a smart new bungalow in an acre of garden, with a patio and a pond. My foster-father had died a year ago. I don't think he ever felt comfortable living in a house that I had paid for, but he had no choice: my mother would probably have left him if he had refused the gift. I took the Metro subway out from the centre of town and then walked a few hundred yards to the house. I had no concern that Mary would be out. She never went out. She had never, so far as I knew, progressed beyond a nodding acquaintance with her neighbours. She was painfully shy. She sat in the lounge, watching television or reading historical novels. Once a week she went out to a book-club lunch, where, I imagine, she sat silent, too intimidated by the other women ever to open her mouth. Years of marriage to my foster-father, who had never allowed anyone to underestimate his intelligence and criticised every other word she spoke, had left her with little self-confidence. His sharp tongue had its effect on me, too.

When I rang the doorbell it chimed, and in a moment Mary opened the door, looking out with timid suspicion. Then her face brightened.

'Oh, it's you! Frankie!'

'Mary.'

We hugged, and then she said with reproach, 'It's been six months since you've been. You ungrateful boy.' She led me into the lounge and made me sit down on the dreadful tangerine-coloured sofa I'd bought them, and then went into the kitchen to make us some tea. I didn't want any tea. I'd been drinking tea, coffee and water all day until I had nearly drowned in liquid. But I knew I had to have a cup of tea with her, so I let her get on with it.

'I'm so sorry, Mary,' I told her. 'I know. But I've been incredibly busy.'

'You're always incredibly busy, Frankie. You only live a mile away. Is it so hard to come over?'

'No, I really have been busy. I've been selling the company. In fact, I sold it today.'

'Oh,' she said. She seemed bemused by the information. 'You've sold it? Why did you do that, dear?'

I found, when it came to it, that I couldn't explain. It had been hard explaining about Francis's wine to Andy; it would be impossible to explain it to my mother.

'Oh, I've been doing it for fifteen years now. It seemed like time for a change.'

'Well, I expect you know best what's good for you, Frankie. You always were a boy who knew what was best for himself, even though your poor father might not always have agreed.'

I drank some tea and watched her. She was trying to think what to say to me next. Mary was a mother who knew all the right responses a mother should have. She knew about them from reading about other mothers, in books. How much of it she felt I never knew. When she kissed me hello or goodbye, or patted my arm, there was something curiously two-dimensional about the gesture – a learned, rather than an instinctive, quality. Perhaps some foster-mothers were like that; perhaps they never really connected with their fostered children. I think, though, that it was just how Mary was.

Now she was running out of things to say to me, after only ten minutes together. For the last fifteen years I had come two or three times a year and told her how hard I was working and she had said, 'Well, it's good to keep busy,' and now we needed a new set of conversational furniture and neither of us could think what it might be.

Then she asked, 'Time for a change to what, dear?'

'I haven't made up my mind yet. I only sold the company an hour ago. I need to get my bearings. I don't want to rush into anything.'

'And that man who works with you – what's he going to do?' she asked.

'Andy? He's going to stay on and run the company. I'm going to leave.'

'Whatever will you do with yourself? I wonder.' Mary thought about this for a while, and I sipped my tea. I was beginning to wish I hadn't come. Instinct, not reason, had brought me here. Reason should have told me that there was nothing Mary could say that would help me; so what was the point of my visit?

Then her face brightened and she said, 'Perhaps now you'll have the time to look about you and find a nice girl. You're getting on. You don't want to be left on the shelf.'

'I'm only thirty-five,' I reminded her.

'You're still a good-looking boy, Frankie. You shouldn't have too much trouble finding a nice girl.'

I wondered what Mary's idea of 'a nice girl' was: someone else who would sit quietly in front of the television; or curl up on the sofa with a Catherine Cookson novel?

'I have found a nice girl,' I said.

'Oh, good,' said Mary. 'Do tell me about her.'

'Well, she's about to get married to another friend of mine.'

Mary looked blank. 'Then you haven't found her. Someone else has found her,' she corrected me.

'That's the problem.'

Mary put her cup of tea down and said, 'Frankie, if she's going to get married to someone else, then it is dreadfully wrong of you even to think about her, except to wish her happiness.'

'Oh, quite so.'

'I would never, ever forgive you,' said Mary, 'if you interfered in an arrangement that had already been made. It would be so wrong.'

I shook my head to indicate that I would never dream of such a thing.

As I stood up to leave I said, 'Mary? When did you last go away on holiday?'

'Oh, I can't remember. I went away for a few days to Bournemouth when your father died. You were going to come, remember?'

'Oh, yes, and then something came up and I couldn't. Well, that was ages ago. Why don't I buy you a plane ticket to somewhere nice and warm?'

Mary asked, 'Would you come, now you're free?'

'I can't get away just at the moment,' I apologised. 'There's quite a lot of tidying up to do in my life at the moment.'

'It's very sweet of you, Frankie, but I don't think I will. The daffodils are out. Have you seen them? It's the only time of the year I really enjoy the garden, and they'd be over by the time I came back, if I went away now.'

I left soon after, walking back to my own flat a mile or so away. It was early April, and a north-easterly wind blew cruel hail showers across the city. Mary was right: the daffodils had been out for a couple of weeks now, and it was spring. I put up the collar of my coat, and turned my face away from the stinging hail as I walked on.

My mobile rang. I recognised the number: it was Francis – or, as it turned out, Francis's nurse, ringing from Caerlyon.

'Mr Black passed away this afternoon, Mr Wilberforce. I thought you'd like to know. He lasted longer than any of us expected.'

I thanked her for ringing and put the phone away. As I walked on through the streets slick with a sheen of melting hail, the sky brightened as the squalls passed overhead, and a pale light lit the eastern sky. Caerlyon was mine, now. The wine was mine, now. Nothing could change that.

I had lost a friend, but gained a wine cellar.

'I am the resurrection and the life, saith the Lord: he that believeth in me, though he were dead, yet shall he live: and whosoever believeth in me shall never die.' As the vicar intoned these words I glanced about the church. It was nearly full. I could see no sign of either Catherine or Ed.

The funeral was at St Oswald's, a small church of Saxon provenance about two miles further up the hill from Caerlyon. Inside, set into rough walls of stone that seemed hewn rather than cut, were brass or marble tablets proclaiming the lives and deaths of generation after generation of Blacks. Some were so faded as to be illegible, dates and inscriptions all in Roman numerals and Latin; others, more recent, testified to soldiers who had died on the North-West Frontier of India, or on the Somme; a judge or two, and the occasional Reverend Black. How would Francis be remembered? As a lover of wine? How would that look on his funeral plaque? On each tablet, without fail, was the family motto: 'Resurgam' – appropriate enough, in the circumstances.

There was the creak of a door, and I turned my head, along with others, to see Catherine slipping into the church. There was no sign of Ed. She looked very pale, and very beautiful, wrapped in a fur coat and with a black hat upon her head with a veil. I turned back to listen to the vicar.

'For man walketh in a vain shadow, and disquieteth himself in vain: he heapeth up riches, and cannot tell who shall gather them.'

A few minutes later Teddy Shildon stood up to read the lesson from Corinthians. I was thinking about Catherine now, no longer following the words. Could we speak together after the service? Would she let me approach her? Was she married now? The wind had got up outside and it howled around the church in fitful gusts, and a door banged somewhere. Teddy raised his voice to make himself heard and, as he did so, the wind dropped again so that his voice boomed out in the now silent church: 'If after the manner of men I have fought with beasts at Ephesus, what advantageth it me, if the dead rise or not? Let us eat and drink, for tomorrow we die.'

Soon after, the service was over. It was very simple: no poems, no readings, no memorial speeches. Francis had insisted in his wishes that everything should be short and to the point.

Then the coffin-bearers came. Eck was one of them. I think the others were mostly professional pall-bearers. We followed them out into the churchyard and walked down a mossy avenue between great yew trees until we came to the freshly dug grave. The coffin was lowered into it. Then Teddy Shildon stepped forward, now clad in a long navy-blue overcoat, and flung a handful of earth down on to the coffin.

The vicar read the last few words of the service: 'Earth to earth, ashes to ashes, dust to dust; in sure and certain hope of the Resurrection . . .'

About us, the storm had passed over, and its dark bulk now hung over the Pennines. The air was warmer again, and the wind had dropped. Blue gaps appeared in the cloud above and then a shaft of sunlight beamed down on the churchyard, illuminating us in its light, and, as it did so, the solemn, stationary group of dark-clad figures suddenly broke ranks, formed little groups, and conversation, even laughter, filled the churchyard. The service was over.

I saw Catherine talking to Teddy Shildon, and saw him shake his head, then put his hand out and pat her shoulder. I saw Eck, in a double-breasted tweed overcoat, roaring with laughter at something. Then we were all walking back to the cars, and in a few minutes a long convoy of vehicles was winding its way down the hillside to Caerlyon. Inside the undercroft a very noisy drinks party was soon under way. With callous disregard for Francis's eclectic filing system, Teddy Shildon had caused the columns and aisles of cases to be re-formed into a hollow square, in the middle of which stood a trestle table laden with bottles and glasses. Teddy had lit candles everywhere, and the bottles threw back a thousand points of light from their flames. Two black-clad maids, presumably also supplied by Teddy, circulated with trays of bits and pieces to eat. Francis would have been horrified if he could have seen it all. I wondered if his ghost was watching us, from somewhere in the shadows.

Teddy clapped me on the back as I appeared. 'Well, Wilberforce, all yours now, lucky man. Come and see me tomorrow. Come and have lunch and we'll discuss the arrangements. But meanwhile, have a glass of wine.' He handed me a glass of white burgundy, and added, 'Oh, by the way, have you heard? Simon Hartlepool died this morning. That's why Ed Simmonds wasn't at the service. Catherine came for them both. Very good of her, in the circumstances.'

I stood in a corner of the square, sipping my wine. Catherine was talking to Annabel on the other side. She had not so much as glanced in my direction; it was as if I was not there.

Eck came up to me and said, 'I've heard you're the new heir to Caerlyon.'

'I promised Francis I'd take it on.'

Eck looked at me, with his measuring blue eyes. 'And you've sold your company, I hear?'

'You hear everything, Eck,' I told him.

'Ah well, you know what this county is like for gossip. So what are you going to do? Are you going to come and live here? If it was me, I'd have drunk myself to death within a couple of months. Too much temptation all around,' said Eck, waving his hands at the wooden city of wine cases, and the light glancing off the bottles. 'I've never been much good at resisting temptation,' he added.

'Francis managed not to fall into that trap,' I pointed out.

'Yes, you're right. He was very moderate in his old age. He was a bit wilder when he was young, but that was women and cards, not wine. I don't think he went in for song much. Well, if ever you're stuck for someone to share a bottle with, you know where I am.' Then Eck moved on, enveloping his next victim in a gale of laughter.

I found myself talking to Catherine's mother, Helen Plender. She was a small, icy woman, not at all like her daughter.

'We flew back from Bermuda especially for this,' she told me with great emphasis on the word 'Bermuda'.

'I am sure Francis would have appreciated it.'

'Well, he was an old friend. Anyway, I needed to come home to help Catherine with her preparations for the wedding. She's so disorganised. She's made no lists, the invitations haven't even been printed. If Ed hadn't booked the caterers, then there probably wouldn't have been a wedding at all, this year.' Every word she spoke was like a stab wound to me.

I managed to say, 'And when is the wedding?'

'At the beginning of July; of course the whole thing is dictated by Ed's shooting arrangements. He had to make sure he was back from the honeymoon by the twelfth of August. Ah, Teddy, there you are,' said Mrs Plender, turning away from me.

I wondered how much of that conversation had been accidental. Perhaps she had heard something about Catherine and me that she did not like, or perhaps she had seen me looking at Catherine. I felt as if I had been given a warning of some sort. I had never liked Catherine's mother much, and I am sure she never understood why Catherine and Ed had taken me up.

The party seemed to me to last for ever, but perhaps it was only an hour altogether. Then, in the way these things happen, suddenly everyone was looking at their watch and muttering about lunch or an appointment. The place emptied within five minutes of the first few people beginning to leave. Teddy Shildon saw me and gave me the keys.

'Wilberforce, as luck would have it, I'm one of Ed Simmonds's trustees as well as executor here. I'm working overtime this week. I said I'd go over to Hartlepool Hall to offer my condolences and have some lunch. Do you mind locking up for me? Of course, we'll meet tomorrow.'

'That will be fine, Teddy,' I told him.

'Have you seen Catherine anywhere?'

'I saw her earlier on – not to speak to.'

'She must have left already then. See you tomorrow. Come about noon if you can, and we can get our business out of the way before we have our lunch.' Then he was gone.

I went around the undercroft, collecting glasses and putting them on the table. Then I started to blow the candles out.

'Don't leave me in the dark,' said a soft voice.

I turned and saw Catherine standing behind me. She had emerged from some corner away from the light.

'I'm sorry,' I said, 'I didn't see you.'

'You didn't see me, because I was hiding.'

'Hiding from whom?'

'My mother. Teddy. The whole lot of them. I wanted to see you.'

I stood and stared at her. Then I said, 'And I wanted to see you.'

She stepped towards me so that she was standing only a foot or so away.

'I haven't been allowed to talk to you, or ring you up. Ed doesn't want me to,' she told me.

'What do *you* want?'

'I don't know,' she said. 'It's wrong for me to be here now, with you – I know that.'

That was when, finally, I found the courage to take her into my arms and say, 'No. It's not wrong, if it's what we both want.'

She said nothing for a while, as we stood together, surrounded by wine and darkness and the few guttering candles I had not yet extinguished. We held each other and I could feel her breathing, at first quick and fluttering like a bird's, then finally, the slow and steady breathing of a swimmer who has reached the shore.

After a while she said, 'Poor Ed.'

A few minutes later Catherine was gone. She had to go to lunch at Hartlepool Hall.

'Will you come back here later?'

'I don't know – will you be here?'

'Probably. I've nowhere else particular to go, so I might as well put all the cases of wine back in their proper places and tidy this lot up.'

'If I can, I will,' she promised, but I wondered if she would.

As soon as she left the spell of the undercroft and Caerlyon and got herself outside into the sunshine, common sense would reassert itself. She would go back to Hartlepool Hall as if nothing had happened. She would go back to the groove of her life and run along it, through to marriage, and childbirth, and beyond.

'When will you tell Ed?' I asked.

'I don't know,' she said. 'Not today. His father's just died.' Then she was gone, and I was alone in the undercroft.

For an hour or so I struggled with wooden cases. My memory was not Francis's, but somehow the place re-arranged itself. By some instinct I put this case back on top of that one, a Pomerol next to a Sauternes, in no especial order except I think that, in its very randomness, the place was almost as it had been before Teddy Shildon had dis-turbed it. It was as if Francis was whispering in my ear, telling me which case to put on top of which other, until it was as he remembered it. Then I sat down and found a half-empty bottle of white wine and poured myself a glass.

The candles were all out, and put away, and I had turned the lights on. I felt like the verger of a cathedral after the congregation has gone, when the echoing space has fallen quiet, and the saints stare blindly from the stained-glass windows, and the knights lie quiet on their tombs. The peace of the undercroft washed through me, and I felt calm – calmer than I had felt for days and weeks.

I wondered if Catherine would come back. But it was no longer the burning anxiety I had felt before, that she had forgotten me and settled down with Ed, and closed the door on the secret garden that I had wandered into one spring evening many months ago. Now I knew that she had, at least, not forgotten me. Very probably, if she tried to break her engagement with Ed, she would be overwhelmed by the emotional forces of the two families combined against her:

Simmondses and Plenders. Whatever was going to happen next would happen; I did not feel there was anything more I could do except await events.

I sat and sipped my wine and thought about Francis. He was still so real to me – not the emaciated old man who had been lying upstairs on his bed until a few days ago. I remembered Francis as he had been when I had first met him: tall, elegant, saturnine. I felt that that version of Francis was still somewhere in the cellar, watching me, approving of me as I embraced Catherine, guiding me, as I reorganised the cases of wine.

I shook my head. I wasn't going to last long if I allowed myself such fancies as that. I decided to take a few bottles of Bordeaux upstairs, select one and have a glass of wine while I waited to see whether Catherine would return.

I went upstairs into the shop and sat down at Francis's desk, found a bottle of Lynch-Bages on the rack at the side of the shop, opened it and poured myself a large glass. As I sipped it, I realised for the first time the immensity of my inheritance. There were a hundred thousand bottles downstairs, a lifetime's consumption, even if I never added to the collection. But what bottles I had inherited: there was nothing common, nothing ordinary about any of them. Every single one of them had been chosen with a care, a love of wine, a profound knowledge. Not one of them would be anything less than an exceptional experience. This, that I was drinking, was delicious. Its fragrance filled my brain. I poured myself a second glass.

As the wine infused my blood, as I tasted the first glass of the second bottle, I wondered what transubstantiation was taking place here. I was drinking the same wines on which Francis had lived; as I consumed them, and they became part of me, would I become more like Francis? Would I become Francis?

I laughed out loud at myself, and poured more wine into my glass. I realised I was on my way to becoming properly drunk, for perhaps the first time in my life. I had occasionally drunk more wine than I should have done, in my evenings with Francis in the latter days of his life. I had explored the edges of inebriation with him; now I was penetrating further into that territory.

I didn't care. My whole life had changed beyond recognition in twenty-four hours. If I couldn't have a few drinks to mark the rite of passage, when would I ever learn how life should be lived?

It was getting dark. Unsteadily I rose to my feet and switched the shop lights on. I looked at my watch and thought that it said half past seven. Where had the time gone? I remembered Francis telling me, 'This place steals your time.' He was right. I splashed a little more wine into a glass and then reproached myself for not pouring it properly. Catherine obviously wasn't coming back. They had got the better of her between them.

I stood up and went and opened the door, feeling the need of some fresh air. Suddenly the whole place had begun to feel unbearably stuffy. I didn't want to drink any more for the moment. I went outside into the courtyard. It was dusk, cool and quiet. That sweet smell from the hills was all around me: a scent of distant heather; the wine – who knows? I looked up at the sky and saw it was a moonless night. A million stars glittered in the firmament. I craned my neck, looking at all the constellations, as if I had never seen them before. I could not ever remember the night sky looking so bright, so full of hope.

Then I saw the lights of a car coming down the lane; Catherine's car turned into the courtyard and stopped. She got out, still wearing the fur coat she had had on earlier in the day, but now she was hatless and, as she walked towards me, her fair hair shone in the light from the shop. She looked at me standing in the doorway of the shop and said, 'Are you all right?'

'I'm drunk,' I told her. 'I've drunk at least two and a half bottles of wine. I didn't think you were coming back.'

'Well, I have,' said Catherine. 'It wasn't easy to get away, believe you me, with Ed and my mother watching me like hawks. I'm sure they suspect something.'

'Suspect what?' I asked. I felt as if I wasn't making much sense.

'About you and me.'

'About you and me?' I swayed as I spoke, and caught the doorway to steady myself.

'Come along,' said Catherine. 'I'll get you inside the flat. I've never seen you drunk before, Wilberforce; it's rather sweet. You don't do this sort of thing very often, do you?'

I watched her whilst, with quick efficiency, she switched off the lights and locked up the shop. Then she took my arm and guided me across the courtyard into the flat.

'You're in no condition to drive tonight,' said Catherine. 'You might as well stay here. I'll make up the bed in Francis's spare bedroom.'

She steered me into an armchair and then ran quickly and lightly upstairs. I lay in the chair and started to fall asleep. Everything was being paid for at once: fifteen years of unremitting work; Francis's death; the wine. I felt tired beyond knowing. I was just aware of Catherine taking me upstairs into Francis's second bedroom and undressing me, and somehow managing to help me into my bed. I lay tucked up, like a child waiting to be read a story.

'I must go,' said Catherine. 'My mother will be wondering where I am. I can't tell her too many lies in one day; she's too sharp.'

'Don't go,' I said, but my eyelids were closing, even as I spoke.

'I must,' said Catherine, 'but I will be with you in the morning, as soon as I can.'

Then she was gone and I fell into a deep sleep.

I awoke to the sound of birdsong and to sunlight coming in through the undrawn curtains. For a while I had not the least idea where I was. Then fragments of memory came back to me: the funeral, the drinks party, Catherine leading me upstairs. She must have had to put me to bed, I realised. She must have undressed me.

I went downstairs and found that the hot water worked in the shower room, and then found Francis's razor and shaved. When I had finished, I wandered into the kitchen with a towel around my waist to look for the kettle and the coffee jar. Catherine was standing in the kitchen. She was wearing a pullover and jeans, with a handbag slung over her shoulder.

'My mother thinks I'm at Fenwick's,' she said, 'organising my wedding list.'

I pulled the towel around myself tightly, feeling embarrassed.

'Don't be silly,' she laughed. 'I had to take all your clothes off last night and put you to bed. It's too late to blush now.'

'I know,' I said. 'Thank you.'

'You'd do the same for me, wouldn't you, Wilberforce?' she asked, coming up to me.

'Yes,' I said.

'Then do it now.'

2002

One

The first time I entered Francis's shop I did not see the undercroft.

Inspired by some unaccustomed lightness of heart, some unaccountable impulse to see what was beyond the valley where I had worked for so many years, I had driven past the shopping mall and up the hillside and discovered Caerlyon. Maybe it was something in the evening light: a hint, in the colours of a spring sky at evening, of undiscovered country. I drove up the hillside and came at last to the house and saw the sign, placed on the edge of a quiet little country lane, that invited passers-by who were interested in fine Bordeaux wines to drop in to the shop in the courtyard. Whoever had caused the sign to be written and placed there had suffered from an excess of optimism; or pessimism; or both.

I crossed a cobbled courtyard in which three cars were parked, opened the door of the shop and went inside. In front of me was a large desk, and behind it a man with his feet propped up on the desk top was reclining in a swivel chair. On my side of the desk two other, younger men sat with their backs to me. All three were swirling a pale-coloured liquid around in their glasses and going through the motions of sniffing the contents of the glass. Beyond the desk a wide and ancient stone staircase led downwards to some interior darkness. The rest of the room was filled with wooden cases of wine, with bottles stacked singly or in pairs upon them. The walls were lined with racks on which more bottles gleamed. A half-empty bottle of white wine sat on the floor.

As I entered, a bell rang above the door, the man with his feet up looked up, and the other two turned to see who had come into the shop. A small brown spaniel pattered around the desk from where it had been sitting in a basket and inspected my trouser leg. One of the two men on my side of the desk, who had gingery receding hair and red cheeks and blue eyes said, 'Good heavens! A customer! Things are looking up, Francis.'

I felt I had intruded into a private party.

'I'm sorry,' I said, 'I just wanted to have a look, but I think I'm interrupting you.'

The man behind the desk swung his feet from the desk top to the floor and stood up. He was very tall and thin, and I guessed he was the far side of sixty. He was wearing a baggy grey cardigan, out at the elbows, and very old fawn corduroys. His face was sad and handsome, with bags under his brown eyes and arched eyebrows. His black hair, streaked with silver, was brushed straight back from his forehead. Despite the scruffiness of his clothes he wore them with an air of ineffable elegance.

'Come in, come in,' he said, and to the spaniel, 'Campbell, go and sit down. We are certainly open, and you are very welcome. Eck, find the gentleman a chair.'

The ginger-haired man went and started to drag a chair towards the desk. The third man, still seated, now rose and introduced himself. 'Hello,' he said, 'I'm Ed Simmonds.'

Ed Simmonds was also tall and thin, but much younger than the man behind the desk. He had a mass of curly blond hair spiking in every direction and a friendly, open face.

'I'm Wilberforce,' I said.

We shook hands. Ed turned and indicated the older man with a wave of his hand. 'That is Francis Black, the proprietor of this shop, and the man struggling with that chair is Hector Chetwode-Talbot. We call him Eck.'

'Very pleased to meet you,' I said, 'but I feel as if I'm intruding.'

'Then the fault is ours,' said Francis Black. He produced a tall-stemmed wine glass from somewhere, like a magician bringing a rabbit out of a hat, and reached down to pick up the bottle of wine on the floor. He poured a measure into the glass and then handed it to me.

'We are trying out some Condrieu I have just got in,' he said. 'Sit down and taste it. No obligation to buy anything.'

'No one ever buys anything from Francis,' the man called Eck said to me. 'If you hang around here long enough he gives you a glass of something anyway. Francis is the last of the world's great wine bores, aren't you, Francis?'

'I have an interest in the subject,' said the older man modestly. 'But you haven't tasted the wine, Mr . . .' He paused, evidently having forgotten my name.

'Wilberforce,' I said. 'Please just call me Wilberforce. That's what everybody else does.'

'No relation to the great liberator of slaves, I suppose?'

'I shouldn't think so.'

I realised that I was expected to taste the wine, so I took a sip. I managed to stop myself from making a grimace. I very rarely drank wine and did not really enjoy it. The wine tasted tart at first, then a little sweeter. I took a second sip.

'Very nice,' I said.

'I don't think you drink wine very often,' said Francis Black.

'Is it that obvious?' I asked.

'Oh, I can always tell. Nothing gives me more pleasure than introducing newcomers to the art of tasting wine.'

'Watch out,' said Ed Simmonds. 'He'll sell you a case before you know about it.'

'I should never take advantage of anyone like that,' said Francis Black seriously. Then he asked, 'How did you happen to come across the shop tonight? Had you heard about us from somebody?'

'I'm afraid not,' I said. 'The truth is, I work down in the valley. I was on my way home but it was such a lovely evening I decided to go for a drive. I'd never come up the hill before, you see. And then I saw the sign to your shop and I thought I would just come and have a look.'

I tasted the wine again. A fragrance like honey filled my mouth, and infused itself into me.

Francis watched me and said, 'You're beginning to find the taste of the wine, aren't you? How long have you worked in the valley?'

'About twelve years,' I said.

'And this is the first time you've been up here? You must keep your head down,' said Eck. 'What do you do, if you don't mind me asking?'

'I work in computer software,' I said.

'Really,' said Ed Simmonds. 'You must be enormously brainy. I am absolutely baffled by computers. I've just had to buy one for my office at home and I simply can't get it to work at all. I don't even know how to work the email. I can hardly turn the computer on. Waiting for it to start up is as exciting as watching paint dry.'

'It's probably not set up quite right,' I said. 'It's a common enough problem.'

'I'm sure,' agreed Ed Simmonds, 'and it's got me beat.'

'Well, if you like,' I said, 'I'll come across and see if I can fix it up for you.'

Ed said, 'Would you really? That's nice of you. I tell you what: come over on Saturday if you're free and have a look at it, and then I'll give you a spot of lunch. Could you bear to do that?'

'I'd be very happy to try and help,' I said, 'and Saturday would be fine.'

'Well, this is my lucky day,' said Ed.

'But where do you live?' I asked Ed.

Eck laughed and said, 'Ed always imagines everyone knows where he lives.'

Ed Simmonds blushed and said, 'Do you know where Hartlepool Hall is?'

Of course I did: Hartlepool Hall was an enormous stately home a few miles away, which was open to the public. I had never been there, but I knew exactly where it was. 'Yes,' I said. 'Where at Hartlepool Hall should I come to?' I imagined he must have a cottage on the estate or work in one of the estate offices there: I knew it was a huge set-up.

'Just come to the front door and ask for me,' said Ed. He stood up and said, 'Thanks for the wine, Francis. I'll pick up a couple of cases later on in the week, if you can get them up from the cellar. I think my pa would like it. No, no, don't bother now: I'm going out to dinner and I must get moving – I'm late as it is.'

He turned to me and said, 'See you on Saturday morning about twelve, Wilberforce. And don't forget, you're expected to stay for lunch.' Then he was gone.

I said, 'Does he really live at Hartlepool Hall?'

'Oh yes,' said Eck. 'His father is the Marquess of Hartlepool, and Ed will be Ed Hartlepool one day. Sooner rather than later, from the look of his father.'

Then Eck also stood up and said, 'I must go too, Francis. I can't afford to buy any wine today, but thank you for the free sample. I'll look in again soon.' Eck turned to me and said, 'Glad to have met you, Wilberforce. Perhaps we'll meet again here if you decide to make a return visit. I'm often hanging around about the place.'

He left and I stood up too and put the glass that had

contained the Condrieu down on the desk. 'Thank you,' I said to Francis Black. 'That was very kind of you.'

'Not at all,' he said, 'I hope you enjoyed it.'

'I'm not much of a wine drinker, as you can see,' I said.

'But you might become one,' said Francis. 'I think you appreciated the taste of that wine. I hope so, anyway. It's one of life's most civilised pleasures.'

On an impulse, wanting to appear civilised, I said, 'I'd like to buy a bottle of wine to take home with me.'

'Certainly,' said Francis Black. 'What a good idea. What did you have in mind?'

'Oh, I don't really know,' I said. 'Do you have any red wine?'

A ghost of a smile flitted across Francis Black's sad face. He said, 'I have red, pink, and white. But what I have most of is red wine.'

He went across to one of the racks along the wall of his shop, took a bottle down and looked at it for a moment, then brought it across to me. 'This is a Château Gloria,' he said. 'It's a good wine, not a great wine, but a good, well-made red Bordeaux. Take it and make sure you open it an hour before you drink it.'

'Oh, thanks very much,' I said. 'What do I owe you?'

'Nothing,' said Francis Black. I began to object, but he held up his hand. 'I won't hear of your paying. It is a gift. Only one obligation comes with it.'

'What?' I asked, though I knew before he told me.

'You must come back here soon and tell me exactly what you thought of it.'

On Saturday I drove to Hartlepool Hall. Most people have been there on open days and will have seen its vast lodge gates and the drive, nearly a mile long, that runs between a row of ancient limes, then avenues of Wellingtonia and finally a double row of great blue Atlantic cedars. The house itself is enormous, a great colonnaded front looking out across terraces of rhododendrons and, beyond, a lake. At the top of its four storeys the house is crowned with a stone balustrade, and above the centre of the house is a grey-stone dome. Behind the house are stables, tack rooms, disused brew houses, bakeries, and storehouses and, nowadays, an estate gift shop and tea room. Quarter of a mile from the house are three vast walled gardens, which have now been turned into a garden centre, where once glasshouses full of figs, peaches and nectarines grew.

As I drove past several signs saying 'Private' or 'Not Open to the Public: Trade Vehicles and House Visitors Only', I felt it very likely that someone would stop me and turn me back. Ed Simmonds would have forgotten about asking me and it would all be monumentally embarrassing. No one did stop me and I parked my car at the front door and got out. I wondered for a moment if my car would be towed away.

I went up the steps to the great double doors below the central pediment. After a moment I found a bell pull and tugged at it, hoping it would not come away in my hand. It did not. Nothing happened for a while; I turned and looked at the lake and saw a flock of geese taking off, wheeling overhead, then skimming back down to land on it. I heard a noise behind me and turned, and saw a very distinguished-looking older man with silver hair in a dark suit standing holding the door open for me. I decided it must be Ed's father and put out my hand and said, 'Hello, I'm Wilberforce. I've come to see Ed.'

The man ignored my outstretched hand – not rudely but simply as if it was not there – and inclined himself in a slight bow. 'My name is Horace, sir. If you would like to follow me, Lord Edward is expecting you in his office.'

I realised, feeling stupid, that Horace must be the butler. I followed him into an enormous, gloomy hall. It had dark panelled wood, with obscure portraits of men, mostly in military costume of earlier centuries, half-hidden in the shadow on the walls. Horace led me through this and then onwards through a maze of corridors, up stairs and down them again until we came to a long corridor. At the last of a series of doors we stopped; Horace opened it and gestured to me go in.

Inside was a brightly lit office with two desks, on one of which sat a computer. Ed Simmonds was sitting in front of it, staring blankly at the screen. When he saw me he jumped to his feet and came across and said, 'It's so good of you to come. Thank you, Horace. I'll ring through when I think we're ready for lunch. Wilberforce, this bloody machine has got worse. I think it's sickening for something.'

I sat down at the desk and started to check the settings on the computer. It took me about ten minutes to fix the problem and another twenty minutes to set up an email account. Ed sat opposite me watching me in awe, as if I was a witch doctor. When I had finished, I showed him which buttons to press and how to use his email.

Ed Simmonds was ecstatic. 'That's wonderful,' he said. 'You really are a genius. I've had three people look at that machine and none of them could do a thing with it.'

'What do you need it for?' I asked.

'Well, no modern estate office is without a computer, so I thought I ought to have one in here, and our accountants and our estate manager all insist on sending everything by email these days.'

'Do you spend a lot of time in here?' I asked.

'Not if I can help it,' said Ed. 'I've got a secretary who does most of that for me, but it's a bit shaming if I can't even switch on the machine, or open an email without help. Now, thanks to you, I will be able to impress them all. Come and have some lunch.'

As we walked back through the house I began to appreciate its enormous scale. I glimpsed staircases soaring towards the upper regions of the house. We crossed two halls tiled in black-and-white marble and filled with pale marble and alabaster statuary. We passed rooms labelled 'Billiard Room', 'Smoking Room', 'Lord Simon's Study' and 'Butler's Pantry'. At last we came back to the hall where we had started out. Ed strode across the hall and opened a door.

Inside was a vast dining room, with a table about fifty feet long. The walls were hung with large pictures, this time mostly Venetian scenes, or improbably robust-looking women clutching suckling children to their breasts. At the far end of the room was an alcove, where a small round table was laid for three. Next to the table was a sideboard with a decanter filled with a golden liquid, and two glasses stood next to it. A third glass was being clutched by Eck, who was sipping from it while he stared out of the window.

When he heard us, he turned and said, 'You took so long I thought I would help myself to some of your sherry.'

'You did the right thing, Eck,' said Ed. 'Wilberforce, can I offer you a glass?'

'No thanks,' I said. 'I don't really drink.'

Lunch was served from a trolley, which was wheeled in by Horace: soup and then lamb chops. Ed and Eck drank wine and I drank water. Afterwards we went through to a small sitting room, where Horace brought us coffee. The conversation was mostly carried on between Ed and Eck, but I never felt left out. They treated me like an old friend, not as if I had appeared in their lives barely five minutes ago. I felt an odd sensation as I sat there, which I tried but failed at first to define. Then I realised what it was: I was enjoying myself.

The door of the sitting room opened, and an elderly man shuffled in wearing a threadbare crimson-velvet smoking jacket and a velvet tasselled cap. On his feet he wore scuffed slippers covered in a tweed check.

Ed sprang to his feet. 'Hello, Pa,' he said. 'You know Eck, but you haven't met Wilberforce.'

'Who?' asked the old gentleman, chewing at the corner of a ragged moustache while he gazed at me.

'Wilberforce,' Ed repeated. 'He's lunching with us.'

'Never lunch myself,' said Ed's father. He turned to me and said, 'Well done. Well done. Splendid effort. A marvellous innings. Showed those Aussies how to play cricket.' Having delivered that encomium he left the room again without further words.

'He must think that you're someone else,' explained Ed to me. 'Don't mind him. He gets ideas into his head.'

A little later Ed announced that he had promised to go and call on a girl called Catherine. 'Don't hurry away,' he said. 'Horace will see you out when you want to go. Wilberforce, thank you so much for coming. Will you come again soon? Will you write a telephone number on the pad by this phone? You really mustn't disappear out of our lives now we've all met. It would be so nice if you could come over again. I'll be in touch.' He was gone.

'Who's Catherine?' I asked Eck.

'His squeeze. She's very nice. You'll like her,' said Eck. He went over to a table where a humidor sat, and helped himself to a large cigar. 'You don't mind if I smoke, do you?'

'No.'

'Want one?'

I thought Eck seemed remarkably at home in Ed's house. 'No, I don't.'

Eck saw me looking at him as he trimmed the cigar. 'This house is the next best thing to Liberty Hall. Ed expects his friends to make free with all the good things he has. I try never to let him down.'

'What does Ed do all day?' I asked, thinking of the office and the computer. 'Does he manage the whole estate on his own?'

'No,' said Eck. 'He's got people to do all that for him. No, what Ed does when he's not going racing, or hunting, or the occasional day's shooting, is read the papers. When he can be bothered.'

I thought this sounded rather severe. Then I realised that to Eck and Ed leisure was a natural state of being and employment was not. I said to Eck, out of curiosity to see if my theory was right, 'What do you do, Eck?'

'I can tell you what I did do. I was a soldier for ten years or so; a Grenadier. I come from a family of soldiers. My father was a colonel; my uncle is General Chetwode-Talbot. You've probably never heard of him, but there it is – if you were ever in the army you would know the name. Soldiering is all that our lot know how to do. After about ten years I decided I wanted to make a bit of money, so I switched to the private sector. I worked for quite a while for Risk Management. Have you heard of them?'

I admitted that I had not.

'What we did was manage kidnaps, for Lloyd's of London. The idea is that if you are working in a dodgy part of the world, your company can insure you against ransom demands with an underwriter at Lloyd's. There are a few of them that make a market in that kind of cover. Our job was, if the worst happened, to get involved in negotiating the ransom and to make sure the hostage came out alive if we could get him out at a sensible price.'

'Goodness,' I said. 'I had no idea all that went on.'

'That, and more,' said Eck, exhaling a cloud of cigar smoke as he sat in his armchair. I understood all of a sudden that, although Eck had cast himself in the role of the joker, behind his teasing and his charm, he was enormously tough.

'So why did you stop?' I asked.

'I was working on a slow case in Medellín in Colombia. A chap from BP had been lifted by FARC. They are a bunch of very professional narco-terrorists, who finance themselves and their revolution through kidnapping and drug deals. But something didn't ring true on this deal. I was getting nowhere. I had no idea if the chap from BP was still alive. Then I came to the unpleasant conclusion that he was not and, worse, that whoever I was talking to – and I'm still not sure whether it was FARC or some other group – had in mind to use me as a bargaining chip instead. I started to feel I was being followed. Then I was sure I was, by some very unpleasant people. So I took off.'

'You left?'

'I took a flight to Bogotá and rang my office on the satellite phone. They advised me to get out of the country and I did. When I got back I found my aunt had died while I was in country and had left my cousin Harriet and me a decent legacy. So I quit. I couldn't see the point in going on, fun as it had been. One day or another it was going to go wrong, and I decided it would be a clever idea to leave before it did.'

I was fascinated; I had never met anyone like Eck before. He stubbed his cigar out and we went out into the hall. Horace appeared from somewhere and opened the front door for us and we walked down the steps to where Eck's car was parked next to mine.

'Well, good to meet you again,' said Eck, putting out his hand. I shook it and then he said, 'Are you going to get in touch with Ed?'

'I might. I don't know. What do you think?' I spoke as if I had known Eck for years. He had that effect on people, at any rate upon me.

'He's a very old friend of mine. If he said he wants you to get in touch, then he definitely meant it. Ed always means what he says. He is the most delightful man on the planet so long as he is getting his own way. When he doesn't, it can be quite bruising for people around him. He likes to get what he wants.'

This didn't seem much of a problem to me. Why shouldn't Ed Simmonds get what he wanted? It was all the same to me.

Ed Simmonds didn't get in touch and I didn't feel able to ring him. After all, why should he? He'd given me lunch and I had fixed his computer. The trade was done. Why on earth should he bother to want to see me again? It shouldn't have mattered to me. I was, as always, very busy at work and I had no time to contemplate a social life of any sort. All the same, there had been something pleasant to me in the brief glimpse I had seen of Ed's world.

I did go back up the hill to see Francis Black again. I felt I owed it to him. After all, he had given me a bottle of very good wine. I had opened the Château Gloria the night he had given it to me. I drank a glass with the Chinese takeaway I had bought, as the shopping mall had been shut by the time I went back down into the valley. It had not been a happy mixture of tastes. Then I had had a second glass the next night, with a pizza. That had been more of a success, although the wine tasted murky. I wondered if you were meant to keep the cork in the bottle. The third night I thought there was something definitely wrong with the wine, and poured the rest of it into the sink.

When I appeared again in Francis's shop he was sitting behind his desk, filling in a form. He didn't recognise me for a moment, but then his face cleared and he put his pen down and said, 'Wilberforce. I hoped you would call in. How was the Château Gloria?'

Campbell the spaniel came to greet me, and I bent down and stroked his head. Then I explained to Francis, rather apologetically, how I had got on with his present of a bottle of wine. I said that by the third day the wine had not really tasted of much at all.

Francis listened, and then said, 'Well, in an ideal world you would drink it all the same night. But perhaps that isn't practical for one man who is not accustomed to drinking wine.'

'I don't really drink, to tell you the truth.'

Francis said, 'Would you mind witnessing my signature on this document?'

I took a pen out and Francis showed me where to sign. I noticed that where he had to fill in his occupation, Francis had written the single word: 'Gentleman'. When I had scrawled my name he asked, 'Would you like to see the undercroft?'

'The undercroft?'

He stood up and said, 'Yes, the undercroft. It is a very large space underneath the house. When I let off the main building, which is far too big for me, to the Council, I did not include the undercroft in the lease. It was part of the old Elizabethan house and we have always used it as a storage space, mostly for the purpose of cellaring wine. Would you like to see it? It might interest you.'

I said, 'Yes, of course. I'd love to.' What else could I have said?

I followed Francis down the wide, worn stone steps that led from a few yards behind his desk down into the gloom. Halfway down the staircase was an old black light switch, which Francis flicked on. Below me I could see an ancient door of black oak. From underneath came a gleam of light.

Francis pushed opened the door, and we were in the undercroft.

It was a large space, as he had said. The electric lights were fitted into old sconces along the wall, rusting metal holders that would once have held candles. The light from the bulbs was weak and yellow and they did not fully illuminate the room. I saw the vaulted ceiling above disappearing into gloom; I saw dark side chambers protected by grilles, behind which a few bottles could be seen. In the centre of the room were piles of wooden cases of wine. We had to manoeuvre between these in order to complete our tour. It was interesting, but for some reason I had been expecting something more.

Francis picked up a bottle here, and a bottle there, and told me the names of the wines, and the places they came from, and the people who had grown them. He certainly knew his subject, but it was all a foreign language to me. I was relieved when we went back into the shop, where the air was fresher. There was something overpowering and stuffy about the room below.

When we reached the shop Francis gestured for me to take a seat and said, 'So, what is it you do down in the valley?'

I told him again I worked for a software company.

'Is it an American company? Aren't those sorts of businesses usually American?'

'No, it's my own company. I started it about ten years ago and now we employ fifty people.'

Francis was absolutely fascinated by this information. He cross-questioned me for a while about how someone of twenty or so could possibly have started a business. 'I could never possibly have done a thing like that,' said Francis. 'I simply wasn't brought up to the idea one ought to work for a living. Now I have had to learn the hard way, if you can call sitting here all day waiting for the odd customer earning one's living.'

'I wasn't particularly brought up to it either,' I said. 'My foster-father was a university lecturer. He thought very little of computers and computer programmers, and probably understood less.'

'Oh, you were adopted, were you?' said Francis. For a moment, for some reason I did not understand, we looked at each other in discomfort. Then Francis went and took another bottle from a rack and gave it to me, saying, 'Take this, and drink it, and if you can't drink it all, throw the rest away the same night. The wine starts to die as soon as you open it. It oxidises after a while and all its qualities disappear. That is the most wonderful and the most frustrating thing about wine: it is a work of art, sometimes a work of genius, that has taken a lifetime of experience to create and has matured for ten or fifteen years in the bottle in order to be ready for you to drink. Then, as soon as the wine is opened, it begins to die. In twenty-four hours it is dead.'

I tried to pay again, but Francis wouldn't let me. 'Take it, drink it; it is a gift from me. When I see that you really enjoy the wine I give you, then I will make you pay for it.' He handed me the bottle and added, 'Once you learn to love my wine, you will pay the full market price.'

Two

I wasn't good with people. How could I have been?

My foster-parents had adopted me because Mary could not have children of her own. That was what she told me, although I have since wondered whether my foster-father had been too busy reading about the politics of Germany and the Hapsburg Empire in the mid-nineteenth century to find time to take her to bed. Mary often told me what a beautiful baby I had been. She used to speak wistfully about how enchanting I had been, looking past me as she recalled the first time she saw me, the one moment in the entire process of my adoption she seemed able to recall with pleasure.

She treated me well, though. I cannot remember ever having been beaten, or even any really hard words. It was simply that she found, quite soon after taking me in, that she did not really love me: indeed she did not seem even to like me.

My foster-father was quite straightforward in his attitude towards me. I had been brought into the house as an indulgence for Mary. After that, it was best if I kept out of his way. That was easy enough. He spent most of his time when he was not at the university locked up in a small room he called sometimes his 'library' and at other times his 'office'.

We led a quiet life together. My foster-father's social life was limited to the Senior Common Room at the university, or wherever else political-history lecturers gather together to graze in the fields of learning. People rarely came to our house for any form of entertainment and, when they did, it did not tempt them to stay long.

I grew up a solitary child. I did not have much opportunity to meet other children outside school, but perhaps that was just as well: I found it difficult enough to talk to them in school. I kept my thoughts to myself. I was a very neat and tidy child. No one could ever complain about that. Sometimes I looked up to the sky and saw stars, even in the daylight. No one else ever seemed to see the stars that I saw, so I did not mention them to anyone else. I think I was about sixteen when I discovered I had an aptitude for numbers. I was not particularly good at any subject until, suddenly, I began to excel at mathematics. My foster-father thought this was a waste of time.

'What is the use of knowing how to add up,' he asked me, 'unless you are planning on working as a shop assistant. Are you planning on working as a shop assistant, Frankie?'

'Not particularly,' I mumbled.

'I hope you are planning on doing something,' he said. 'Bringing you up has been a considerable financial burden. I wish you could appreciate the sacrifices we have made. I hope you do not expect this largesse to last for ever.'

I did not know then what 'largesse' meant. My foster-father enjoyed using words like that.

I said, 'I'm interested in computers, though.'

'Oh, *computers*,' said my foster-father.

When I was awarded a scholarship at a local university to read Computer Sciences, I went and knocked on the door of my foster-father's office. It was unheard of for anyone to interrupt him while he was working on his book. The projected *Life of Bismarck* occupied a great deal of his time. A publisher in Augsburg in Germany was said to be keenly interested in the German rights.

'Who is it?' he called.

'It's me,' I said. 'It's Frankie.'

'What do you want? I'm very busy.'

'I just wanted to tell you something.'

He called me in. The weariness in his voice made me feel tired. I opened the door. He looked up from his desk. His hands were covered in printing ink from the ribbon of his Remington typewriter.

'What is it, Frankie? You can see how busy I am.'

'Let me help,' I said, and quickly untangled the ribbon for him and clicked the spool back into place. Then I said, 'I've been given a scholarship, to read Computer Sciences at Durham University.'

My foster-father said, 'Oh. Well, I don't see why you couldn't have waited until dinner to tell me that. And I suppose you expect me to pay for your maintenance, do you?'

My father was right: my news could have waited until dinner.

I never finished the university course. I absorbed knowledge so fast that I soon knew more than most of the lecturers, at least about the things that interested me. After eighteen months I left, and with some help from one of the lecturers, who gave me some contraband 'obsolete' equipment from one of the computer labs, I started my own business.

Of course, since setting up my own company I had learned the necessity of meeting people and getting on with them. Customers in particular needed careful handling. I had learned that you had to talk to them, before you could ask them for money. Until Andy joined the business I found the selling side rather painful and, if it had not been that the software I had developed was really rather good, I would never have made a sale. When Andy joined, even though he was employed as finance director, his natural social skills meant that he took over a lot of the customer work, until we grew big enough to employ full-time salesmen. Even then he kept up the relationships with our bigger customers. He was a natural. He laughed, he made jokes, and he teased them about their football teams. Everyone liked Andy.

I don't know how much any of them liked me, except for Andy himself. They knew, though, that the business wouldn't be there if it wasn't for me. I was the person who had developed the original software on which the business had been built, and I still knew more about it than anyone else. When the staff or the customers needed more than jokes, they came to me for the explanations and the answers.

I knew how to talk to people, but I had never got to the point of doing it for fun.

The day that I left Hartlepool Hall, after having had lunch there, I believed that I would never see Ed or Eck again. Why would I? All that had happened was that there had been a transaction: one hour of IT support, provided by Wilberforce, value say £100; one lamb chop, and a cup of coffee, provided by Ed Simmonds, value say £10. On the face of it Ed Simmonds still owed me something, but then he had given me, if only for a couple of hours, the countenance of his friendship, value probably rather more than £90.

Andy used to tell me he was my friend, usually in the context of a discussion about salaries or share options, and in many ways he was my friend. We used to have supper together in a little Indian restaurant sometimes after work; we shared moments of triumph and crisis in the business; and we plotted and schemed together. All of those things I thought amounted to friendship. I supposed that that was what friendship was. But after my visit to Hartlepool Hall I began to speculate that there might be other modes of life, where people passed time together and did not talk about their work but about other things: about each other; about

266

forms of activity of which I knew nothing, such as racing or hunting; even about wine. I imagined the world inhabited by these people to be like a garden surrounded by a high wall: inside the garden, the few inhabitants allowed to enter it enjoyed a life of leisure, in surroundings that were pleasant to the eye; outside, the world trudged about its weary business. I had been allowed a glimpse of the garden through the railings, had even stepped inside for a moment, and it had unsettled me. In the garden there were fewer transactions than on the outside: instead relationships flourished, which the word 'transaction' was not always adequate to describe. I had thought that relationships with other people, if you had to have them, were based on mutual need: I have something you want; you have something I want. The possibility that people could spend time together with no other object in mind than enjoyment of one another's company was a new idea to me.

My life, which before had seemed full, now seemed empty.

My routine went on as before. I worked until seven or seven thirty, then drove to the food mall at the shopping centre, bought a takeaway and took it home. I would sit at the kitchen table in my flat, eating the food without really knowing what it was I was eating, and sipping the giant Diet Coke I usually bought to wash down the food. Sometimes I had the television on when I did this; sometimes I did not. I never took much notice of what the programmes were about, anyway. While the television was on, the picture and the sound gave an illusion of activity to the flat which I liked, for some reason.

After I had finished eating I used to tidy up. A cleaning lady who did the other flats in the building came in three times a week, and did the laundry as well, so there was never very much to do. I liked rearranging things: I used to rearrange the books in the bookcase, a mixture of a few novels bought at the supermarket checkout and manuals for software developers. I would sometimes arrange them by size and at other times by colour. I used to wash and dry the foil cartons in which my takeaways came and keep them in neat piles, in case they could be of use some day. I rearranged the piles of cartons now and then. I found it soothing. At other times I would empty everything from the fridge and clean the fridge out, a job the cleaning lady often neglected to do. There was never much in it: a block of processed Cheddar, a tub of instantly spreadable butter, a carton of orange juice or two, and a few eggs.

If there was nothing to tidy up, I would sit and do large sums in my head. It was an ability I had been born with: numbers were to me like words to other people. Thinking up algorithms was a form of passing the time that I found particularly satisfactory. When I had completed these recreations, it would be time to turn on the computer, call up the office file server, and do a couple of hours work on whatever project was engaging me at the time. Some time before midnight I would go to bed and sleep for a few hours before driving to the office at five or six in the morning.

For more than ten years this routine had satisfied me, and I had needed no other distraction in my life. I loved doing what I did. I was good at it – better than most people. My work was everything to me: Andy used to say I was obsessive about it, but then he earned a salary of seventy thousand a year on the back of my obsessions, so he really couldn't complain.

Now, like dawn creeping through the drawn curtains of a darkened room, a pale light was beginning to grow, and as it grew it illuminated the austere and lonely nature of my world. It hadn't just been the visit to Hartlepool Hall that had unsettled me. One morning I woke up with a haunting sense of loss. I awoke from a dream, and as I awoke, its shreds and tatters of memory drifted away and evaporated into nothingness even as my conscious mind reached out to grasp them. I awoke from a dream in which someone very close to me had died, and yet in the dream he or she was still able to reproach me, to call out to me for help. It had been a she, I felt sure. As my mind struggled with the remains of sleep, for a moment the image in my dream came back to me. I saw a dim figure on the far shore of a pale lake, with her arms reaching out to me. It seemed to me that if I could have reached out and touched her outstretched fingers, and grasped her hands, I might have brought her back; but the pale lake stood between us and I knew I could never cross it. Then the figure receded into darkness, and as it disappeared, its silent cry of anguish and despair reached inside me and twisted itself around my heart. Then I was truly awake, and tears stood in the corners of my eyes.

A dream is a dream, and most of the few dreams I had ever had involved the development of a new bit of software. Once I dreamed I had found a new prime number. I had never had a dream like this before. Its memory stayed with me for days, like a wound deep within my brain that would not heal.

The existence that I had led, sitting in front of a computer for fourteen hours out of every twenty-four, once seemed to have sufficient rigour and clarity to be the complete answer to any question that I might ask myself about the point of my existence. Now, I began to appreciate that life and software development could not be balanced in the same scales. I began to imagine that my life was itself like an insoluble equation, and there was an 'x' in the middle of the equation that I had to understand and could not quantify.

Ed Simmonds didn't ring me back. Once I would have been grateful not to have the problem of knowing how to refuse further invitations. Now I regretted that he had ever allowed me to think that he would be in touch again. I had written my telephone number down for him because he had asked me to, and I had left it by the telephone in his sitting room. It would not have required a moment of his time to pick up the phone and call me, and he appeared to have no shortage of time available to him. He did not ring, and I knew exactly what he must think about it all, as if I could hear him in the next room speaking to Eck about me: 'Such an odd chap, that Wilberforce; he's awfully clever with computers. He must live and breathe them. He doesn't tell many jokes, though, does he?' and Eck would reply, 'True. Still, it's probably better to keep his number in case your machine breaks down or something?'

Ed Simmonds didn't ring. I did go back to see Francis Black now and then. He did not seem to mind me dropping in and he did not expect me to buy anything. We sat and talked and I was surprised how easy it was to talk to Francis; or to listen, for Francis was quite apt to suddenly recall some piece of family history, or some incident from his own past, which he would decide it would suit me to hear about. I began to form a disconnected picture of Francis's past. He had been wild in his youth – almost to the point of self-destruction. The death of his parents and the inheritance of what remained of his family estate had steadied him up. Now wine was his one reason for living. It was almost an obsession with him.

I did not visit Francis very often. I was afraid of imposing myself on him. From time to time I bought a bottle of his wine, because I thought it might be expected of me, in order to give him the pleasure of telling me all about the grower, the vintage or the appellation. Francis's shop had been where I had met Ed and Eck, and whenever I went up to Caerlyon I half-expected and half-hoped I would see another car parked in the courtyard. I never did.

After each visit, if I had bought some wine, I would put the bottle away somewhere. There were quite a few of them after a while, lining my shelves. Very occasionally I opened a bottle and drank a glass. I had to admit that I could see why people sometimes drank wine. The taste was strangely interesting, certainly more interesting than Diet Coke. If I ever drank a second glass I felt, for a moment, disinclined to do any tidying up or count up to very large numbers in my head. Oddly enough, the most readily identifiable feeling I had after drinking the second glass was that it might be nice to drink a third. I never did; I poured the rest of the bottle down the sink, as Francis had told me I should, so that the wine should not die.

It was odd to think that wine could die so quickly. What had Francis's words been? A lifetime of experience to create, ten years in the bottle to become ready to drink, and a few hours of drinkable life before the wine was drunk or extinguished.

One's own life, too, was finite. I had once read in a science magazine that we start to die as soon as our cells stop dividing and growing, in our late teens or early twenties. The same article said that we lost most of our ability to learn at around the age of five, when our ability to absorb new information reduced by at least three-quarters. On that basis I was on the way out. I was well over thirty, my brain was vanishing in an exponential decay of brain cells, my body had stopped growing and started ageing, and all I had ever done was write some clever software.

I expressed this view to Andy one night in Al Diwan, the Indian restaurant we used to eat in.

He piled a spoonful or two of chopped onion on to a flake of poppadum, added a good-sized amount of hot lime pickle and said, 'Yes, well, in your case, Wilberforce, it is very likely that you are either already dead, or else in a state of suspended animation.'

'That's not particularly funny,' I said. Andy enjoyed winding me up, I knew, and he indulged himself quite often enough for me.

'No, but seriously, you don't allow yourself much of a life. Why don't you ever go on holiday?'

'Where to?'

'Majorca? Florida? The Maldives? You could afford to go anywhere in the world, but you never bother.'

Andy went on holiday a lot. He worked hard, but he went to France or Spain with his girlfriend at least three times a year, and dreamed of owning his own villa next door to a golf course.

'What would I do on holiday?' I asked him.

'Nothing – that's the whole point,' explained Andy. He drank from his glass of lager. 'And then there's the question of your social life.'

'What social life?'

'Exactly,' said Andy. 'What social life? Other people have friends. They even have girlfriends. They go to bed with their girlfriends sometimes and have sex with them. Did you do sex at school, or did you leave before they got to that bit?'

I didn't like Andy teasing me, but then again I did like him talking about me. No one else had ever spent any time on the subject, apart from the teachers who wrote my school reports. He had an attractive girlfriend called Clare whom he had once told me he might marry when he had the time.

'I got a GSCE in Biology,' I said, 'I got a C. I got an A-star in Mathematics and—'

'We're not writing your CV,' said Andy. 'I'm just saying that most people, when they get to your age, probably have a few friends. They might belong to the rugby club, or the tennis club, or the golf club. They might not even belong to a club at all, but just might get out and meet people. They might be going out with someone, or they might even be married. Wilberforce, did you know quite a lot of people got married before they were thirty? You and I are still single and at our ages we are the exception rather than the rule. But at least I can say I have a girl in my life.'

'A very nice one too,' I said, thinking of Clare.

'She is, isn't she?' agreed Andy, with a complacent smile. 'I don't mean to lecture you – ah, mine is the lamb vindaloo; my friend is having the chicken madras,' he said to the waiter as the food began to arrive. 'But it was you that brought up the subject of a social life.'

There was a pause while we helped ourselves to curry.

'Yes, I've been thinking about having a social life myself,' I said. 'But I'm not sure how to go about it, or what I would do with it if I got one.'

'A social life', explained Andy, 'isn't like a takeaway. You can't buy it. Well, some people can, but I don't think that you are one of them. You have to work at it. You have to meet people, you have to like them, and they have to like you. That's how it works.'

'I met some people the other day,' I said, as casually as I could.

'People? What people?' he asked. He seemed slightly put out by my initiative.

'Oh, some people at the top of the hill.' Then I had to explain that my remark was not about their social status, but more to do with geography.

He said, 'Well, there you are. It just shows how these things can happen. Will you be seeing them again?'

'I don't know,' I answered. 'It depends.'

Then he became bored with teasing me and we spent the rest of the evening, as usual, talking about the business. Andy wanted me to float it on the stock market one day and I said, 'That's more or less the same as selling it, isn't it? I don't think I could ever sell it. What would I do with the money? What would be the point?'

It depends, I had said, when Andy had asked me if I would see my new friends again. It depends on what? I wondered, as I drove home that evening. On what would it depend that Ed Simmonds, whom I hardly knew, or Eck, or Francis, or anyone whom I would ever meet, would want, having once met me, to repeat the experience? I couldn't think of a single reason. What could he gain from seeing me a second time, if his computer still worked?

Once again the image of a secret garden came into my mind. Everybody else in the world was in on the secret and had a key to its iron door. Only I, a child of no known mother, a person of no accomplishments except being able to add up large numbers in his head, prowled around on the outside and was never to be admitted.

I did not sleep much that night. It takes someone to tell you about what you might be missing before you realise you are missing it. That was what Andy had just done. I lay awake staring at the invisible ceiling in the darkness, and thought about prime numbers and counted in my head up to some impossibly large number. At four in the morning, I fell into a sleep like drowning. I awoke with a start at half past seven, feeling dreadful, and rushed into the office without stopping to shave.

Andy was already there. 'Morning, Wilberforce,' he said. 'You look ghastly. I told you the chicken madras would be too hot for you.'

Three

A few weeks later, to my surprise, Ed Simmonds did ring. When my secretary asked if she could put the call through, I had to think for a moment before I placed the name.

Ed was on the line. 'Wilberforce, is that you? How are you?'

'Ed, how nice to hear you,' I said. I really meant it. His voice, not heard for several weeks, was as familiar to me when I heard it as if I had been listening to it every day. In a way, I had been listening to it, in my memory, wondering and doubting whether he would ever be in touch again. Now he was, and all the doubts I had of his sincerity when he'd promised to be in touch again flapped away like a flock of crows when someone claps his hands.

'I'd have rung before,' Ed told me, 'but I've been away, fishing in Iceland with some friends.'

'How was it?'

'It was bloody cold. But we took a few cases of Francis's claret to warm us.'

'I didn't know anything about fishing, but I thought I ought to say something, so I asked, 'Did you catch any fish?'

'Lots, but to tell the truth, after fish number ten it became quite hard work.'

I wondered in that case why he had bothered to go. I was not then familiar with the language of understatement, irony and self-depreciation that formed the vocabulary of Ed Simmonds and his friends.

As if guessing my thoughts he said, 'An old friend asked me last year to go with his party. I'm not much of a fisherman, but I must have accepted after drinking too much at dinner, and I didn't feel I could jack out of it when he told me it had all been fixed up. Anyway, the way I'm droning on about Iceland, I shouldn't be surprised to find I was showing you my holiday snaps next. I didn't call you to bore you to death with my fishing stories. I was wondering whether you could come and have supper tonight. Sorry it's such short notice and all that, but I thought I'd see what you said.'

I hesitated. I had half-promised to go and have supper after work with Andy, to kick around some idea he had for growing the business. Then I thought, he won't mind, and I said, 'I'd love to. Thank you very much. What time?'

'Eight, here, if that suits you; and just scruff. It's only me and Catherine; we'll probably eat in the kitchen.'

I went next door to Andy's office and said, 'Were we supposed to be having supper together after work this evening?'

He looked up and said, 'Sure. It's in your diary.'

'Can I cancel? I mean, can we do it another night? Something's come up.'

Andy looked irritated. 'Well, OK, if you must. What's come up? Is there a problem?'

'No,' I said. I felt a little awkward. 'Actually, some friends have asked me out to supper and I seem to have double-booked myself.'

He stopped looking irritated and started to grin. 'Friends, Wilberforce? What is this *friends* business?'

Now it was my turn to be irritated. 'I do have friends, you know.'

'First I've heard of it,' said Andy, cheerfully. 'No, go for it, Wilberforce. Lighten up. Have a social life for an evening. We'll do our thing some other night.'

*

I arrived at Hartlepool Hall at eight, and Horace opened the great hall door almost before I had tugged the bell pull. When he saw me he inclined his head, as he had before, but this time smiled as well. He seemed genuinely pleased to see me.

'Good evening, Mr Wilberforce. Lord Edward and Miss Plender are in the kitchen. If you will follow me, sir?'

We crossed the hall and found a staircase into the lower parts of the house. Horace opened a door on to a large and surprisingly modern kitchen. It appeared to be filled with every sort of device known to modern catering: ovens, microwaves, a double Aga, an industrial-sized dishwasher, racks from which stainless-steel pans hung, and endless glass cupboards around the walls filled with wine glasses and different dinner services. In the centre of the room was a square marble worktop, with a sauce boat and some chopped-up vegetables sitting on it. A bottle of white wine stood there, with two half-full glasses beside it. There was no one in the room. Then another door opened at the other end of the kitchen and Ed came in carrying some objects on a tin tray, followed by a girl. They were both laughing, but stopped when they saw me.

'Wilberforce,' said Ed, 'you made it! Well done. Horace, bring Wilberforce a glass of champagne. Or perhaps you'd prefer wine?'

I was going to ask for a glass of water but decided that would not do, so I just said, 'Whatever's open.'

'No, no,' said Ed. 'Horace loves opening bottles. Horace, please bring Mr Wilberforce a glass of champagne.'

The girl behind Ed came forward and put her hand in mine. 'Hello,' she said. 'I'm Catherine Plender. Ed always expects everyone to know everyone. He's useless at introductions.' She was about five foot six, with thick blonde hair and grey eyes. I thought she was absolutely beautiful and I found that I could hardly look her in the eyes. I shook her hand. I felt myself blushing.

I was saved by Horace touching my arm and saying, 'Champagne, sir?'

I turned and took the glass, turned back and saw Catherine Plender smiling at me. I think she knew the effect she had had on me, and was gaining some slight amusement from it.

Ed held up a small brown carcass and said, 'Any objection to roast grouse, Wilberforce?'

'I've never had it.'

'Then now's the moment,' said Ed. 'Darling, can you shove them in the Aga, and we'll all go next door.'

'It nearly wasn't the moment,' explained Catherine. 'Ed only remembered to get them out of the deep freeze about half an hour ago. Then I had to show him how to defrost them in the microwave. Then I had to show him how to peel a potato. Then I had to show him how to open a bag of frozen peas. Now I've got to finish making the bread sauce. All this because he told me it was cook's night off, so he would get our dinner.'

The moment of awkwardness passed and we all laughed, Ed in a slightly abashed way.

Then he said, 'Bring your drink, Wilberforce. Darling, we'll be in the library.'

I followed Ed out of the kitchen and after a few minutes' traverse of the house we came to a large book-lined room, the rows of books broken at intervals by glass display cases containing various bedraggled-looking stuffed birds. A log fire was burning in a stone hearth and, although it was not a cold night, we wandered towards it and sat on the fender.

'You'll love grouse,' said Ed enthusiastically, as we sipped our drinks. 'Have you never shot them?'

I was surprised that he would think that I ever would have, but then I realised that Ed expected everyone else in the world either to be like him, fishing in Iceland or shooting grouse in the Pennines. Or else he expected them to be like

Horace, opening bottles of champagne for other people when required.

'No,' I said. 'I never have. I don't shoot.'

'You *don't shoot*? Why ever not?' asked Ed. Then he blushed and said, 'I'm so sorry. Perhaps you're one of those anti-what-do-you-call-'ems. Quite all right with me if you are. Nothing against racing, I hope?'

'I'm not anti-anything, as far as I know,' I told him. 'It's just that I've never done it.'

'Oh dear,' said Ed. He looked chastened, as if I had told him I was sickening for something. Then he brightened up. 'Well, there must be something you like doing. Do you ride? Do you fish? You can't spend your entire time with computers, I suppose?'

'I don't do anything like that,' I said. 'I don't ever seem to have had the time.'

Ed Simmonds was gripped by this revelation. 'Seriously?' he asked. 'You really mean that all you do is work?'

'I'm afraid so,' I said. I wondered why I sounded so apologetic.

'That is absolutely amazing,' said Ed. 'I mean – how old are you. I'm twenty-nine. You might be a year or two older, I imagine.'

'I'm thirty-four,' I said.

'Well, it's not too late then. You need taking in hand, Wilberforce. I'm going to instruct you in the art of having a good time. You don't mind, do you? It will be very good for you; and, apart from Eck, there isn't anybody better than me for knowing about that sort of thing.'

'That's what my friend at work says,' I told him. 'He says I ought to have a social life.'

Ed started to laugh, and his laughter was so infectious that I began to laugh with him.

'A social life? Is that what it's called? Don't worry, Wilberforce, we'll make sure you have a *social* life.'

He was still laughing when Catherine came into the room.
My eyes left Ed without my willing them to, and turned to
her.

'Dinner is served,' she said, giving a mock curtsey to Ed.

'That's Horace's job, you know,' Ed told her. 'Union
rules.'

The next morning Andy wandered into my office with two
cups of coffee and handed one to me. As usual he sat on the
corner of my desk.

He said, 'We beat forecast again last month. About fifty
thousand above budget profit.'

'Good.'

'Good? It's bloody wonderful.'

'Well, yes, I suppose it is.'

He looked at me with curiosity. 'Have you got a hangover?'

'No, you know I don't drink.'

'Then what is it?'

I wished he would go away. I didn't feel up to his banter
this morning.

'Didn't you enjoy your evening with your friends?' he
persisted. What made Andy a good finance director was that
he kept asking questions. I wished for once he would stop.

'On the contrary,' I said. 'It was very pleasant.'

'Good,' said Andy. 'It's good for you to have a social life,
Wilberforce, so long as it doesn't get in the way of business.
All play and no work, and all that sort of thing.'

I said nothing, waiting for him to go.

He looked at me again and said, 'You met a girl, didn't
you?'

'Well, there was a girl there.'

'And did you manage to meet her? Or did you do that

famous Wilberforce thing you do with our best customers sometimes, and pretend they are not in the same room as you?'

'I met her,' I admitted. 'Look, I've got some work to do . . .'

'You met a girl.'

'Yes, someone else's girlfriend, that's all.'

He started to laugh. 'Really, you shouldn't be allowed out on your own,' he said. 'You go out to dinner for the first time almost since I've known you, and you fall in love on your first outing.' He went on laughing and then stood up, crooning. 'Wilberforce is in *lurve* . . .'

He left the room, thank God. I was not in love. He was talking absolute rubbish, winding me up for his own amusement, as he liked to do. I had liked Catherine. She was very amusing, and lively, and probably a good deal brighter than Ed. Why shouldn't I like her? I put my head in my hands for a moment and shook it to clear from my mind the image of her laughing as we sat in the kitchen last night, the muscles moving in her throat. Out with the images of Catherine laughing, in with the software, I told my brain.

Only she had looked, as she sat there, like an angel.

The next weekend I drove out to Hartlepool Hall again. Ed had invited me to have a shooting lesson, on clay pigeons. It was part of his grand new scheme of Educating Wilberforce. I knew, or I thought I knew, that I represented a diversion for Ed. I was his project. He was going to teach me to shoot, or to fish, or to ride. He was going to take me racing. There was even a half-promise that I could go and stay at the end of August at the family's other house in the county, Blubberwick Lodge, to watch a day's grouse-shooting. I still could not really believe that there might be a simpler explanation: that Ed Simmonds actually enjoyed the company of someone so different from his usual circle, and that he wanted nothing more from me than my company.

When I drove to Hartlepool Hall I half-hoped Catherine Plender would be there, and I half-hoped that she would not. When I arrived at the house, and Horace took me through to meet Ed, it was soon clear that she was not. I felt a strong sense of disappointment. Ed took me out through the back quarters of the house, through stable yards, and coach yards, and down a path behind the kitchen gardens, beside a long brick wall with a lean-to structure running along it.

'This used to be our bakery,' said Ed. 'I remember it was still going when I was a child. It was fuelled by coal from our drift mine. The bread was baked in here and the heat was used to heat up water, which was taken away in pipes to warm the peach house. The bread was like rock. If you dropped your slice of toast you were quite likely to break something with it. I was so relieved when they decided to pack it in and I was allowed to eat Mother's Pride like everyone else.'

We came out past the bottom of the kitchen garden, and into a field that fell steeply away to a small stream at the bottom. At the top of a grassy bank stood a man beside a contraption I realised was a clay-pigeon trap.

'Morning, George,' said Ed. 'This is Mr Wilberforce I told you about. I want you to help him a bit with his shooting.'

'Done it before, sir?' enquired George.

'No, it's my first time,' I told him.

'Don't worry, we'll soon have you hitting clays just as good as his lordship there.'

'Now then, George,' said Ed, 'I'm not sure if you meant that as a compliment.'

The keeper grinned and then bent down to open a leather gun case that lay on the ground at his feet. He opened it up, took out the disassembled parts of a shotgun and quickly put the gun together. It was a thing of beauty: a walnut stock, silver chasings on the sidelock, and a number one in gold on the barrel, showing that it was one of a pair.

'Try that for size,' George suggested, and showed me how to fit the gun tight into my shoulder and how to swing with it on to an imaginary target.

'Don't drop it, for heaven's sake,' said Ed. 'A pair of those guns costs about fifty thousand to replace.'

After a lecture about gun safety I was allowed to walk down the slope with Ed and try my luck at shooting clays. George the keeper sat on a seat behind the clay-pigeon trap at the top of the bank, protected from any inaccurate or careless shot of mine by a sheet of corrugated iron.

'Remember, Wilberforce,' said Ed: 'blot the clay out with the end of the barrel as it comes over you, and fire, all at the same time.' Then he shouted, 'Pull,' and two black discs sailed overhead and glided harmlessly into the trees beyond.

'Was I meant to shoot them?' I asked.

'Next time I shout, "Pull," get your gun up to your shoulder and fire as soon as you like. Remember, you've got two barrels, one trigger for each.'

He shouted, 'Pull,' again and before I knew what was happening I had fired two shots.

'What happened?' I asked.

'You powdered both of them,' said Ed ecstatically. 'Well done! A right and a left first time you've ever shot. I can't believe it. Did you see that, George?'

'He's a natural, sir,' shouted George from the top of the bank.

For the next hour they made me fire at clay after clay. I missed some of them, but hit a few.

We walked back to the house, leaving George to pick up the empty cartridge cases and undamaged clays. The sky was brightening, there were patches of blue everywhere now, and the day was warm. The dew was nearly off the grass. I felt pleased I had done so well, and Ed was delighted by my newly acquired shooting skills.

'Well done, Wilberforce,' he said. 'I tell you what we'll do. If we've got any grouse this year, you shall come out to Blubberwick with us one day in August. You can watch how it all works and, if you'd like, we'll give you a minder and you can try a few shots yourself.'

A little while later we parted, as Ed was going to Thirsk Races for lunch and the afternoon, and I was going back to the office. I thanked him again, and he replied by asking me to come to dinner the following week. 'Eck's coming,' he said, 'and Annabel Gazebee. You'll like Annabel. Oh, and Catherine, of course.'

I accepted. All of a sudden I had new friends, a new life. It felt very odd, but as I drove back to the office I decided it was a good feeling.

So began a long summer different from all the other summers I had ever known. That was the summer when I passed from being frozen in permanent adolescence, like some juvenile mammoth overtaken by the ice sheets, into a new state of being. As I thawed, new emotions overtook me, and new longings. Now, instead of begrudging time not spent in my office I began to count the hours, on those evenings when I had an invitation from one or other of my new friends, until I should be out of the office and once again driving up the little road that wound up the side of the hill. There were many such invitations. It seemed as if I spent every spare moment with people, no longer always on my own. Each time I went out to dinner, or to Sunday lunch, I met more and more new faces. I discovered after a while that there was an inner circle. Whether the circle had formed itself around Ed, or whether it had formed itself around Francis Black, I was not quite sure. The inner circle was Ed Simmonds himself, Francis Black, Annabel

Gazebee, Catherine Plender and Eck Chetwode-Talbot. Sometimes we met at Eck's large and rambling farmhouse, where Eck, who was a surprisingly good cook, entertained us. We dined several times at the Plenders' house, Coalheugh.

Catherine's parents were rather forbidding, but as they spent most of the year in Bermuda or Antibes, I only met them once that summer. One night we had kitchen supper with Francis, at his flat at the back of Caerlyon, and after supper went down to inspect the undercroft. It seemed fuller of wine and more impressive than I had remembered it. Most of all we lunched, dined or simply sat around and talked, at Hartlepool Hall. Maybe it was on the occasion that Ed first asked me to meet Annabel Gazebee that I had an odd conversation with Eck.

I was seated next to Annabel at dinner. She was a tall, angular girl with long brown hair, a sharp beak of a nose and a brittle manner of speech. She was easy enough to talk to, though. She seemed to find it fascinating that I went to an office every day and worked there.

'I think that's so good,' she told me. 'Such a good example to people like Eck and Ed, who do absolutely nothing all day long.'

'I'm very busy,' said Ed indignantly. 'I'm going to be a steward at Kelso races next year.'

Annabel herself sat on a committee that raised money for the Red Cross and considered herself to be second to no one in the matter of being busy.

Another person joined us unexpectedly for dinner: a family friend of the Simmondses, the Earl of Shildon, whom I had heard Francis talk about. He had been visiting Ed's father, who was unwell, and confined to his bedroom.

'He's one of my trustees,' explained Ed, while we waited for Teddy Shildon to join us before dinner. 'So I've got to be civil to him. Anyway, even though he's only ten years younger than my pa, you'd never guess it to look at him. He's great fun. You'll like him, I know you will.'

We went into the library after dinner. Ed, Annabel, Catherine and Teddy Shildon were sitting at a table near the fire. Bridge had been proposed and rejected and instead they had begun to play a noisy game of racing demon. Eck refused to join in, saying that he hated cards, and I didn't know how. Card games had not been on my foster-father's list of acceptable entertainments.

'Mind if I help myself to one of your stogies, Ed?' asked Eck, reaching for the humidor as he spoke.

'Help yourself,' cried Ed; 'you too, Wilberforce. Oh, Catherine, you cheat!'

Eck trimmed his cigar and lit it. 'Let's go outside,' he suggested. 'It's a warm enough night.'

At the far end of the library were double glass doors that led out on to a terrace. We went outside and seated ourselves on a stone balustrade that led the length of the terrace and looked out on to a corner of the lake and the dark woods beyond that girdled Hartlepool Hall. It was a green and pink dusk, and the moon was rising.

'Perfect evening,' said Eck, puffing on his cigar. Two bats skittered past, chasing insects in the twilight.

'Eck,' I said, 'why does Francis look so sad all the time?' We had both been with Francis a few nights before.

'Does he?' asked Eck, in surprise. 'Is that how he strikes you? Well, maybe you are right. We're all so used to him that I don't suppose we ever notice anything like that. I suppose he might well look sad. He's had a disappointing life, in some ways.'

'In what way?' I asked.

'Well, Francis is very intelligent – much brighter than any of us. You know he's my godfather, don't you?'

'You said.'

'So I know him as well as I know anyone of that generation. He was born with brains and good looks; he inherited a good few acres and a decent-sized house. He's ended up with next to nothing, and no one to leave it to. That's why I think he might feel disappointed. Anyone would.'

'What happened?' I asked. Francis fascinated me. I wanted to know. I knew Eck loved talking about other people's lives. I knew he would tell me almost anything.

'Francis was very wild when he was young. I think it was a reaction to his mother. She was very much the *grande dame*. My father once said she was the most frightening woman he had ever met. Francis's own father was a brave soldier when he was in the army, but he used to creep about and keep out of trouble at home. Then Francis had the most horrendous falling-out with his mother.'

Eck paused, and puffed on his cigar until the end glowed an even red in the gloom. I said nothing. I wanted Eck to go on with the story.

'Francis fell head over heels in love with a girl who lived in one of the cottages and worked as a daily maid in the house. At first everyone thought Francis was just having a fling. But my father told me that it had been the real thing. Francis had absolutely fallen in love with the girl who did the ironing for his mother. Then it got worse. The girl became pregnant and, of course, Francis's mother found out. She got the whole story out of her maid. She called Francis in, who said he was going to marry the girl. There was a huge shouting match.'

Eck paused to puff on his cigar again. It was very quiet outside. I could hear frogs croaking down by the lake, and a firefly went past.

'So Francis fell in love?'

'The one and only real passion of his life, as far as anyone knows,' agreed Eck. 'Then he went away to London, and he got in with Johnny . . . well, with a whole lot of people you probably don't know, who played cards for pretty high stakes at the Clermont and those sorts of places. Francis dropped a serious amount of money. I mean an enormous amount of money. He was playing with people who could afford to sit down and lose a hundred thousand in a night. Unfortunately, he couldn't. Then his parents paid off his debts, which cost them a fortune, and sent him off travelling, to get him out of the way. When he came back he'd acquired an interest in wine. He'd been staying in Austria with a friend of his parents, Heinrich Carinthia, a sort of Hapsburg relation who's a prince and owns vineyards all over the place. He still comes once a year to shoot at Blubberwick. Francis caught the wine bug from him. He started collecting wine around then, and he's been at it ever since. It's become rather an expensive obsession, in fact. He's tried being a wine broker, and a wine merchant, and none of it has ever worked. Francis is simply completely uncommercial. He talks a good game. You would think he would be the world's best wine salesman, to hear him. But if anyone knows more about buying dear and selling cheap than Francis does, I haven't met them. Apart from the money he lost gambling, he's lost another fortune speculating in wine. He can't afford to buy proper wine any more. Now all he can do is buy the odd parcel of bin ends, from time to time. He's cashed in just about every farm and house he inherited in order to stay in the game, except for Caerlyon, and even that's on a long lease to Gateshead Council.'

'But he has a marvellous collection of wine,' I said with enthusiasm.

'Well, maybe. There's quite a lot of it, I know, but it all seems to me to be bits and pieces and odds and ends. It's become an obsession for Francis. In some ways, it's tragic. He has no children to leave anything to, and he has nothing to leave – except, of course, his wine. So, you're absolutely right: Francis has a reason to look sad. But we all look after him, you know. Everybody loves Francis, for some reason.'

Eck stood up and stretched himself.

'What happened to the girl?' I asked.

'What girl? Oh, Francis's girl. She had the child and had to give it away for adoption. Poor mite.'

The thought of adoption made me uncomfortable, and to change the subject I said, 'Annabel's nice, isn't she?'

'Yes,' said Eck. He took a last puff at his cigar and flung it over the balustrade in a trail of sparks. 'She's very nice. She and I had a fling, once.'

'Really?'

'It was very jolly. The leg-over part of it was very jolly indeed. But then there was so much talking beforehand and afterwards, I found it all rather tiring, and in the end we decided to give it up and just be friends.' Eck started to stroll back towards the lighted windows through which we had walked earlier. The sound of laughter could be heard from within as the card game reached its climax.

'Some people think I'm an incurable romantic,' said Eck. 'But in all honesty I've found this love business is rather an effort, don't you agree? A quick bonk and a large gin and tonic satisfy most of life's wants, in my opinion.'

I could not think of an adequate comment.

'Why don't you have a crack at Annabel?' suggested Eck, stopping and turning to face me.

'Me? I don't think so,' I replied.

'I don't know, Wilberforce. I think she quite fancied you at dinner. I can tell. I should ask her out if I were you. You might be just her cup of tea: brainy sort of chap that you are.'

'No, I don't think I will, Eck.'

He didn't move, but stared at me. It was full night now, but in the light from the windows, and in the moonlight from above, we could see each other's face clearly enough.

'You're sweet on Catherine, aren't you,' said Eck. It was not a question.

'No,' I said in a hoarse voice. I was absolutely taken aback by the sudden change in Eck's tone, and by the question. He was no longer bantering.

'There's nothing to be ashamed of, if you are,' said Eck. 'I was pretty gone about her at one time. It's easy enough to understand, with a girl who looks like that. But it's a lost cause.'

'I've no intention of interfering between her and Ed,' I said. 'They're my friends.'

'Yes, of course,' said Eck. 'But friendship has a funny way of going up in smoke in these situations. Ed and Catherine are going to get married. It's all been arranged. Old Simon Hartlepool and Robin Plender made plans for them both long ago, and Ed and Catherine have been brainwashed into the idea they will be married one day, almost since they could walk. So don't waste too much time on that idea.'

I did not reply and Eck said, 'Come on. It's gone quiet inside. They must have finished playing that dreadful game. I think it'll be safe to go back in.'

Four

In late August, Ed asked me to go and stay at Blubberwick Lodge. There was to be a shooting party there for a couple of days. Ed and his guests were going up the day before, to shoot on the Friday. They were staying that night at the lodge. Francis and I were asked to go and watch the shooting and then stay for dinner on the Saturday night. It was half understood that Ed would lend me a gun for the last drive, arrange for me to stand with a minder and have a go at shooting a grouse. Francis wanted a chance to work Campbell, and pick up grouse behind the line.

Eck had told me about Blubberwick Lodge. It had been built by the first Marquess of Gateshead in the 1860s, when the moors around Blubberwick were no longer mined for the lead that had founded the fortunes of the Simmonds family in the last two centuries. Now the moors were harvested for grouse, not lead.

It was considered inconvenient to ride twenty miles from Hartlepool Hall to Blubberwick Moor, so a lodge or shooting box had been built closer to hand. 'It is a very comfortable set-up,' Eck told me. 'Enormous soft beds, huge old bathtubs, very comfortable armchairs you can fall asleep in without cricking your neck. The only concession to modern life has been the installation of an ice-making machine to speed up the production of cocktails after shooting.'

I arranged to meet Francis at Caerlyon at eight o'clock in the morning on the Saturday on which we had been invited.

Francis, Campbell and I drove to Blubberwick together in Francis's old Land Rover. I wasn't allowed to take my Range Rover.

'Too smart,' said Francis, shaking his head. 'White leather seats. Campbell will get mud everywhere.'

So we drove, early one morning in late August, deep into the Pennine uplands at about twenty miles an hour. The air had a sharp feeling to it and was so clear that one had the impression of seeing the wide horizons through a telescope. Everything seemed nearer than it really was. The heather was still in flower: its purple bloom covered every hill.

'Will I know anyone there?' I asked Francis, as we drove along the narrow roads across the moorland.

'Eck will be there, of course. No party ever takes place that Eck isn't invited to. There's someone called Heini Carinthia, who comes every year. He's an old friend of mine. He started my interest in wine. I'd like you to meet him. Ask him about Château Trébuchet: that's his property, in Pomerol, in Bordeaux. He says it produces the best Pomerol after Pétrus. I myself think it is a moderate wine. Then there's Philippe de Bargemon, a very charming Frenchman, who spends his life shooting: grouse in the Pennines, doves in Argentina, quail in Texas, pheasants in Hungary. He's never without a gun in his hand. Nice man. The others are mainly locals. You'll know some of them, I expect.'

We drove on and then Francis said, 'You're very privileged, you know. Getting an invitation to Blubberwick isn't something that happens every day. It's one of the best grouse moors in the North of England.'

'I don't know how I feel about shooting those poor grouse.'

Francis smiled. 'Well, of course you have to hit one first. But if they are not shot, they get diseased. Once the number of grouse on the moor gets beyond a certain density, they start passing a parasite to one another. I believe they pick it up from sheep. That kills them off faster than anything. The only way to preserve grouse is to shoot them.'

I did not follow the logic of this, but Francis spoke as if he knew what he was talking about, so I said nothing more.

'There is no sport like it,' said Francis. 'You go and stand on the roof of the world, and the grouse come at you from all directions, faster than you would believe possible. All other forms of shooting come a distant second. Few people ever get the chance to do it. You don't know how lucky you are.'

We were now driving along a narrow single-track road that wound through the heather. Then I saw my first grouse. A brown bird with a red comb on its head whirred out of a clump of heather close to the side of the road calling, 'Go back, G'back, g'back.' We came over the crest of a hill and saw Blubberwick Lodge below us. It was a large rambling building, covered in a fading cream-coloured rendering to protect it from the constant drizzle and wind of the dales. As we drove down the bank towards it, I could see activity: beaters climbing into two big ex-army lorries, guns coming out of the house and straggling towards a line of four-wheel-drive vehicles drawn up on the gravel. We drove through the lodge gates.

Ed was waiting for us on the gravel. When he saw us he tapped his watch with his finger and said, 'Francis, if I'd known you were coming in that old banger I'd have told you to set out yesterday. What was wrong with Wilberforce's Range Rover?'

We stopped and got out.

Ed said to me, 'Wilberforce, I don't think you know Heinrich Carinthia? Or Philippe de Bargemon?' I shook hands with a large, smiling elderly man and then a younger, dark-haired Frenchman. The other guns I knew. Eck greeted me with a wave of his hand. One of the party, to my surprise, was Annabel Gazebee.

'Hello, Annabel,' I said. 'I didn't know you would be shooting.'

'We rely on her to get our bag,' said Ed. 'She's a top gun.'

Then Ed introduced me to my minder, Bob. 'Go and stand with Francis this morning. You'll get a better idea of what goes on from behind the line. Then, if you feel like it, you can have a go yourself this afternoon, and Bob will show you what to do. He'll stand with you and make sure you're safe.' Bob had the gun that Ed was lending me slung in a sleeve over his shoulder.

'Francis, why aren't you shooting?' I asked.

'I gave up shooting years ago,' he said. 'It's an expensive sport, and anyway I much prefer working my dog nowadays.'

'It's a pity,' said Ed to me, 'because Francis was one of the best shots in the county in his day.'

'I was about average,' said Francis modestly. 'Now, my father was what you would call a good shot. And my grand-father was one of the great shots.'

Ed laughed and said, 'It runs in the family, I expect.'

Then we climbed into our vehicles and set off towards the moor. We drove in a convoy up a moorland track towards the first line of butts. An undulating landscape of heather and peat hags and small pools opened before us and we stopped and parked the vehicles on a dry bit of ground in the lee of a small hill. Then the guns and the followers, including Catherine and Francis and myself, walked slowly along the line of the wooden butts, Ed indicating to each gun in turn which butt to occupy.

Francis turned away from the line and strode across the heather with Campbell dancing at his heels. I followed him, and when we were about three hundred yards back from the line, we stopped and hunkered down in the heather.

The silence was, for a time, absolute. Francis did not speak, and Campbell sat quivering beside him, once letting out a small moan of excitement. A great white sky arched over us. In every direction the moors rolled away, like a huge sea. Not a house or a road could be seen, nor any human figure. Then I saw a line of moving dots on the distant horizon. They did not appear to get any closer for a while, but then I realised it must be the beating line, and I began to hear, in the stillness, the snap of the flags they carried to drive forward the grouse. Occasionally shouts would arise from the line of 'Flag up! Flag up!'

'They're trying to stop the grouse flying back over the beaters, and turn them back towards the guns,' Francis explained. 'Things should start to happen soon.'

Now I saw a cloud of birds in the sky wheel and turn over the beating line, and then drop low again so that I could not pick them out against the heather. Then a shot rang out from one end of the row of butts; then shots were being fired up and down the line. I saw a pack of grouse coming straight towards us and, as it flew over the butts, I saw two or three birds tumble and then those that were not hit went past us in a rush of wings almost before I had realised they were coming.

At the end of the drive Francis stood up and Campbell sat up, a paw raised, waiting for orders. Francis gestured with his arm. 'Go on, Campbell,' he said. 'Hi lost. Hi lost!'

The little dog surged through the heather, his head appearing from time to time with its ears flapping as he searched for fallen birds. In a few minutes he came back with one in his mouth.

'There, Wilberforce,' said Francis, handing me the soft, still-warm creature with its brown plumage and downy white leggings: 'your first grouse.'

I held the bird gingerly for a moment and then gave it back to Francis. He smiled, and went back to working his dog.

After everything had been picked up, we walked on to the next drive, and then a third. Each was as exciting to watch as the first one and, by the time the last drive was over, it was afternoon. A pale sun was trying to burn its way through the overcast and not succeeding. It was warm and still. Francis and I walked back to the line of butts and joined up with the guns, and then we all walked together for a few hundred yards down the hill to where a small burn trickled between soft, grassy banks where the sheep had grazed off the heather. There we had a picnic beside the stream, and the keepers and the beaters took themselves off into a huddle with their Thermoses and sandwiches fifty yards away. The rest of us sat or lay on the grass surrounded by wicker hampers and wine coolers from which Horace, clad in a tweed jacket and twill trousers instead of his customary dark suit, dispensed all manner of good things.

Catherine came and sat down beside Ed and Eck and me and said, 'What did you think of it all, Wilberforce?'

'Very exciting, but I don't see how anyone ever hits anything. The birds fly so fast.'

She laughed. 'You'll soon find out for yourself. I expect you'll hit something. You are going to shoot after lunch, aren't you? Try to remember not to shoot more than Ed. He won't like it if you do.'

Ed, who was reclining in the heather munching on a chicken leg said, with some asperity, 'On the contrary, Catherine, I would be absolutely thrilled if he did.'

'I know you would, darling,' said Catherine. She went and sat down nearer to him and stroked his hair. 'You're so good.'

Before we finished lunch Ed pulled a camera out from his pocket and took photographs of everybody sitting on the grass, eating their lunch. Then Catherine asked me to take a photograph of herself with Francis and Ed. The three of them got to their feet for the picture. Francis stood in the middle with an arm around Ed and an arm around Catherine. The heather stretched behind them to the milky sky, and the air was so clear that whenever I looked at that photograph afterwards – for Ed gave me a copy – it seemed to me as if the three of them might at any instant step out of the picture, or that I might step into it and return to the innocent happiness of that moment.

The shooting began again after lunch. Bob the minder followed behind me, carrying my gun in its sleeve and a bag of cartridges slung over his shoulder. We followed Ed towards another line of butts, about half a mile from where we had sat and eaten our picnic. As we came to the butts Ed directed the guns where to stand. Halfway along the line he stopped and said, 'This'll do for you, Wilberforce. You should get some shooting here. There are plenty of grouse about on this bit of the moor this year.'

I could hear them all around us, their liquid bubbling music occasionally broken as a cock bird would flutter up for a moment to see what was going on, uttering its cackling admonition: 'Go back! G'back!'

Bob and I entered the butt, and Bob took the gun out of its sleeve and began to instruct me. 'Now then, sir,' he said, 'I'll put these two canes on either side of the front of the butt. Never swing your gun past them, otherwise you'll shoot one of the other gentlemen in the line, and they never enjoy being shot, sir. And when you hear horns blowing, that will mean the beating line will be within range, and then you must only shoot grouse that have gone past us and are behind the butt, otherwise you'll shoot one of the keepers, and they definitely dislike being shot, sir.'

Then he showed me how to break the gun and present it to him so that he could reload for me after I had fired it, and we settled down to wait. Various other pickers up and flankers walked past, and the flankers settled themselves in the heather at each end of the line of butts, with sticks on to which were stapled sheets of white plastic from old bags of fertiliser.

'What are those men going to do?' I asked Bob.

'When the grouse start coming through, they'll get up and flag them to make sure they go over the line of guns and don't get out the side. There'll be a bit of a wait now, sir. The beating line starts the drive quite a long way away.'

I stood in my butt, a wooden hurdle with heather along the top to give the illusion of camouflage, with my gun resting on the lip, waiting for the grouse to appear. My heart was beating faster than usual. I half-hoped I wouldn't hit anything; but a deeper urge made itself felt: I knew I would want to shoot the grouse when at last they came.

The silence was absolute. The limitless horizons of the Pennines opened up before me. A huge grey bird wheeled in the sky above us.

'Look at that, sir,' said Bob: 'that's a hen harrier. They eat the grouse chicks in the breeding season and pick off any wounded birds we don't find. They know what's going on today, sir.'

The great raptor soared and wheeled against the pale sky, waiting for its chance. Strange-looking flies drifted past in front of the butt, locked in amorous embraces. A solitary bumblebee droned past in search of heather honey. The milky sky and the horizon seemed indivisible, as if the land rose up to meet the white light of heaven, as if it went on for ever. Somewhere far to the east were the urban sprawls of Tyneside and Wearside: now it seemed as if those places, and everything in them – my work, my life so far – were an unguessable distance away.

I saw a line of dots appear on the horizon.

'That's the beating line,' said Bob. 'In a few minutes we should start to get busy. Remember, when you see the grouse, pick your bird and stay on it. Shoot it in front as far out as you dare. They travel that fast, if you wait, it'll be on you and past you before you can shoot.'

A moment or two ticked by. I could hear the occasional flap of a flag, as the beating line snapped them to and fro, to move the packs of grouse forward. Once or twice I heard again the screams of 'Flag up! Flag up!'

Bob said, 'Any minute now.'

My heart started to beat a little faster. I still had not seen a grouse on the moor. I wondered whether we would draw a blank. Perhaps Ed was wrong. The grouse I had heard earlier had all gone quiet. There didn't seem to be a bird anywhere except for the hen harrier, still circling above the beating line. Then there was a shot from further down the line, then a ragged fusillade and then, before I had a chance to do anything about it, a pack of small brown birds was rocketing past the butt on every side, swarming in every direction. The birds were moving at an incredible speed. They were gone before I had even thought to raise my gun to my shoulder.

'Don't worry,' said Bob. 'It takes getting used to. Just keep your eyes open and – now, there in front: do you see that single bird?'

A lone grouse was darting this way and that along the gullies in front. It was about two hundred yards away. I put my gun up and Bob said, 'Now. Now, sir!'

I swung on it and fired and everything slowed down: the grouse, which had already closed the gap to less than forty yards, seemed to tumble in the air in front of me, and then something whizzed past my head at great speed, and I turned and saw it bounce as it hit the ground ten yards behind me, in a cloud of white and brown feathers. After that I fired shot after shot, and by the end of the drive six more birds had fallen. Bob had made me wear ear protectors, but even so, by the time the beaters arrived at the butts and the drive was over, my head ached, my shoulder felt bruised from when I had fired before nesting the gun properly into my shoulder, and my throat was dry with the pollen from the heather.

As we walked back from the last line of butts towards the vehicles, I found myself beside Catherine. 'Did you enjoy yourself today?' she asked.

'It was unforgettable. I don't know if I'll ever do it again, but I'm so glad to have tried it once.'

'Oh, you'll do it again,' said Catherine. 'Ed will see to that. You're his mascot now.'

Suddenly she bent and picked something from the ground. When she straightened up, she was holding a sprig of white heather. She gave it to me and said, 'Wear this in your cap, Wilberforce. It brings good luck.'

I thanked her and stuck it into the tweed cap that Francis had lent me. Then she walked on and I found myself beside Heinrich Carinthia.

'You have shot your first grouse, I hear. Then, I should say, you have had a very good day.'

'It has been memorable.'

'It is always a special moment when you shoot your first grouse. Of course, we have none at home in Austria. I still remember my first grouse. It was here, many years ago, just after the war, almost the first year they started shooting the moors again. I was sixteen years old, and Ed's grandfather and Francis's father were still alive. I still remember that little bird coming down, just as if it was yesterday. You arrived here with Francis. He is a friend of yours?'

'Yes,' I said.

'He used to shoot so well, before he gave it up. It is a great shame that he does not shoot any more. His obsession with wine, I fear, has cost him his fortune. I feel a little bit responsible, for it was I who started his interest in wine.'

Heinrich stopped walking, and so I stopped as well. 'I must catch my breath. I am not so young. Walking over this heather is hard work for an old man. Yes, Francis came to me for some months when his parents wanted him out of the way of some trouble. He never told me what it was, but I expect a girl. Francis was so good-looking in those days. I looked after him for his father's sake. His father had been in the army and had stopped Russian troops from burning down my family's house at the end of the war, so I felt that I owed the Black family some favours. I took Francis to see my new winery in California that I had just bought. In those days it was very brave for Europeans to try to make wine in California, but it has been my best investment. Then I took him to my little property in Bordeaux. You have heard of Château Trébuchet?'

I said that Francis had mentioned it to me. We started walking again, moving slowly across the heather to where the vehicles had been parked.

Heinrich Carinthia said, 'He is so rude about it. Francis knows a lot about wine, but I still ask myself whether he truly understands it. You must try the Château Trébuchet. I will find your address from Francis and send you a case.'

'Oh, please don't go to the trouble.'

'You will drink it to celebrate your first grouse, and then you will tell Francis that, after all, my Trébuchet is a very good wine. If you are a friend of Francis, you must also be an amateur of wine.'

I said, 'I don't really drink that much. But he is trying to get me interested.'

Heinrich Carinthia shook his head. 'Be careful. It is good to like wine; it is acceptable to love it, as I do; but what Francis feels for wine is beyond love. You must be careful to

301

stop at liking. Even loving is a little dangerous. Ah, here we are, and we have kept them all waiting.'

'Finished your nature ramble, Heini?' called Ed, who was standing next to Francis and waiting for us. 'Right, everybody into the vehicles. Let's get back to the house.'

When we arrived back at the Lodge, Ed told everyone to do whatever they liked with the rest of the afternoon, but to be ready for drinks and dinner by eight. There was a race for the three bathrooms as soon as he had finished speaking. I decided I could wait my turn, and I went into the rough garden and looked about the Lodge. I came around the side of the house and found the keepers still tying up the grouse into braces with lengths of red twine, and hanging them in the game larder. There were dozens of birds still in there from the previous day's shooting.

I saw Bob, and went over to him and said, 'What happens to these birds now?'

'They go down to London, sir, to the restaurants and hotels. The dealers pay a good price for them, at this time of the year.'

I went on with my tour and finally sat down on a bench looking over the dale, beneath an open upstairs window. I sat there for a minute or two. Then, to my surprise, I heard voices just above my head. I realised after a second that I must be sitting beneath the open window of Ed's bedroom.

I heard him say, 'He's quite hard work.'

Catherine's voice replied, 'I think he's sweet. He was so thrilled to have shot his first grouse.'

'I don't know why I asked him,' said Ed. 'I know nothing more about him than when I first met him. He seems to have wandered into our lives from nowhere. He's Mr Nobody.'

'Well, you do get your enthusiasms for people, Ed, and then you get bored with them.'

'What's that supposed to mean?' said Ed angrily.

I didn't want to hear any more of this. I was eavesdropping against my will, but I knew if I stirred they might hear or see me.

'You know.'

There was a pause and then Ed spoke again: 'And another thing, I don't like the way he looks at you.'

Catherine's voice said sharply, 'Looks at me like what, Ed? He can look at me if he likes. You don't own me. You're just in a bad mood because you didn't shoot well today.'

'Please don't talk to me like that in my own house,' said Ed. There was some muttering from further away that I could not hear, and then the loud slam of a door. It sounded as if there had been a row.

I sat there until the silence from above persuaded me that there was no longer anyone close to the window. At any rate, I could not sit there for ever. I stood up. Tears were smarting at the corners of my eyes. I could not believe what Ed had just said. Every time I had ever met him he had been so kind to me, so friendly, so full of charm and thoughtfulness. What was it I had just heard him call me: 'Mr Nobody'?

I walked down to the bottom of the garden where the shaggy lawn ran into a spinney of Scots pine. I thought there might be tears running down my cheeks and I did not want to meet anyone just then. I felt humiliated and disappointed at the same time, but within me a reasonable voice said, 'Mr Nobody: that sums it up very well.' After all, I didn't even know who my real father and mother were, or had been. All I knew of life had been learned by sitting in front of a computer for the last ten or fifteen years. No wonder Ed got bored with me. Everyone was bored by me, after a while. I bored myself. Everyone who ought to love me abandoned me.

I stood amongst the trees for quarter of an hour feeling sorry for myself, until at last a sense of calm returned. After all, what did it matter? I would get through the evening and drive back the next morning with Francis, and then I need never see any of them again. I practised a smile and found I could stretch my lips into some semblance of a grin. I could at least look normal, even if I did not feel it.

I walked back to the house and made my way upstairs to my bedroom. In a corridor I met Ed, returning from the bathroom with a towel round his waist.

'Bathroom's free, Wilberforce,' he said, 'if you don't mind a few pools of water on the floor.'

'Thanks,' I said, and began to go past him.

He stopped me by gripping my arm and giving me his most charming smile. 'Wilberforce, I'm so pleased you shot your first grouse today. We'll definitely get you out again. You shot so well today. Bob told me. You'll be shooting as straight as the best of us before long – I know you will.'

'I'm very grateful to you, Ed,' I found myself saying, 'for giving me the chance.'

He loosened his grip, his eyes still holding mine, dancing, wanting to be loved, wanting to be admired, demanding my tribute. He was still smiling.

'Oh, we'll get you out again,' he promised. 'Huge fun, to see someone get their first bird. It's always a special moment.' He gave me two quick pats on the shoulder and went on to his bedroom.

I went to my bedroom and undressed for my bath. As I did so, I wondered if I had really overheard that conversation below Ed's bedroom window.

Ed could be so charming, when he wanted to be.

Five

It is evening now, and I am sitting outside on a stone bench on a terrace outside the Lodge. Heinrich Carinthia is sitting in a deckchair a few feet away, reading a newspaper. The others are all still inside, awakening after their afternoon sleep, and thinking about changing for dinner. I am dressed in rented evening clothes that do not fit me very well. Heinrich is wearing a huge green-velvet tent of a smoking jacket over trousers of a mysterious tartan, and velvet slippers with stags' heads embroidered on them in gold thread. We exchange nods when I come out, but he is absorbed in his paper, so I sit and stare at this alien landscape.

The deep fold of the dale below is shrouded in shadow and dark fir woods. Above the woods small green compartments of pasture are marked out by stone dykes. Sheep are streaming down the hillside towards one such field where there is a circular sheep fold, rounded up by two dogs and followed by a farmer on a quad bike. I can hear the sheep shouting in complaint, as they are gathered in. Above the pasture is the heather, the beginnings of the moor where I have spent the day. A year ago, a few months ago, it would have been unthinkable that I would ever have been in such a place, and had such a day.

The overcast that has covered the sky all day has gone. Now the sky is streaked with red and gold. The air is warm, with that familiar sweet smell I remember from my first visit to Caerlyon. My life has been transformed in these four months. Now, as dusk approaches, a great golden light drenches the summits and ridges of the hills, suggesting infinite distances of undiscovered country, and endless possibilities. A line of cloud sits on the horizon, its domes and pillars catching the evening sun, so that it resembles a distant range of Himalayan peaks. I turn to look at the house, and see Catherine coming towards us along the terrace, carrying two misting glasses of white wine. She is wearing a dark-rose-coloured evening dress that suits her perfectly, and once again, as on the very first time that I met her, I am overwhelmed by her beauty.

She walks across to Heinrich Carinthia in his deckchair and says, 'A glass of wine, Heini?'

'*Was? Was denn?* Ach, it is you, Catherine. I was miles away, watching this glorious sunset. A glass of wine would be very good.'

Catherine hands him the wine and then walks across to me with the other glass.

'And you, Wilberforce?'

And me?

The question has many possibilities. I take the glass of wine from her, and as I do so her fingers, cool from holding the glass, briefly touch mine. She does not at once withdraw her hand, but glances at me, and our eyes meet for a moment. I see a look of curiosity, of puzzlement, in her expression. Then she leaves the glass in my hand. I do not speak, not even to thank her. I cannot speak. She does not smile, nor say anything, but after a moment longer she turns and walks slowly back to the house.

Who are you? her glance asks. What are you?

I know the answer to that one. I am nobody. I am anybody. I can choose to be whom I like. I turn back with my glass in my hand to watch the golden sky.

'*Was für ein himmlischer Abend*,' says Heinrich Carinthia. 'So heavenly a night.'

I nod in a friendly way, but do not speak. I still cannot. Heinrich understands how I feel. There is no need for either of us to speak again. The sheep are grazing quietly again. The great silence of the dales has fallen again, a peacefulness that is not like any other, and the two of us watch the sun sinking further down in the sky, in a silent companionship. A single bright star is gleaming, low in the sky. Then another, and another comes out, as the sun goes below the horizon. My heart is choked by my great discovery, the truth I have just seen in this wonderful sunset, the truth I have just felt in the touch of Catherine's hand.

Because I am nobody, I can choose to be whom I like. I can choose my life to be what I want it to be. I can become anybody; I can do anything.

For the first time in my life, I feel that things, after all, might change for the better. I have been a prisoner for too long, a prisoner of my own self-doubt, a prisoner of a loveless childhood, and a life without experience and without joy. Now I feel an absolute certainty that my life is about to change and become so different from what it has been up until now. It is so simple. It has always been so simple. It is a matter of choice, a matter of understanding that one's freedom to choose is limited only by courage and imagination. I have enough courage to choose, I hope; enough imagination to understand that life may have more possibilities than I can tell. So I have that freedom. I've always had that freedom, but it has taken until tonight to realise it. All I have to do is stretch out my hand and take the things I want. At this moment, on this heavenly evening, I feel absolutely certain in my new sense of optimism. I will learn to have fun; I will learn to have friends, real friends; perhaps one day I will even learn how to love somebody – not Catherine, of course, for she belongs to Ed, but someone like her.

Do you ever have that feeling? Have you had that absolute sense of conviction: that, after all, life is going to turn out really well for you?

With grateful acknowledgement to Robert Parker, author of *Bordeaux: The Comprehensive Guide* published by Dorling Kindersley, whose writing enabled me to imagine the many clarets I could not afford to buy, but wanted to describe, whilst writing this book.